Poverty and Development
in Latin America

D0095777

Poverty and Development in Latin America

Public Policies and Development Pathways

edited by
Henry Veltmeyer
and Darcy Tetreault

Kumarian Press

A Division of Lynne Rienner Publishers, Inc. • Boulder & London

Published in the United States of America in 2013 by
Kumarian Press
A division of Lynne Rienner Publishers, Inc.
1800 30th Street, Boulder, Colorado 80301
www.kpbooks.com
www.rienner.com

and in the United Kingdom by
Kumarian Press
A division of Lynne Rienner Publishers, Inc.
3 Henrietta Street, Covent Garden, London WC2E 8LU

Library of Congress Cataloging-in-Publication Data
Poverty and development in Latin America : public policies and development pathways /
edited by Henry Veltmeyer and Darcy Tetreault. — 1st ed.
    p. cm.
  Includes bibliographical references and index.
  ISBN 978-1-56549-507-4 (cloth : alk. paper)
  ISBN 978-1-56549-508-1 (pbk. : alk. paper)
    1. Poverty—Latin America. 2. Poor—Latin America. 3. Economic development—
Latin America. 4. Latin America—Economic policy. I. Veltmeyer, Henry.
II. Tetreault, Darcy Victor.
HC130.P6P677 2012
339.4'6098—dc23
                                                                    2012025267

British Cataloguing in Publication Data
A Cataloguing in Publication record for this book
is available from the British Library.

Printed and bound in the United States of America

∞ The paper used in this publication meets the requirements
of the American National Standard for Permanence of
Paper for Printed Library Materials Z39.48-1992.

5 4 3 2 1

Contents

Introduction

The Economic Commission for Latin America and the Caribbean (ECLAC), the major UN agency to track the social panorama of Latin America and to monitor progress over the years regarding poverty and inequality, recently reported "substantive achievements" (over the past decade) regarding poverty. After a decade lost to development, during which the rate of poverty in the region climbed from 40 percent of the population to 48 percent, and then "the difficult 1990s" characterized by slow to negligible economic growth and a marginal decrease in poverty (down to 44.3 percent), the new millennium opened with a commodities-export-led boom and an appreciable reduction in the rate of poverty (down to 33 percent) and the incidence of indigence (ECLAC 2009).

This achievement, in a region characterized by some of the widest and deepest social inequalities in the world, with a substantial part of the population unable to meet their basic needs, was a cause of relief or comfort for some and celebration by others. Most of the poor, however, are blisslessly unaware of this "achievement." As for the officials in the international development community who had declared a renewal of the war on poverty at the opening of the millennium—promising to halve the rate of extreme poverty by 2015—many saw this evident progress on the poverty front as a testament to their efforts and the correctness of their approach.

Nevertheless, rather than providing answers to questions that bedeviled at least three generations of development experts and practitioners, the publication of diverse official reports and the statistics on this progress and "achievement" raised more questions. It is these questions that concern the authors of this book. They include, first, how "real" is the recorded progress? Is it perhaps more apparent than real? Second, what or whose actions are responsible for the achievement: those of the international community? The governments in the region? The myriad nongovernmental organizations that joined the war against global poverty at the outset of the new world order? Or, as some have suggested, is it the result of actions taken by the poor themselves? Third, what are the theoretical implications in regard to understanding the root causes and factors that contribute to the problem of poverty, and that resisted over five decades of efforts to reduce it, eradicating poverty in its most extreme forms and conditions and alleviating the pain of the many millions still mired in poverty? And fourth, what are the practical or political implications in regard to the actions that need to be taken to redress the problems that continue to affect over 180 million people in the region?

The answer to these questions depends on a clear understanding of the agency or agencies responsible for the apparent or real progress made over the past decade—to be exact, from 2002 to 2008, the years of the primary commodity boom. Was it, in effect, changed conditions in the arena of the global economy—for example, the ascension of China and a spike in the demand for the resources and commodities that the region is able to provide? Or is the apparent success in the war on poverty the result of public policy and actions taken in pursuit of a strategy consciously formulated to tackle the problem—the poverty reduction strategy pursued by many governments in the new millennium in the context of a new consensus on the need for a more inclusive form of development? If so, what specific strategy and policy mix? And whose actions?

In response to these and other such questions, the authors of this book met a number of times to exchange ideas about the problem, to design various lines of research and conduct both a systematic review of the voluminous literature that surrounds it and field research in a number of locations in the Latin American context—on the diverse and complicated dynamics of what we choose to term "the poverty problematic." This book is the result of this research—of our collective research effort and findings.

The book is organized into three parts. Part I concerns primarily the World Bank in its self-appointed role as guardian of the world order and the headquarters of the war on global poverty. In this connection chapter 1 provides a summary overview of the poverty problematic in its most important dimensions. It traces out major shifts in understanding and the strategy designed to tackle the problem in the context of a decades-long war against poverty declared by the World Bank in 1973 and fought in diverse theaters, with different and improved weapons and changing strategy and tactics ever since. It also traces out the different actions taken on the Latin American stage of this war over the past three decades of neoliberal globalization under the auspices of the Washington Consensus, within the new world order established in the early 1980s.

These actions implicated the policy and institutional framework established by the development community to prosecute the war on global poverty. They also point toward the various pathways open to the poor—and the possibilities for them to take action. In this connection, for example, at least one study, published in 2000, suggested that the progress recorded in the 1990s (a reduction of 5 percentage points in the regional poverty rate) was entirely the result of actions taken by the poor themselves, not the efforts and the strategies pursued by the development community or the governments in the region. The question is (one among several), is this also the case for the subsequent period in the opening decade of the new millennium? Or was the achievement recorded over this period (a 8.7 percent reduction in the regional poverty rate) the result, in part anyway, of actions taken by governments and international and nongovernmental cooperants? Also, what was the role—effect, rather—of changed international conditions? For example, what was the impact of the global crisis that brought an abrupt end to the primary commodities boom in the second half of 2008? Chapter 1 addresses these and other questions about the regional dynamics of the war on global poverty. These dynamics implicate the actions taken by diverse actors in this war—the international organizations engaged in the project of international cooperation for development, the governments in the region, the political Left, civil society in its diverse expressions, and the grassroots organizations and social movements formed in the context of changing conditions in the new world order.

João Márcio Mendes Pereira in chapter 2 provides a critical analysis of the way in which the war on global poverty has been fought over four decades of changing conditions in the capitalist world order. The war on poverty was officially launched by the World Bank in 1973 in a directive from Robert McNamara, the president of the Bank. The chapter discusses the reasons and means of the initiative taken by the Bank. The focus is on the incontrovertible fact that the problem of poverty has defeated all of the efforts and all of the resources that the Bank and the "world community" of concerned organizations marshaled in this war, raising serious questions about if not the nature of the problem, which has been endlessly studied and is well enough understood, then the dynamics of the war itself. Is the failure one of understanding—an inability to theoretically grasp the true nature of the problem, the obstacles involved, or the forces at play? Or is the matter one of inadequate or misdirected, improperly targeted, resources? In all the twists and turns of the war against world poverty, fought as it has been in so many diverse theaters and contexts all over the world, without (it seems) any tangible results, no dint has been made in the scope and devastating social effects of a problem lived today by more than a billion people worldwide, more than when the problem was first "discovered."

Chapter 3 focuses on the World Bank's pathbreaking study on the role of agriculture in the development process and the available pathways out of rural poverty. The chapter provides a critique of the World Bank's *2008 World Development Report* on the role of agriculture in the development process, specifically its conception of capitalist farming as a pathway out of rural poverty. It has been argued that the report is unable to overcome a fundamental deficit in development thinking based on modernization theory and an ideological predisposition toward (and belief in) the agency and working of the market. Another argument advanced in the chapter is that the failure of the report to propose radical land redistributive measures for tackling rural poverty derives from its failure to grasp the fundamental cause and dynamics of rural poverty.

In chapter 4 Darcy Tetreault dissects in the context of Mexico the major policy response made to the poverty problematic by governments in the region in the context of what has been termed the "post-Washington Consensus" on the need to "bring the state back in" and establish "a better balance between the market and the state" in the rural front on the war on poverty. The policy response took the form of social programs that transferred income directly to the rural poor to assist them in their self-development efforts and to provide social security and a minimum standard of welfare. Permutations of this program can be found across the region in virtually every country. In Mexico the program is titled *Oportunidades*. Tetreault provides a nuanced analysis of this poverty reduction program, drawing out its theoretical and political implications and its relevance for the regional war on global poverty.

Part II deconstructs and dissects the three most important modalities of the Poverty Reduction Strategy pursued by governments and the international development community over the past two decades. At issue in this strategy is the question of whether poverty is basically a matter of social exclusion, the lack of opportunity and resources, and deficits attributed to the poor (lack of an appropriate mind-set, etc.); or whether it is the product of what ECLAC (2010a) terms "the structure of inequality," a structure rooted in and maintained by relations of political and economic power. If poverty is basically understood, as it is in all official reports prior to 2010, as a matter of exclusion and a deficit of opportunities and resources, then it can be redressed via a policy of social inclusion, economic assistance, and institutional reform. However, were poverty rooted in the social and economic structures of the system, then the solution is substantive social change, not just reform designed to improve the level of participation in existing institutions (remove barriers such as discrimination and exclusion) but actions and policies leading to structural change—change in the social relations of production and power.

In chapter 5 Anthony O'Malley identifies four main schools of thought, each with its pros and cons in terms of understanding the poverty problematic and policy implications. With reference to these different ways of understanding the poverty problematic, he dissects the Rural Poverty Reduction Programs (RPRPs) pursued by governments in Latin America over the past decade, with international cooperation. He begins with the finding that over this period, from 1990 to 2008, the urban poverty rate was reduced from 42 percent to 33 percent (a reduction of 9 percentage points) while the rural poverty rate was reduced only 5 percentage points from 66 percent to 61 percent. What this suggests to O'Malley is that rural poverty is more entrenched and resistant to policy intervention for that reason, or the war on rural poverty is misconceived as to its structural roots, and fought with inappropriate or ineffective strategies, possibly based on a misunderstanding of the impact of the policies. The chapter provides a systematic and critical analysis of the strategies pursued by the governments in the region and the international development community in the cause of war, in order to get at the bottom of the failure, which, as O'Malley points out, requires rethinking the entire rural poverty problematic— the way that it is conceived, theorized, and practiced, and the policy regime and the institutional framework established to combat it.

In addressing this issue chapter 6 focuses on the microfinance and credit strategy designed and pursued by the World Bank in one context (the closing of the labor pathway out of rural poverty) and by nongovernmental organizations, in a movement led by the Grameen Bank in another (the retreat of the state from the responsibility for social development). Chapters 7 and 8 turn to the two poverty reduction strategies designed by the World Bank and allied international organizations and launched in 1999, on the eve of the new millennium. The PRSP has been widely implemented in the new millennium in the context of the least developed and most heavily indebted countries of the global South. The strategy entails the requirement of aid recipients that they lay out on paper the specific measures they propose to implement in progressing toward the Millennium Development Goal (MDG) #1, which is to reduce by one-half the rate of extreme poverty by 2015.

Another poverty reduction strategy that has achieved considerable traction in recent years, even described (by Nancy Birdsall, president of the Center for Global Development) as "close to a magic bullet in development," takes the form of direct transfers of cash to the poor conditional on the children of the poor participating in educational programs and health services. Conditional cash transfer (CCT) programs have spread throughout Latin America and, more recently, throughout the world (at least thirty countries have implemented a CCT program). As heavily criticized in some circles as they are widely admired in others, CCT programs have become a key subject of debate within contemporary global social policy. Some early findings suggest their potential to overcome poverty and create human capital, but other studies are much less sanguine, pointing to serious shortcomings and few or insignificant improvements.

In chapter 8 Enrique Valencia Lomelí undertakes an assessment of CCT programs and the conventional theory that has evolved to justify them. He concludes that despite the fanfare the actual successes to date are rather limited, albeit with positive effects on schooling and some aspects of health and nutrition in poor households. Overall, he concludes, CCT programs have relatively weak effects on reducing and alleviating poverty in the short term and uncertain effects on educational aspects of human capital formation and poverty reduction in the long term. The reason, it could be concluded, is that while the direct transfer of cash to the poor does indeed provide the poor a needed lifeline of income support, it does not alter the fundamental structure of social inequality.

Part III of the book turns to the pathways out of poverty available to Latin America's rural poor. In chapter 9 Darcy Tetreault conceptualizes the complex issues involved in the poverty problematic before proceeding to critically analyze the pathways out of rural poverty proposed by the World Bank in its *2008 World Development Report* (farming, labor, and migration). With reference to the Bank's study of the role played by agriculture in the development process, he raises the following questions, which are then discussed in some detail: Has there been a reduction in the incidence of income poverty in rural Mexico during the era of neoliberal globalization? And if so, what are the main contributing factors? Is labor migration the best pathway out of income poverty, taking into consideration the labor conditions faced by rural migrants (on both the national and the international levels)? To what extent does fair trade and organic production represent a pathway out of poverty for Mexico's small-scale "peasant" farmers? Should the Mexican government (and Mexico's trading partners) pursue policies that would make farming a more viable alternative for Mexico's rural poor? If so, what would these policies be? Finally, and tellingly, Tetreault looks beyond and moves away from the strategies and policies pursued in the context of the "development project" and turns our attention to the actual responses of the poor to the forces of change that impinge upon them.

In chapter 10 Darcy Tetreault argues that an alternative pathway out of poverty is needed, a pathway paved by the small landholding peasant farmers who are at the center of the poverty-rural development problematic and the main targets (and presumed beneficiaries) of the World Bank's orchestrated solution to rural poverty. It is extremely unlikely, he argues, that the corporate-led continuation of the Green Revolution proposed by the Bank will redress Third World hunger and rural poverty. He argues that an alternative approach based on the principles of agroecology and food sovereignty is needed. This alternative, advanced by *Vía Campesina* and proponents of radical agrarian change, assigns agriculture a multifunctional role that goes far beyond mere commodity production. It includes overcoming poverty, reducing social and gender inequality, reversing environmental degradation, stabilizing rural communities, and stopping the hemorrhage of emigration.

In its entirety, this book seeks to move consideration of the poverty-development problematic beyond the framework established by the World Bank and the architects of the post-Washington Consensus (PWC) for the pathways paved by the agencies of development and available to the poor. The economists and officials at the World Bank assume that the poor essentially have no choice but to adjust to the forces of change released in the process of global capitalist development. However, there are in fact alternative pathways out of poverty that are predicated on resisting rather than adjusting to these supposed forces of progressive change. From this critical perspective a number of rural development and agrarian change analysts, including the authors of this volume, argue the need to

- reject the neoliberal policy of structural reform and strengthen the capacity of the state to advance the forces of national production and protect local producers from the so-called "forces of (economic) freedom" that distort and prevent the development of these forces;
- reject the dogma concerning free trade and market-led development and strengthen the capacity of the state to guide national production; control strategic sectors of the economy; protect and nurture small-scale producers and ecological modes of production; provide high-quality health care, education, and social security to the entire population; and use the instrumentalities and the power of the state to allocate returns to diverse factors of production and to ensure a more equitable distribution of national income;

- truly empower the poor by improving their access to the country's stock of natural, financial, and physical capital, implying collective local control over local natural resources and respect for indigenous autonomy;
- reject the antiagriculture bias of the prevailing and dominant development policy and also the corporate capitalist model for developing the forces of agricultural development, substituting for it an alternative model of small-scale agriculture oriented toward the domestic market;
- abandon the poverty-targeted social policy of the PWC with a return to a universalistic approach to social policy—to construct a basic universal welfare system in the areas of health and social security, consolidating existing programs into one homogenous system that provides universally available quality services;
- finance these social and development programs via restoration of a system of progressive taxation and by controlling strategic sectors of the national economy; and above all
- pursue the pathway out of poverty advanced by the poor themselves in the form proposed by *Vía Campesina*, that is, on the basis of organizing the peasant farmers or small-holding agricultural producers for small-scale production of food for the local, regional, and global markets.

The major conclusion reached by Tetreault and shared by the other authors of this book is that poverty reduction cannot be sustained with a strategy of the rural poor abandoning direct agricultural production supported by government action (an antipoverty strategy) in the form of inclusive development (social inclusion and economic assistance). Sustainable poverty reduction and social development requires a substantive change in the structure of social inequality in regard to both land and income distribution, and a direct confrontation (and change) of the relations of production and power that sustain this structure. A second conclusion is that neither the prevailing model of economic development—pragmatic neoliberalism: boosting economic growth via macroeconomic "structural reform"—nor the strategy (poverty reduction and inclusive development) and social policies prescribed under the PWC are sustainable. The reason is that they are predicated on institutional reforms and policies designed to maintain productive and power relations that inhibit or prevent the realization of a truly inclusive and equitable social order. To achieve such an order—that is, to bring about "another world"—requires an alternative economic model, a different strategy, and different social policies. Several chapters in this book discuss possible elements of this strategy based on the agency of social movements. Ultimately, substantive social change will depend on the ability and strength of radically progressive social movements to impose their agenda on the state. In other words, diverse social movements must unite or work together and find sufficient confluence in order to take control of the state apparatus and keep the governments accountable.

Part I

The World Bank and the Fight Against Poverty

The Poverty-Development Problematic

Henry Veltmeyer

No problem has troubled the international development community as much, or has engaged so many resources and effort, as poverty—a problem that has assumed global proportions with diverse regional, national, and local permutations. The "problem," "discovered" as it were in 1973 by the economists at the World Bank and then placed on the agenda of the organizations and development associations, remains a central concern of the international development community today at the end of the first decade in the new millennium. The World Bank, for example, defines its mandate as "working for a world free of poverty."

In the 1970s, when poverty was placed at the center of the development agenda, it was estimated to encompass some two-fifths of the world's total population. Toward the end of the century and the beginning of the new millennium, notwithstanding four decades of concerted effort and diverse strategies aimed at poverty reduction and alleviation, neither the scale nor the dimensions of the problem had diminished. As a percentage of the world's population, a slight improvement was recorded (perhaps 37 percent rather than 40 percent in 1980), but given four decades of population growth, the magnitude of the problem in terms of the sheer number of people who were still living in poverty or destitute was hardly diminished, if at all.

Nevertheless, over the course of the first decade in the new millennium, some progress was recorded, with an apparent substantial decline in the rate of extreme poverty in some places and also a reduction in the global scale of the problem. According to the Economic Commission for Latin America and the Caribbean (ECLAC 2009), the regional poverty rate in Latin America and the Caribbean for 2008 was 33 percent (equivalent to 180 million), which is high enough but down from 44 percent in 2000, 48 percent in 1990, and 40 percent in 1980. According to ECLAC's (2010a) *Social Panorama of Latin America*, the financial crisis of 2009 added only a tenth of a percentage point to the rate of poverty in the region (from 33 percent to 33.1 percent). The next year, the regional poverty rate fell by 1.6 percentage points (to 31.4 percent) (ECLAC 2011), thus it is hoped (and predicted) that the region has returned to the downward trend in the incidence and virulence of poverty that began in the early years of the new millennium. It is unclear whether this belated and rather uneven progress in the war on poverty in the twenty-first century is the result of efforts exerted by different agencies and stakeholders in the development enterprise in response to the United Nations' declaration of the "Millennium Development Goals" (MDGs), which included the stated goal and operational objective of halving the rate of extreme poverty by 2015. Or whether it is the result of policies implemented by governments within the framework of the post-Washington Consensus (PWC) on the need to "bring the state back in" and the search for a more inclusive and equitable form of development. There are also those who continue to argue, albeit with little evidence, that the best way to reduce poverty is to boost economic growth via the time-honored path of productive investment, technological innovation, human resource development, trade, and market-oriented structural reform.

It has also been suggested that the main reason for the recorded and reported "success" in reducing the global poverty rate was a change in international conditions in the world economy for a number of countries on the south of the development divide. The so-called "global financial crisis," which put an end to the short-lived boom in the export of primary commodities from the developing and less developed countries to the more developed, has given some credence to the argument about the importance of changes in the global economy in the reduction of global poverty.

It has even been suggested that most of the progress made in regard to alleviating and reducing poverty is not the result of international cooperation, government intervention, or changes in the global economy but should be attributed to actions taken by the poor themselves, especially their decision to migrate in the search for better opportunities and a more secure livelihood. For example, De Janvry and Sadoulet in 2000 argued that any progress made to that date in the war on poverty was the result not of development in one form or the other but of actions taken by the poor themselves.

Even so it is still unclear as to what the best explanation is or what weight to attach to the different factors involved in these explanations. Is the persistence of global poverty in diverse contexts, and the recorded or apparent progress made on the poverty front, the result of conditions over which governments and other "actors," including the poor themselves, have little or no control? Or is it the result of a failure to understand or address the root causes of the problem? Is it a matter of conflicting interests between the powerful few and the powerless many? Of policies that favor the rich or that are biased or work against the poor? Of "structures" or policies that make and keep people poor? Of misinformed actions or counterproductive strategies?

The research on these and other such questions will be discussed in this chapter and in other chapters of this volume. Much of this research is inconclusive or dependent on assumptions, predilections, or perspectives that have not yet been reconciled. What is nevertheless clear is the connection between social inequality and poverty, between poverty and the "pro-growth" policies of the post-Washington Consensus that have been shown to increase social inequality, and between the failure of the war on poverty waged by international organizations over the past fifty years and the prevailing relations of economic and political power. In this regard, the United Nations Development Programme (UNDP), for example, in its most recent report on human development in Latin America and the Caribbean (UNDP 2010), argued that there is a direct correlation between structured social inequalities (in power and production relations) and the persistence of poverty.

As for the source of the problem (the inequality-poverty nexus), the UNDP report is clear enough. It is located and can be found in the institutionalized practices and structures brought about by powerful economic interests that have advanced with the policies instituted under the post-Washington Consensus. In the words of the report, there exists a "direct correspondence between the advance of globalization, neoliberalism, and the advance of poverty social inequality, social inequity" (UNDP 2010, xv). "The most explosive contradictions," the report adds, "are given because the advance of [neoliberal] globalization marches hand in hand with the advance of poverty and social polarization." "It is undeniable," the report continues, "that the 1980s and 1990s [were] the creation of an abysmal gap between wealth and poverty" and that this gap constitutes the most formidable obstacle to achieving human development (UNDP 2010, xv).

Undeniable it might be, but it was not until 2010 that the UNDP— and also the economists at ECLAC (2010b)—finally made the connection between structured social inequalities and poverty, a connection long made in the scholarly literature critical of capitalist development in its neoliberal form. UNDP Regional Director Heraldo Muñoz in this regard notes, "[i]nequality is inherently an impediment to progress in the area of human development (the proposed 'solution' to the poverty problematic), and efforts to reduce inequality must be explicitly mainstreamed in the public agenda." For the UNDP, he adds, "Equality is instrumental in ensuring meaningful liberties; that is to say, in terms of helping all people to share in meaningful life options so that they can make autonomous choices."[1]

Posing the Problem: Poverty Matters

Poverty alleviation and reduction is a central feature of the international development agenda and has been for over three decades, ever since the World Bank, under the presidency of Robert McNamara, discovered that around two out of every five people in the world were unable to satisfy their basic needs as human beings. To redress this problem, which had scarcely been diminished in its awesome magnitude since its initial determination, the world leaders meeting at the UN Millennium Summit in 2000 agreed to a number of key social development objectives, including the goal of significantly reducing poverty by 2015—reducing by one-half the rate of extreme poverty [MDG #1]. However, the question arises—a question that oddly enough was not even raised at the Millennium Summit—as to how it is possible for a problem identified and diagnosed three and a half decades ago to be with us still.

What then accounts for the persistence of poverty in its most extreme forms and debilitating conditions even with and after a four-decades-long global war waged against it by so many powerful organizations such as the World Bank? How is it that so many dedicated people, so many resources, and so much effort have resulted in so little by way of solution to the problem? Is it because the war on poverty has been waged irresolutely or poorly targeted, fought with misguided ideas and the wrong weapons? Or is it perhaps, as some have suggested, that the war has been fought at cross-purposes, with a perverse insistence on macroeconomic policies that by some accounts exacerbate the problem if not reproduce some of its most perverse conditions? Is it perhaps because the war on poverty was fundamentally flawed in its conception and in the way that it has been conducted and led by international financial institutions such as the World Bank that have various masters to serve at once, both those organizations genuinely concerned to bring about an improvement in the human condition and the guardians of the capitalist world order who are at the beck and call of the rich and powerful in the pursuit of private profit? In any case, the persistence of poverty in a world of plentiful resources remains a serious challenge to us all.

Research Findings: Poverty at Issue

It is estimated, on the basis of a methodology elaborated by the World Bank, that anywhere from 950 million to 1.3 billion people across the world live in conditions of extreme poverty, that is, on less than a dollar a day, and are unable to meet their basic human needs; at least another 1.7 billion (depending on how "poverty" is defined) are "poor" according to the World Bank's measurement standards. In fact, other estimates of the world's poor are much higher, as much as double. But even by the more conservative World Bank proxy measure of extreme poverty, it means that nearly 800 million people each day do not get enough food, and about 500 million people are chronically malnourished. According to UN data and calculations, close to a billion people go to bed each night hungry and are vulnerable to life-threatening disease, malnutrition, and starvation. Also, according to the World Bank, close to one-half of the world's children are surrounded by wealth but live in poverty, and more than a third are malnourished. More than 840 million adults (538 million of whom are women) are illiterate, 640 million live without adequate shelter, 400 million have no access to safe water, and 270 million have no access to basic health services. In 2003, 10.6 million died before they reached the age of five years (roughly 29,000 children a day). According to UNICEF, 24,000 children die each day because of poverty.

Current and Recent Trends

Research shows that over the past five decades, the rate of poverty has hardly responded at all to the rate of economic growth—which system-wide averaged 5 percent from 1960 to 1980 under the aegis of the development state, 2.3 percent in the era of neoliberal globalization (1983–99), and around 3 percent from 2002 to 2008 (with wide dispersals from the average in some regions and countries) in the context of a global commodity export boom from 2002 to 2008. Over the course of these "development" decades, the percentage of the world's population living in poverty hardly changed at all, and the overall number steadily grew. Only in the first decade of the new millennium was some progress made in reducing the incidence of extreme poverty—and this only in some few places (mainly, it turns out, in China, Brazil, and Chile) and in conditions of a primary commodity boom. When this boom went bust in October 2008, and with the onset of a global financial crisis (that coincided with a global food crisis for many of the world's poor), much of this progress was reversed.

In explaining this progress and the recent trend toward a reduction in the incidence of extreme poverty, researchers have pointed toward three main factors: (1) the ascension of China in the world economy, with rates of economic growth averaging over 10 percent for a decade and a half (if one were to take China out of the equation, a different picture emerges—one of growing social and economic inequality between the global North and South, that is, rich and poor); (2) the shift from free-market capitalism and neoliberal policies toward a new consensus on the need to bring the state back in; and (3) actions taken by the poor themselves, such as to migrate in search of a more viable livelihood or labor market opportunities.

The China Factor

Aggregate economic performance, arguably a necessary condition of poverty reduction (a more equitable redistribution of society's productive resources and global output would be another), improved significantly in the developing world in the 1990s and particularly the 2000s, and over the same period average poverty rates decreased even faster. However, China's success was responsible for much of this (see, for example, the OECD report *Perspectives on Global Development*, 2010). China's economy has grown at an average annual rate of almost 10 percent over the past three decades. "Poverty in China," the OECD reports, "stood at 84% of the population in 1981 but had dropped to 16% by 2005. Excluding China, the picture is more mixed. Poverty in India—home to a sixth of the world's population—also fell fairly steadily from 60% to 42% over the same period" (2010, 98). This, the authors of the OECD report point out, "is certainly a worthwhile improvement but it will not be fast enough to eradicate poverty in a lifetime" (2010, 98). As for the rest of the developing world, the rate of poverty reduction during the 1990s was marginal.

Nevertheless, there has been some improvement since the early 2000s, particularly in "emerging economies" like China and India but also in parts of Latin America beset with some of the worst inequalities and bulwarks of poverty in the world. As earlier mentioned, according to ECLAC (2009), the regional poverty rate dropped from 44 percent to 33 percent between the years 2000 and 2008. In terms of these statistics, poverty in the region worsened significantly in the 1980s under the weight of the inequalities engendered by the Washington Consensus (with the incidence of poverty increasing from 40 percent of the population to 48 percent), improved marginally in the 1990s under the policy conditions of the so-called "post-Washington Consensus" (dropping from 48 percent to 44 percent), and then improved markedly in the following decade—raising questions that are very much at issue in this book. What lies behind and can be seen as responsible for this belated reduction in the incidence of poverty in the region? And can this improvement in the social condition of the poor be sustained?

As for the global trend regarding poverty, there is some dispute as to whether the trend is toward convergence, or a lessening of the global divide, or divergence, a deepening or extension of this divide. At issue here is China. When China is taken out of the equation, the global trend takes a different form than the convergence identified by *The Economist* in its January 22, 2011, thematic issue on what the editor termed "the Davos Consensus" on the relationship between economic growth and social inequality. In fact, by different accounts the extraordinarily rapid rate of economic growth sustained over two decades in China by itself explains most, if not all, of the observed trend toward convergence in regional and national incomes and the reported success in achieving global poverty reduction over the past decade.

However, there is a downside to this "development" in regard to or within China. Although large numbers of Chinese, some 40 million of mostly rural migrants, have been lifted out of poverty in the sense of increased access to work-related income, this has entailed the separation of many millions of rural Chinese from their means of production, pushing many of them into other nonincome forms and conditions of poverty—leading also to numerous almost daily outbreaks of political protest and conflict in rural society, inducing a mass exodus from the countryside, and leading many to replace rural poverty (in income terms) with urban poverty (not captured by official figures using the Chinese government's poverty line or the World Bank measure of $2.50/$1.25 a day). Although the scale of magnitude is very different, what is happening in China today in terms of the push and pull and the dynamics of rural-urban migration is comparable to the process of capitalist development that unfolded in Latin America in the 1960s and 1970s and especially the 1980s and 1990s.

Another downside that bears mentioning is the extraordinary degree of environmental degradation that has accompanied China's rapid economic growth. In a comprehensive assessment of the country's environmental record, Elizabeth Economy (2004) argues that air and water pollution, depletion of natural resources, and social environmental conflicts are undermining the long-term sustainability of the Chinese economy, not to mention the demand it makes on global resources.

The Feminization of Poverty[2]
Poverty in Focus is a regular publication of the International Poverty Centre (IPC). Its purpose is to present the results of research on poverty and inequality

in the developing world. It specializes in the analysis of poverty and inequality and in offering research-based policy recommendations on how to reduce them. IPC is directly linked to the Poverty Group of the Bureau for Development Policy, the UNDP, and the Brazilian government's Institute for Applied Economic Research (IPEA).

The January 2008 issue of *Poverty in Focus* highlights the importance of improving gender equity for pro-poor growth and improved well-being of poor families, with references to recent research literature and sharing of important and policy-relevant results. Naila Kabeer leads the issue with a summary of current knowledge about the relation between gender, labor markets, and poverty, explaining why there are no easy generalizations about the poverty implications of women's paid work. Gita Sen, for her part, approaches poverty as a gendered experience that has to be addressed with due consideration to its various impacts, responses, and policy implications. Joana Costa and Elydia Silva underline the burdens of gender inequalities for society as a whole and show how paid work by women reduces overall poverty and inequality. And Andrew Morrison, Dhushyanth Raju, and Nistha Sinha summarize a World Bank study that shows a robust relationship between gender inequality and poverty; poor women's paid work plays a key role in getting their families out of poverty. The prospects for achieving the Millennium Development Goals are both directly and indirectly improved by enhancing gender equity. Thus, there are close links between the reduction of both gender inequalities and multidimensional poverty. The empirical evidence suggests that developing countries with less gender inequality tend to have lower poverty rates.

Addressing gender inequality represents an untapped source for stimulating economic growth and promoting social development. This is particularly true in the developing world, where women are often systematically deprived of equal access to social services and to physical and social capital. Hence, empowering women by improving their living conditions and enabling them to actively participate in the social and economic life of a country may well be the key for long-term sustainable development.

John Sender, in the same issue of *Poverty in Focus*, presents data indicating that when women in rural Mozambique have greater autonomy, daughters are less likely to be neglected; rural wages provide an escape route from poverty for a new generation of women. Ranjula Bali Swain and Fan Yang Wallentin use evidence from India that microfinance may lead to increased empowerment, self-confidence, respect, and esteem for women. Irene K. B. Mutalima reports on the experience of microfinance in Africa and warns that gender concerns often take a secondary role to the financial sustainability of the credit institutions. Marcelo Medeiros and Joana Costa examine the claims of a "feminization of poverty," making the distinction between static levels and dynamic change, and argue that current poverty measures underestimate the real levels of women's poverty. Sylvia Chant also finds that the scant data on intrahousehold inequalities prevent certain knowledge about the feminization of poverty and that the focus should be on women's privation beyond incomes.

Food for Thought—and Action

In the vortex of a multifaceted crisis of global proportions, and at the precipice of a disastrously vulnerable economic situation, hundreds of millions of the world's poor are on the verge of hunger and starvation. According to the United Nations, for the first time in history more than a billion people face starvation worldwide. Secretary-General Ban Ki-moon announced his intention to fast for twenty-four hours in "solidarity" with the planet's one billion people who do not have enough to eat.

If only the secretary-general and others within the project of international cooperation would take more serious and consequential action in redressing this and other dimensions of the crisis as it affects the world's poor—according to the World Bank, close to three billion people, almost one-half of the world's population. Such action, to be effective or consequential, would have to take a very different form and truly require a global partnership of diverse organizations in the governmental, nongovernmental, and intergovernmental sectors—all directed against the world capitalist system and its operational agencies and agents and the guardians of the world order, which, unfortunately, includes some of the very same organizations that are leading the war on global poverty.

It might be said that this is the same as giving responsibility for guarding the chicken coop to the fox in the belief that the fox has both the wherewithal and the public concern to secure the survival, if not the well-being, of the poor chickens, all too vulnerable to climate change and other natural disasters. At issue in the threat of widespread hunger and mass starvation, a poignant expression of the situation faced by a large number of the world's poor—and a major indictment of the system that governs global production—is a fundamental change in the capitalist world order and the system of global food production and not merely regulatory reform in the search for good governance (Akram-Lodhi 2011).

As for the urgent need of many of the world's poor to access food and water—not to mention shelter, health care, and other conditions of human welfare—the issue is not to expand production or to increase the supply of goods and services on the market. The issue is that many of the world's poor do not have the income to afford to buy what is for them a need but for the system is a commodity. Katie Allen of *The Guardian* (Allen 2010) reports that food prices in many parts of the developing world are poised for a 40 percent rise.

In this connection, research suggests that the conditions of malnutrition, food insecurity, hunger, and starvation are often not caused by natural disasters such as drought; more often than not, and increasingly so, they can be attributed to (they are caused by) the dominant system of global food production and the dynamics of global finance and so-called "free trade"—and also, according to a recent UN report, due to the growing demand for commodities and natural resources from emerging markets and biofuel production (McMichael 2010).

The Financialization of Production, Crisis, and Poverty

A major trend offset by neoliberal globalization during 1980s and 1990s was a growing chasm between the economy based on financial transactions—many of them speculative or unproductive—and the real economy where most people work, engage in productive activity of one sort or another, and live. It is estimated that while in the 1970s the international flows of global capital served to an important extent to expand production and finance development, by the 1990s and into the new millennium these "international resource flows" were largely disconnected from the development process, resulting in a highly polarized world economy and society characterized by huge concentrations of wealth at one pole and deepening regional and localized pockets of poverty at the other (Petras and Veltmeyer 2011b).

Another issue behind the current global food crisis is the financialization of global production: the separation of the real economy in which people are engaged in productive activity from the money economy based on financial transactions increasingly divorced from the production process (Bello 2009). In this connection, it is estimated that the value of total financial transactions in just one capital market (the London currency exchange) is twenty times greater than the value of world trade. It is also calculated that by the mid-1990s, only 5 percent of total international capital flows had any productive function at all.

Under these and such conditions of profit-seeking capital, the financialization of development and deregulated capital markets (what some have dubbed "casino capitalism"), there has emerged a crisis in global food production, which, combined with an expanding process of "primitive accumulation" (forcing small-scale producers off the land), has deprived millions of the world's poor of the capacity to access the food they need to avoid going hungry or starving (Bello 2008).

Another factor in this "development" has been the conversion of land for food production into biofuels. A secret study by the World Bank, which reportedly has not been made public on pressure from the Bush administration, concludes that biofuel cultivation was directly responsible for the current explosion in grain and food prices worldwide. The US government at the recent Rome UN Food Summit claimed that "only three percent of food prices" were due to biofuels, but the World Bank secret report states that at least 75 percent of the then recent price rises were due to land being removed from agriculture—mainly maize in North America and rape seed and corn in the EU—in order to grow crops to be burned for vehicle fuel. The World Bank study confirmed what many critics have written about the madness of biofuels. It fits the agenda described in the 1970s by Henry Kissinger, namely, "If you control the food you control the people"—again substantiating the point made by UNRISD regarding the centrality of power relations in the poverty-development problematic.

An even greater factor concerns the speculative profit-seeking operations of finance capital. The machinations of global speculative capital and its role in global speculative frenzy—controlling something everybody needs or desires, then holding back the supply to drive up prices and capture windfall profits—is described in detail by Frederick Kaufman, contributing editor of *Harper's Magazine* (Kaufman 2010). The "food bubble" purposively created by Wall Street financers to create a "killing" on the market sparked riots in more than thirty countries and drove the number of the world's "food insecure" to more than a billion. In 2008, for the first time since such statistics had been kept, the proportion of the world's population without enough to eat ratcheted upward.

In a study of the impact of the global financial crisis on poverty, World Bank economists Martin Ravallion and Shaohua Chen (2009) calculate that the crisis in 2008 added another 94 million to the poverty head count just in Latin America, reversing a decade-long trend decline both in the region and worldwide. Moreover, they calculate that globally the ensuing production and food crises in 2009 added another 53 million people to the count of the number of people living below $1.25 a day and 64 million to the count of the number of people living under $2.00 a day. Given current growth projections for 2010, they argue, "there will be a further impact on poverty in that year, with the cumulative impacts rising to an extra 73 million people living under $1.25 a day and 91 million more under $2 a day by 2010."

Inequality and the Washington Consensus

A number of studies by World Bank and other economists concluded that the deeply entrenched and growing inequality in the global distribution of wealth and income is a major source of poverty and a major obstacle in the war on global poverty. The data regarding social inequality are astounding. For example, the poorest 40 percent of the world's population accounts for just 5 percent of global income (and the distribution of wealth is much more unequal!). On the other hand, the richest 20 percent account for three-quarters of world income, and the richest 10 percent consume about 60 percent of the world social product (World Bank 2008). Reducing inequality, concludes Oxfam International's Duncan Green, is essential to reducing poverty. Not only is inequality a fundamental source of poverty, but "the world's yawning social and economic divide" is morally repugnant (2008, 4). There is something deeply unjust, Green observes, "about a system that allows 800 million people to go hungry while an epidemic of obesity blights millions of lives in rich countries" (2008, 4). Extreme inequality, he continues, "provokes outrage and condemnation because it violates the widely held notion that all people, wherever they are, enjoy certain basic rights" (Green 2008, 5). Addressing social inequality and inequity, Green opines, "is essential if countries are to live up to their obligations under the international human rights framework established by the UN" (Green 2008, 5). Yet, he observes, "inequality and redistribution have been out of fashion with rich country decision-makers for many years and warrant barely a mention in the Millennium Development Goals (MDGs), which emerged during the course of the 1990s" (Green 2008, 5).

"In sway to the Washington Consensus view that 'a rising tide lifts all boats,' rich country leaders believed that economic growth alone would be enough to address poverty" (Green 2008, 5). Yet "by 2005 the manifest failure of this approach prompted a rash of high-profile publications from the World Bank, and the UN argued that tackling inequality is one of the most urgent tasks of our time" (Green 2008, 5). The virtual consensus of the economists at the World Bank, ECLAC, and the UNDP is that equality is good for growth and makes that growth more effective at reducing poverty. As Duncan Green argues (2008), reducing inequality is essential to reducing poverty.

More recently, a number of UN organizations have begun to focus more sharply on what the United Nations Department of Economic and Social Affairs (UNDESA) in its 1995 report on the world social situation termed the "inequality predicament." Both ECLAC's (2010a) *Social Panorama of Latin America* and the UNDP's *Regional Human Development Report for Latin America and the Caribbean 2010* identified social inequalities in the access to vital resources and services, the grossly inequitable global distribution of wealth and income, and the free-market policies that exacerbated these inequalities, as the fundamental obstacles to achieving the MDG #1.

In the words of the UNDP's 2010 report, there exists a "direct correspondence between the advance of globalization, neoliberalism, and the advance of poverty social inequality, social inequity. . . . The most explosive contradictions . . . are given because the advance of [neoliberal] globalization marches hand in hand with the advance of poverty and social polarization. It is undeniable that the 1980s and 1990s [were] the creation of an abysmal gap between wealth and poverty" (UNDP 2010, xv). Undeniable it might be, but it was not until very recently that the annual development reports of the UNDP, or the periodic official reports on the poverty problematic over the past decade, made the now obvious connection between inequality and poverty, a connection long made in the scholarly literature critical of capitalist development and globalization in its neoliberal form. ECLAC, in both the 2010 *Social Panorama of Latin America* and its 2010 report on Latin American development (*Time for Equality*), concludes that it is "time for equality: closing gaps, opening trails" and that the agency for doing so is the state, with "international cooperation" and "social participation."

Capitalist development, whether the market is free or regulated, generates social inequality in access to productive resources (which tend to be concentrated), wealth, and the distribution of income. Under these conditions of uneven global capitalist development, poverty can be attenuated by means of government intervention in the market but is nevertheless inevitable. Thus, the ideas and policy prescriptions advanced by Jeffrey Sachs (2005) for putting an end to poverty are not realistic or practical; they are not based on any evidence or social science. The issue for him and for those who reflect the same paradigm is as follows: what institutional and policy frameworks provide the optimum conditions for social welfare and human development, that is, for the alleviation (not the eradication) of poverty?

Recent experience with the macroeconomic and social policies established under the PWC suggest that what is required is to "bring the state back in"—to assign the state a substantive and leading role in establishing an institutional and policy framework for an inclusive and more equitable form of development (Wilson, Kanji, and Braathen 2001). What is required is a "development state" and "a mixed system," that is, a combination of capitalism and socialism—policies that combine regulation of the market and capitalist development with the social inclusion of the poor in public policy formulation, and the empowerment of the poor with a disempowerment of the rich.

A major finding of social scientific research, tacitly acknowledged by the economists at the UNDP and other operational agencies of the UN system, is that the existing distribution of wealth and income is based on power, on the capacity of the rich and powerful to set up a system that works in their interest. Given this economic and political power, and the unavoidable constraints of the macroeconomic policy regime that it sustains, the theorists and practitioners of development in the 1990s counseled reform—social reform in the direction of a new social policy (NSP), economic reform in the direction of a more nuanced macroeconomic policy (pro-poor redistributive growth), and political reform in the direction of decentralized governance and the strengthening of civil society (Ocampo 2007).

The proposed new institutional and policy framework is designed for a socially inclusive and equitable form of local development that builds on the one asset that the poor are deemed to have in abundance: social capital (Ocampo 2004; Uphoff 2004).

Bringing the State Back In: The Post-Washington Consensus

Liberalization through privatization and structural adjustment to reduce fiscal deficits has meant not only less intervention by the state in rural matters but also the dismantling of the institutions traditionally responsible for the sector, making rural development more difficult until these can be replaced with institutions devised by civil society at the local level. The reduction or withdrawal of public sector services has been particularly noticeable in some areas of rural life such as social spending (education, health), the financial system, and infrastructure (Echeverria 1998, 5).

Most countries in Latin America in the 1980s and 1990s complied with the requirements for macroeconomic equilibrium set out in what became known as the Washington Consensus. The results in terms of economic growth and social equity were paltry, although the upturn in 2004–2008 (due to a primary commodities boom) did bring some improvement. Annual growth averaged barely 3.2 percent in 1990–2008 (ECLAC 2010b, 52).

As for poverty, "an over-reliance on market forces and economic liberalization led to neglect of nationally designed and developmentally-oriented strategies, to the detriment of the world's poor."[3] Only at the turn of the new millennium was there any progress in reducing the incidence of absolute or extreme poverty. Research by the economists and sociologists at UNRISD and the IDB (1998d) suggests that this progress "occurred principally through state-directed strategies which combined economic development objectives with active social policies in ways that were complementary and synergistic."[4] As the authors of this study argued, "[i]t was only at the dawn of the new century that the social role of the State came to be seen in a new light, shifting from a focus on poverty (and the segmentation of services according to ability to pay) towards a more integrated vision" (UNRISD 2010, 176). In this connection, the ECLAC (2010b, 171) report on social inequality notes, "the reforms of the 1980s and the impact of the debt crisis actually widened income gaps, and it was only in the past decade that this trend was reversed, thanks to more inclusive labor market dynamics and the State's assumption of a more active role in income transfer."

The most important lesson drawn by the authors from their findings—although they did not take into account steps and actions taken by the poor themselves (migrant remittances, etc.) or the effect of changed conditions in the world market—is that "governments need to play a developmental role, integrating economic and social policies that support inclusive output and employment growth, while attacking inequality and promoting justice" (UNDESA 2009, iii). This is essentially the post-Washington Consensus.

Implications for Public Policy

A major finding and conclusion reached by the academic community is that poverty fundamentally is a structural problem rooted in the social, rather than the institutional, structure of an economic system and that the problem (structured inequalities) has been seriously exacerbated by the policies implemented by virtually all governments over the past three decades under the Washington Consensus. The root cause of poverty can be traced back to the way that society and the economy are organized, with extremes of wealth at one pole and poverty at the other. In the context of this "inequality predicament," the structure and conditions of which can be identified at both the global level and the subnational level, ECLAC (2010b) argues that it is "time for equality—for closing gaps, opening trails." In other words, it is time to act and to do so collectively, with the agency of government intervention, international cooperation and social participation.

The policy framework for this action is constituted by measures designed (1) to substantively change the structure of social inequalities in the global and national distributions of wealth and income and to improve access of the poor to means of production and productive resources (land, capital, technology, etc.) and (2) to ensure democratic governance and a participatory form of development that empowers the poor. This means, above all, allowing the poor to take charge of, and take ownership of, their own development effort—to take action for themselves, with the support of their government and the international development community.

The Agency of the State, With International Cooperation and Social Participation

An analysis of the conditions of the relative success in having achieved an appreciable reduction in the incidence of extreme poverty over the past decade, notwithstanding a failure to change the basic social structure of poverty, has demonstrated the importance and the centrality of the agency of the state. By diverse academic accounts and official reports, a major agency of this poverty reduction was government intervention, with international cooperation and social participation, in the form of a strategy formulated and pursued within the framework of a new consensus and a new Comprehensive Development Framework, as well as a new development paradigm.

Pathways Out of Rural Poverty: Where Development Comes In

According to the World Bank in its *World Development Report 2008: Agriculture for Development*, there are three major pathways out of rural poverty: (1) farming, (2) labor, and (3) migration. Each pathway, the report points out, is littered with obstacles and pitfalls that can be removed or overcome with appropriate policy intervention and international cooperation.

Farming. In this sector analysts and theorists have identified two basic models for organizing agricultural production and farming. From the perspective of economists at the World Bank, the forces of productive and social transformation at play in the process of capitalist development point to the need for a model of corporate capitalism. This corporate model of large-scale agricultural production and a global food regime (see Akram-Lodhi 2011) is geared to the forces of change at work in the global economy and links the producer to the system of capital, markets, and technology needed to expand production and is designed to ensure the increased productivity of agricultural labor and the capacity of producers to compete on the world market.

However, farming on this model provides a pathway for very few of the rural poor; the vast majority are unable to take this pathway. For one thing, it requires that the small-holder "peasant" farmer be converted into a capitalist entrepreneur, able to access capital, modern technology, and the world market. Thus, many analysts conclude that for the rural poor, the more appropriate model—a model more likely able to sustain rural livelihoods and reverse pressures to abandon farming as a way of life—is one advanced by diverse organizations of peasant producers and articulated in theoretical terms by a growing community of scholars of agrarian change and rural development (Akram-Lodhi, Borras, and Kay 2007). The model is one of small-scale agricultural production based on principles of cooperation, solidarity, and food sovereignty.

The policies prescribed by this model (see Kay 2009) include support for the small-scale producer, including land reform (expropriation of land not in productive or social use, land redistribution, legal security), credit, price support, and protection of local markets from forces of undue foreign competition.

Labor. Labor is regarded by political economists in both the classical tradition and the Marxist tradition to be the major driving force for economic development. However, labor, in one form or the other, is also seen as a, if not the, major pathway out of rural poverty. In this respect it is of critical importance that governments, with international cooperation and social participation, design and implement policies that facilitate the incorporation of the rural poor into the labor force, be it in the formal sector of paid employment (waged or salaried labor) or, as is increasingly the case, in the informal sector. In regard to the former, the policy should include social inclusion in government programs in the areas of education, health, and social security. In regard to the latter, the best or most frequently recommended policy is for governments to provide credit and microfinance. A microcredit or microfinance strategy of local development has been promoted by the Inter-American Development Bank in its interventions over the past two decades. By a number of accounts the strategy has had a measure of success in reducing poverty. However, the strategy has also had its share of critics (see, for example, Weber 2002), and the precise contribution of the strategy and associated policies to redressing poverty is not clear. It awaits a more definitive systematic evaluation.

Migration. Migration to the cities or beyond—to the United States, Canada, Europe, or elsewhere in the region—has also been conceived to be an important pathway out of poverty, both rural and urban (World Bank 2008). In the case of Bolivia, it is estimated that over 50 percent of Bolivians now live and work abroad, and the number of Mexicans who have crossed the border as an escape from rural poverty or in search of better conditions and opportunities is in the many millions. People migrate for all sorts of reasons: poverty to be sure, but also out of landlessness, insecure or unsustainable livelihoods, and the search for new opportunities, employment, and better conditions for themselves and their children. Migration, however, is also a mixed blessing. While providing an avenue for mobility or improved conditions for individuals, it also deprives many rural communities of their most productive members, exacerbating conditions of rural poverty.

On the other hand, it has been argued that migration is a factor of rural development in the form of migrant remittances, which in many communities constitutes a major source of foreign exchange—in the case of Mexico, second only to oil exports and greater than manufactured products.

Currently, governments both in the region and abroad do not actively promote outmigration, that is, they do not have any policies explicitly designed to support or to induce outmigration. But some of them do have policies designed to help migrants adjust to their new situation or to protect their rights (although this is primarily a responsibility assumed by or assigned to the NGOs in the area rather than governments). In this connection, governments should implement policies designed to integrate migrants into city life—to facilitate their incorporation into the labor market and ensure inclusion in social programs and services, particularly education, that facilitate their adjustment to a new life.

It has been discovered by both researchers and governments that on the whole, migrants are disproportionately entrepreneurial—that is, that they have a greater-than-average propensity for innovation, self-employment, and setting up their own enterprises. In this, migrants constitute a major driving force for economic development. To take measures, such as credit provision, designed to take advantage of this propensity would be of benefit to the recipient community or country, as well as the migrants themselves.

Fiscal Expenditures: Investment in People (Human Capital)

A key feature of the PWC is a new social policy targeted at the poor and the inclusion of the poor in social programs designed to (1) provide the infrastructure for social development (health, education, security) and (2) capacitate the poor in taking advantage of existing "opportunities" for self-development and improvement in their social condition.

Regarding the agency of governments within this consensus, the policy entails measures designed for decentralization, greater inclusion in social programs, local development, and targeting of the poor in social expenditures. The problem with this policy, and the entire strategy within which it is framed, is that the policy and the strategy are predicated on the building and mobilization of social capital. The problem is that while a social-capital strategy (Durston 2001) has proven to be relatively effective at the level of community-based local development, it has also proven to have severe limitations. First, in focusing on social capital to the exclusion of improved access to building other forms of capital, improved access to which requires government intervention, it seriously reduces the scope of economic development, which requires improved access to natural, physical, and financial forms of capital as well as social capital. Second, it is predicated on the poor seeking to make improvements and change within the local spaces of the "power structure," which, a number of studies suggest, is a major structural source of poverty and a major impediment to the poor. In this circumstance, a better policy vis-à-vis empowering the poor would be to assist them in their struggle to challenge the rich and the powerful—to intervene in this struggle on the side of the poor, rather than the rich and powerful, who, according to the UNDP in its latest report on human development in Latin America (UNDP 2010), tend to have much greater access to the levers of political power.

UNRISD in its 2010 poverty report makes precisely the same point, one that has been made for decades by scholars in the political economy tradition but that only recently seems to have dawned on the consciousness of the development practitioners within the UN system. With this convergence in academic (theoretical) and policy perspectives, redressing the inequality predicament can be taken as the most effective policy response to the poverty problematic. Unfortunately, neither the academic literature nor the two UN system reports provide any policy guidelines or prescribe any precise policies. At the moment there appears to be no adequate or defined policy response to a problem that is of critical concern to the social movements in the region. On this see Petras and Veltmeyer (2011b).

As for the poverty problematic more generally, in addition to structural change vis-à-vis inequality, an effective policy response has proven to be, or would be, for governments to include the poor in their social programs and to target them in their social polices. Every country in Latin America over the course of the 1990s, in the context of the PWC, has formulated a variation of the NSP and designed a program of measures to implement it. Although there has not been any systematic and comparative evaluation of these policies, it is nevertheless evident that the policy has had positive outcomes and results and is a contributing, if not determinant, factor in the relative success of some countries in the region having reduced the incidence of extreme poverty over the past decade.

Over this period a number of countries, with very different policy regimes that range from the "orthodox neoliberal" (Mexico, Peru, Colombia) and "pragmatic neoliberal/social liberal" (Chile under Bachelet, Argentina, Brazil) to the radical populist/socialist (Bolivia, Ecuador, Venezuela), have had a measure of success in reducing the incidence of extreme poverty. Each country, irrespective of the ideological orientation of the governing regime, essentially pursued the same policies, with different degrees of success. Perhaps the most successful case—widely regarded as an exemplar or the paradigmatic case of the NSP—is Brazil, which has managed to reduce the rate of extreme poverty by 40 percent in just five years. In various scholarly assessments of this record, there are four determinant factors of this success: (1) various policy measures designed to redress the country's inequality predicament (ECLAC 2010b; UNDESA 2005); (2) increased and targeted expenditures on social programs; (3) social inclusion of the poor, and their active participation; and, most notably, (4) direct cash transfers to the poor, conditional on their inclusion and participation. This conditional cash transfer approach (see chapter 8) is now widely touted as the model of the NSP for reducing the incidence of extreme poverty. The policy is a new form of social welfarism in which the poor are expected to, and do, assume a more active role in the development process.

The strategy and policies of poverty reduction in Latin America in the new millennium have generally been constructed and pursued within the framework of a PWC predicated on the institutional framework of a capitalist system of economic production and development—on state-led social reform of these institutions. However, two countries in the region have pursued a different approach: the same strategy and policies but within a different systemic framework: socialism, in the case of Cuba, and a mixed economy (socialism of the twenty-first century) in the case of Venezuela.

In the case of Cuba, poverty in its extreme form (absolute poverty) by 1985 to all intents had been eradicated in a strategy of socialist human development, pursued in the 1960s and 1970s, but the specter of income poverty reemerged in the 1990s in the wake of the collapse of socialism in the USSR and in the context of a major economic downturn, which required of the regime a program of "structural adjustment" (market-oriented policy reform). This structural adjustment strategy and associated policies of economic reform by some accounts (Espina Prieto 2008) generated new forms of structured social inequalities that accentuated the poverty problematic of the economic downturn. However, a continuing policy of socialist human development pursued by the government, not unlike the policy implemented by other governments in the region within a different institutional and systemic framework (although in the case of Cuba, not one school or one clinic has closed down), meant that the emerging inequalities and poverty were kept in check.

As for Venezuela, poverty over the same period in the new millennium was targeted and attacked systematically, not only in the inclusion of the poor in new social programs (*misiones sociales*) and the targeting of expenditures and investments on the poor but also by a policy of engaging the poor directly in decision making at the level of community development. The basic mechanism of this development "from below" was the institution of the Community Council. Again, in regard to the improvement image in social conditions vis-à-vis poverty, the relative contribution of the NSP implemented by the government and broader structural change is not at all clear. This issue needs a closer look and further study.

As for international cooperation in the policy arena of social programs and participatory development, the dominant strategy, formulated by World Bank economists in 1989 and advanced thereafter, has been to require governments to prepare a Poverty Reduction Strategy Paper (PRSP) as a condition of financial and technical assistance (see chapter 7). Although once again there have not been any systematic evaluations of this strategy and the policies that flow from it (existing studies include Dijkstra 2005; Klugman 2002; Morrow 2001), indications are that the policy has been somewhat effective. As to whether the success of countries in the region on the poverty reduction front can be attributed to this strategy, to changed conditions in the global economy, or to actions taken by the poor themselves is not clear. Nevertheless, based on the evidence there is no reason not to pursue this strategy. At the very least, it is a useful part of the multifaceted strategy that is called for in the war on global poverty.

The Academic Pivot: Explaining Poverty Up Close and From Afar

Explanation is a matter of theory, identifying the critical factors involved in making people poor and keeping them poor, preventing effective action. At this level numerous factors have been identified over the years, but they can be sorted into two categories: factors that relate to the type of individual involved or conditions (for example, values and attitudes) for which the individual might be held responsible or could change, and factors that relate to the social or economic system, that is, the predominant form of social and economic organization, the working of which creates conditions that are "objective" in their effects on the individual, essentially determining who is rich and who is or will become poor.

Explanations of poverty given in both academic studies and an array of poverty-watch organizations and research centers have ranged from discriminatory practices and attitudes, lack of equal opportunity, barriers to accessing strategic resources, lack of education, exclusion from essential government services or other resources or assets, policy biases or dysfunctional institutions, and diverse systemic factors such as the capitalist mode of production, neoliberal globalization, exploitation, the policy agenda and institutional framework, systemic forces, location in the social structure or geographical marginalization, and so on.

What is most striking about the explanations given by economists and sociologists over the past sixty years of development efforts, and used by governments and international organizations to inform policy or action, is the lack of congruence between theory and practice—between the type and range of explanations given most often by academics in their studies of poverty and the strategies pursued and actions taken by the governments and organizations that have led the fight against poverty at the global level. Sociologists for the most part, and also those economists oriented toward a structural or some institutional form of analysis, have emphasized structural factors and generally insisted that poverty is a function of the way that the society or economy is organized—the "structure" of institutionalized practices, the dynamics and machinations of economic and political power rather than social exclusion, or a failure of the poor to grasp and act on their "opportunities."

However, policymakers, and also organizations such as the World Bank that define poverty alleviation or reduction as their mandate, generally locate the source of poverty not in the system itself but in the culture of poverty, a culture that traps the poor and prevents them from taking action to seize their opportunities and take one of the available pathways out of poverty. In effect, they blame the poor themselves for their poverty.

The thinking that prevails in the global circuit of policymaking is reflected in a report tabled by the G8 in its 2000 summit. In this study "poverty" is defined as a condition of "multidimensional deprivation" that reflects not only a lack of income and resources but also a dearth of opportunities caused by "low capabilities and geographical and social exclusion" and an inability to access resources and essential services. For example, limited access to education affects the ability of the poor to get jobs and to obtain information that could improve the quality of their lives. Poor health due to inadequate nutrition, hygiene, and health services further limits their prospects for work and from realizing their mental and physical potential.

As for the "structural" (or systemic) explanations of poverty, a large number of studies seek to establish as a fact that poverty is a social condition at one extreme of the unequal distribution of wealth and income, a socioeconomic structure that is undoubtedly the result or "product" of specific social relations of production and power dominated by the rich and powerful and beyond the ability of the poor to control or affect in any way—a structure that arises from actions taken and institutionalized practices, which, as the sociologist Durkheim emphasized, are "external to individuals" and "coercive in their effects" on them.

What the UN in a 2005 report dubbed the "the inequality predicament"—the unequal distribution of wealth and income to such an extreme that just 350 of the world's super rich dispose of more income than all of the world's poor together, some 1.4 billion the world's poorest—is a major source of enduring poverty. In fact, if the poorest 47 percent of the world (about 2.7 billion persons) were to pool their incomes, they could barely purchase the assets of the world's wealthiest 225 individuals (UNDP 1999, 3). The gross domestic product (GDP) of the forty-one Heavily Indebted Poor Countries (567 million people) is less than the wealth of the world's seven richest people combined. Thus, any "solution" to the poverty problematic should take into account and change the system that generates poverty and keeps the poor in their place (Chossudovsky 1997). As noted by Cimadamore, Dean, and Siqueira (2005), it must fall to the state, the greatest repository of power, capacity, and authority—if not the political will—to allocate more equitably the productive resources of the society, or at least to regulate the market, the economic institution that the rich and powerful have used so effectively to advance their economic interests.

A study by Weisbrot et al. (2005) makes this connection clear—that poverty is the indirect consequence of policies and a system that generated a huge concentration of wealth, sprouting an enormous number of billionaires in conditions of deepening and spreading poverty in the developing countries. The Center for Economic Policy and Research, a network of critical economists, put the neoliberal hypothesis—that if the poor countries were to let their economies be dominated by private capital and the free market, they would converge with the rich countries—to the test. It divided countries into five groups, from the poorest to the richest. Then it compared how these countries fared between 1960 and 1980 (before the introduction of neoliberal policies) and 1980 to 2000 (when these policies were widely embraced). The results reveal the impact of neoliberal policies, touted by the World Bank as "pro-poor." The study concludes that the neoliberal policy reform agenda recommended, but not imposed, by the World Bank has a deleterious effect on developing countries, reducing their economic status (and creating new forms of poverty) relative to states (mostly in Asia) that did not embrace the neoliberal policy reform agenda.

Structuralism in its most persuasive form has brought to light the connection between social inequality and poverty on the one hand and policies
pursued over the past two decades under the Washington Consensus, as well
as conditions of global multiple crises generated by these policies, on the other.
In diverse "structuralist" accounts, the world is on the threshold, if not in the
throes, of a crisis that will dramatically reduce the capacity of billions of the
world's population, with few resources and little income, to access potable water and nutritious food and affordable housing, sinking them further into the
morass of hunger. For example, the doubling of world food prices in conditions of a global financial meltdown and recession since 2008 has forced an
added 100 million people below the poverty line, triggering food riots from
Bangladesh and Egypt to Haiti.

A striking if puzzling feature of the many reports on poverty by the World
Bank and other international organizations is that they have documented at
length, and illustrated with tables and graphs, the complex and varied dimensions, forms, and conditions of poverty but yet managed to elude any reference
to its structural sources, attributing it instead to various deficiencies of the
poor themselves or to institutional rigidities, social exclusions, or prejudices
that can be remediated by education, rational argument, or legislation. It is as
if the economists at the Bank know everything there is to know about poverty
but understand nothing.

Who and Where Are the Poor? Measurement Matters

Most of the debate and controversy surrounding the concept of poverty has to
do with matters of methodology and measurement rather than conceptual issues. Poverty is conceptualized by virtual consensus as a state of deprivation, a
condition in which individuals or households lack the capacity or the resources
needed to have a minimally decent standard or quality of life—to meet their
basic needs. Over the years, there has been some discussion as to the range and
number of these needs, ranging from five basic needs to as many as twenty-seven
(Max-Neef 1986), including nonphysical or "spiritual" needs such as freedom
of choice and participation in decisions that affect one's life. This discussion has
been limited, however, compared to the debate surrounding the question of
how to operationalize these "needs"—how to move from conception to measurement (translate a theoretical definition into an empirical indicator).

Where controversy has arisen is at the level of empirical measure—how
to measure the quality of life of the population within different societies and
to measure shortfalls and deficits related to basic needs (Laderchi, Saith, and
Stewart 2003; Streeten 1998). At this level, the center of debate has been on

the use of GDP per capita as a measure of "development" conceptualized as economic "growth" and poverty as a deficit in the distribution of this growth. At issue in a series of unsettled debates is in regard to the World Bank's methodology of a universal standard for a poverty line, adjusted to local purchasing power, in which poverty is defined empirically in income terms as having to subsist on less than $2.00 a day (now $2.50)—extreme poverty as $1.00 (now $1.25) a day. By these measures around 2.4 billion people, around a third of the world population, today are deemed to be poor—about half of them destitute or extremely poor.

This methodology, used by most international development associations, differs from that used by many governments, such as the United States, China, India, and so on, in which the poverty income line is measured in terms of a basket of goods needed to meet basic needs. This measurement methodology has been fraught with controversy, however, and the surrounding debate has not yet been settled. One issue has to do with the rather arbitrary nature of setting the poverty line. The issue has plagued policymakers for years. How should a country define a reasonable poverty line? At issue is who and how many in the population are deserving and in need of government support. In both China and India, the official poverty line is below the World Bank's already conservative $2.00 per day (India's by about 75 percent, and China's by about 25 percent). This is because important basic needs are not being included. India's "basket," for example, specifies three basic meals a day and nominal expenditure on health care and education but does not include expenditures for housing or transport (the same is true of China). In many other countries, even after housing and transport costs are factored in, it is evident that there are large groups and numbers of people just above the official poverty line or the World Bank's poverty line who are in need, even dire need, and in poverty by any reasonable definition or other calculations and judgments.

Academic studies by sociologists or welfare economists on the whole have opted for an alternative methodology for measuring poverty based on the integration of the income factor into a broader measure or index that includes a number of nonincome conditions of poverty such as access to nutritious food, health care, education, housing, transportation, and other vital services that in many countries are "commodities" (not services provided by the government). In this methodology, the concept of poverty is operationalized in terms of variables such as (1) the percentage of the population age fifteen years and older that is illiterate; (2) the percentage of the same population that has not finished primary school; (3) child mortality rates; (4) the percentage of the population with public health insurance and pensions; and, in the area of housing, (5) the percentage of houses with running water or (6) with sewer systems and (7) with electricity.

By using an "integrated" measure of poverty understood in its acute conditions and multidimensional forms, and that includes a number of these "basic needs" variables, the number of the population deemed to be poor can be considerably higher than measured by the poverty line approach. For a systematic analysis of the limitations of conventional measures of poverty, and a proposal for a "new index for developing countries," see Alkire and Santos (2010).

Poverty Reduction Programs and the Rural Poor

There are a number of mutually reinforcing alternatives for addressing the problems of rural poverty. These alternatives cover a wide range of possibilities from overall planning to specific details. Five approaches may be considered central to design of a strategy for reducing rural poverty: (1) a favorable institutional and policy framework, (2) affirmative action programs to assist the poor, (3) sustainability, (4) investments in human capital, and (5) greater participation by communities in designing and carrying out strategies (Echeverria 1998; IDB 1998a, 1998b).

The World Bank, together with the IMF, in 1999 formulated a new approach to its lending policy in regard to promoting Wolfensohn's Comprehensive Development Framework (CDF) and enhancing the implementation by governments of their own poverty reduction strategies. The approach was simple in concept but potentially radical in its implications for development assistance. It was to require all governments, as a condition of accessing official "assistance" from the Bank and the Fund, to prepare a PRSP in which the government outlines the steps it proposes to undertake in the direction of reducing poverty. The PRSP must be prepared through a participatory process involving both domestic stakeholders and external development partners. The PRSP approach, in effect (or at least as the Bank understood or presented it), is based on "country ownership" and "participation" (Dijkstra 2005; Klugman 2002; Morrow 2001).

Anthony O'Malley (see chapter 5) identifies four schools of thought ("perspectives") on how to achieve poverty reduction, each with a number of cons and pros, though the program as a whole awaits a more systematic assessment and evaluation.

Pathways and Public Policies

As Alain De Janvry, one of the leading authors of the World Bank's *World Development Report 2008: Agriculture for Development*, noted in an earlier study on poverty in Latin America, the exodus of the poor to the cities had been, and still was, the primary mechanism of poverty reduction in the region, explaining virtually all of the advances made on the rural front of the global war on poverty. "Reduction in the number of rural relative to urban poor," De Janvry and Sadoulet (2000, 389) argued, "has been mainly the outcome of migration, not of successful rural development."

The authors conceived of four "exit paths" available to the rural poor: exiting (outmigration), agriculture (farming), development (assistance), and pluriactive, with reference here to the livelihood strategies pursued by many if not most of the rural poor, which is to combine farming with off-farm wage labor. Without going into details, then as now (at least in Latin America) most of the rural poor remain poor not because of the low productivity of agricultural activity or their regressive worldview but because they have been rendered landless or near landless in a process of "primitive accumulation" of capital. Dispossessed of their means of social production, they had little choice but to turn from direct production to labor in one form or another, working the land owned by others or, more often, searching for nonfarm employment in the countryside or in the cities. Most of the rural poor had (and still have) no option but to turn from farming to migration and labor, often both.

In this view—entirely, and in many cases quite consciously, ignoring the structural sources of poverty—the only way out of poverty is for the poor to participate in the opportunity structure of modern industrial-urban capitalist society, and the best policy advice that can be given to the poor is for them to adjust to, and not resist, the forces of change. "Development" in this context implies intervention in the form of helping the poor make this adjustment—to capacitate them to take advantage of the opportunities open or made available to them, a policy matter of "equity," "inclusion," "participation," "empowerment," and "good governance" (World Bank 1994a; UNDP 2006; Bebbington, Hickey, and Mitlin 2008).

In the Latin American context, the rural poor include large numbers of landless or near landless peasants, but most, over 50 percent in many cases, are semiproletarianized, that is, in their livelihood strategy they have to combine agricultural production or tenant farming with wage labor—what the World Bank economists conceive of as the labor-migration (De Janvry's pluriactive) pathway out of poverty.

In theory, the labor released from the land would be absorbed by urban industry, incorporated into the labor markets of the growing urban centers. But reality has not confirmed this theory. In practice what has occurred is a process of partial or semiproletarianization. Rather than being converted into a modern urban-centered working class, the vast majority of the rural poor, dispossessed of the land, has been converted into a rural semiproletariat, retaining access to some land but increasingly reliant on wage labor as a means of livelihood and household income, and an urban semiproletariat of informal workers, working "on their own account" on the streets rather than exchanging their labor power against capital. Over 50 percent of the rural poor in Latin America can be categorized as semiproletarianized in these terms, with substantial evidence to suggest that they will never complete the theorized transition—the process of social transformation into a modern wage-earning working class.

The role of the state (the government, to be precise), with international cooperation, is to assist the rural poor in this process of productive and social transformation—to pave their chosen path out of poverty, facilitating access to productive resources such as education and a decent job, and to ensure their inclusion in essential government services, empowering them to act, develop their capabilities, and seize their opportunities for self-advancement.

The Politics of Poverty Reduction

There is an obvious theoretical blind spot in the World Bank's 2008 *World Development Report*, trapped as it is in the old paradigm of modernization theory, which is that the pathways out of poverty identified are conceived entirely in terms of economic adjustment to the presumably irresistible forces of agrarian transformation and capitalist development. In these terms, the opportunities of the rural poor to "farm their way out of poverty" are few, and the majority are expected—and encouraged—to take the pathways of labor and outmigration.

The report's "three world" categorization (agriculture based, transforming, and urban) suggests a remarkably uniform triad pathway out of rural poverty: (1) commercially oriented entrepreneurial smallholder farming, (2) rural nonfarm enterprise development, and, more particularly, (3) rural nonfarm waged labor, outmigration, or both. These pathways can be complementary and mutually reinforcing. In the report's typology of livelihood strategies, it is the latter two (outmigration and rural income diversification) that are usually found to be the normal route out of rural poverty.

What is surprising, considering the extensive field experience of at least one of the report's leading authors (De Janvry) in the contentious area of land reform, is how it entirely ignores the struggle of small-scale agricultural producers and other categories of "peasants" that make up the bulk of the rural poor in each of the "three worlds," the political dynamics of social change that arise out of this struggle, and the "voices of the hitherto excluded"—which the World Bank itself commissioned but subsequently ignored; voices that have been loudly raised by the international peasant movement *Vía Campesina* against the economic model used by the World Bank to guide its thinking and practice.

In Latin America, for example, the struggle for land reform has brought the small-scale producers and the mass of landless and near landless "workers"— generally conceived of as "peasants" in diverse forms—into a relation of political conflict with the big landlords and rural bourgeoisie, who through different means under changing conditions in diverse rural contexts managed to acquire the lion's share of the arable and productive land, and also the state apparatus, which in this context generally assumes responsibility for mediating this conflict.

Conclusion

Few problems have engaged as much attention and concern over the past five decades of capitalist development as poverty—the inability of a substantial part of humanity to satisfy even their basic human needs in a context of unparalleled wealth, the result of an unprecedented global expansion of society's forces of production based on new forms of social cooperation and technological development. Poverty in a world of plenty, it could be said, is a monstrous problem and totally unacceptable because it is incontrovertible that the global community of nations and international organizations has at its disposal the means and more-than-sufficient resources needed to "make poverty history."

The question that then arises, which we tackle in this volume from different angles and perspectives, is, What explains the fact that until recently so much effort and so many resources targeted at the problem in such a long war resulted in so little improvement, so little change? And what, if anything, has changed in the new millennium, when, according to diverse official reports, the problem of global poverty has finally begun to yield signs of improvement? Is it changes in the global economy, as some have argued? Is it because the poor have taken in greater numbers the pathways out of poverty available to them, paved by actions taken by governments with international cooperation? Or is it, as the architects and officials of international cooperation for development allege in their self-congratulatory official "reports," the result of the successful new millennium poverty reduction strategy constructed by the international development community and pursued by governments with international cooperation and social participation?

It is too early in this book to arrive at an indicative or definitive answer to these questions. The one overriding conclusion that we have come to on the basis of a review of the academic literature and the official reports on the poverty-development problematic is that any proposed solution to the problem must address, and come to terms with, what has been described as the "inequality predicament." The predicament is how to ensure a more equitable distribution of the world's wealth and the income-generating assets built up globally on the basis of social cooperation—how to prevent the appropriation of these assets by the super rich, a small number of powerful men acting and free to act in their own interest and at the expense of the many. The problematic of this predicament is the subject matter of subsequent chapters, but we can anticipate the discussion and analysis provided in these chapters with the observation made by the authors of the ECLAC report (2010b) on the war on poverty in the region: "It is time for equality—for closing gaps and opening pathways."

Notes

1. Cited from the UNDP website: http://content.undp.org/go/newsroom/2010/july/pnud-presenta-el-primer-informe-regional-sobre-desarrollo-humano.en.

2. This section can be found in www.ipc-undp.org/pub/IPCPovertyInFocus12.pdf.

3. Cited from the UNDP website, with reference to UNDESA (2009): www.un.org/en/development/desa/newsletter/desanews/publication/2010/02/index.html.

4. Cited from UNRISD's website, with reference to UNRISD (2010): www.unrisd.org/80256B3C005BB128/(httpProjects)/791B1580A0FFF8E5C12574670042C091?OpenDocument.

2

Banking on the Poor

The World Bank and the Assault on Poverty

João Márcio Mendes Pereira

Created in 1944 and in operation since 1946, the World Bank has always worked the synergies between making loans and framing economic thought in order to expand its influence and institutionalize its policy platform on the international level. Recent research argues that the World Bank has acted since its origins as a political, intellectual, and financial agent. The Bank has done so in varying forms via its unique position as a lender, policy formulator, and salesman of ideas. These ideas have largely been generated by the predominant Anglo-Saxon community and disseminated (or produced) by the Bank in conformity with its conventions to determine what, how, and for whom capitalism should be developed (Mendes Pereira 2010a; 2010b).

Since the 1950s, the Bank has been at the center of international debates about development, in which one of the principal dimensions has been poverty reduction. However, few studies have examined the contribution of the Bank's political and intellectual activity to link development to poverty relief and consider these themes as legitimate objects of economic and public policy research. In this sense, this chapter seeks to contribute a historical perspective to understanding the idea of the "assault on poverty" as advocated by the Bank.

The chapter begins with an examination of the introduction and institutional enthronement of the "assault on poverty" directive during the 1968–81 Bank presidency of Robert Strange McNamara. These were years of Cold War tensions and negotiations, US reconsideration of foreign development aid, and debate among mainstream thinkers about such policies. Next, the chapter discusses why the "assault on poverty" idea was gutted from the Bank's operational agenda during the 1980s, only to return at the end of the decade as a means of justifying the implementation of structural adjustment programs in collaboration with the International Monetary Fund. Thereafter, it is argued that the World Bank emphasized the neoliberalization of social policy, prescribing and legitimating palliative relief projects, and focused on getting national states to see a "war on poverty" as a preferential instrument of action for dealing with the "social question." In this context, the research concludes that basic ideological continuities oriented Bank prescriptions from the 1970s to the 1990s, such as confidence in "trickle-down effect" and a social policy vision centered on minimal social goals.

World Bank Expansion during the McNamara Administration (1968–81)

The arrival of Robert McNamara as president of the World Bank in April 1968 profoundly marked the history of the institution. If before his arrival the Bank was "almost an appendage of the US Treasury Department" (Ayres 1983, 7), with McNamara at the Bank it moved closer to the political rather than economic sphere of the US government, taking on an even more central role in the diplomacy of development (Babb 2009, 89–90).

As he was former secretary of the US Department of Defense, it is no surprise that McNamara's tenure at the Bank was marked by his focus on connections between security and development. Growing recognition of the failure of the predominantly military route followed by the United States in the Vietnam War reinforced the idea that the "security" of the United States depended not only on arms but also on the preservation of political order, an order that could be obtained, it was thought, by means of economic growth, improving basic social indicators and reducing socioeconomic inequality. In a book that McNamara published shortly before taking on the World Bank job, he wrote, "Poverty and social injustice may endanger our national security as much as any military threat" (1968, 123). For McNamara, the relationship between poverty and political instability was valid for any society marked by deep inequality.

Reflecting about the post–World War II processes that had increased the gap between rich and poor nations, McNamara considered that the "economic backwardness" of some countries, as well as the contradictions of capitalist modernization in others, would open the door to communist influence (McNamara 1968, 146). Based on this diagnosis, security and development seemed like a dancing couple, one following the other's lead: "In modernizing societies security means development. . . . Without internal development of at least a minimal degree, order and stability are impossible" (McNamara 1968, 149).

From the beginning of his mandate, McNamara was influenced by the impact of the Vietnam War on US foreign policy. At the end of the 1960s, with the bipartisan consensus on foreign policy torn asunder, the political parties abandoned the containment policy that had shaped US actions since 1947. On the domestic political scene, the same wave of fragmentation eroded the bases of support for international development assistance and eliminated congressional acquiescence about foreign topics. The corollary of this was the growing interference of Congress in bilateral and multilateral foreign policy decisions, including closer monitoring of US participation in the World Bank (Gwin 1997; Babb 2009).

The McNamara administration operated in this context, and the objective to consolidate the Bank as a "development agency" arose, to great extent, as a response to these circumstances. The US government actively supported this shift in the Bank's mission. At the end of the 1960s and beginning of the 1970s, with Richard M. Nixon as president of the country, there was growing conviction in Washington that it was necessary to diversify the sources of assistance in the context of bilateral relations. Thus, in a September 1970 message to Congress, Nixon proposed a thorough reorganization of the bilateral assistance programs and reinforcement of multilateral aid. For the government, multilateral development banks (MDBs) could stimulate foreign direct investments for geopolitically important peripheral countries without straining limited domestic support for international aid. Moreover, funds dressed in the clothes of multilateralism would help the United States depoliticize its foreign influence and thus avoid direct conflict with certain governments, a likely outcome of bilateral aid. The emphasis on multilateral assistance would also alleviate the financial costs of foreign policy on the federal budget as North America passed through difficult economic times (Gwin 1997, 211–13). Finally, the multilateral clothing provided by use of the MDBs would permit Washington to shun internal criticism of the Vietnam War and the administration's support for the military coups and dictatorial regimes that it promoted throughout the so-called Third World (Burbach and Flynn 1982, 72–73).

In his first days as president of the Bank, McNamara reflected on "the disenchantment of the rich with the future of development aid" and noted "the disappointing picture of the development world" that many in his circle held (McNamara 1973, 17). According to McNamara, this disappointing picture arose from two main observations: (1) that the rich nations did not have enough surplus to adequately support poor nations and (2) that investment in poor countries was not smart because their governments tended to squander the funds "in waste, incompetence and failure" (McNamara 1973, 9). This evaluation implied a recognition that the dominant model of foreign aid had failed and that the expected "trickle-down effect" had not occurred.[1] Thus, to McNamara, the idea that economic growth necessarily leads to poverty reduction no longer seemed valid. On the one hand, it was necessary to analytically distinguish the two processes, opening the space required to approach both goals separately and directly. On the other, McNamara refused to admit that poverty reduction could come only at the cost of growth, a position held by the great majority of Bank economists at the time. During his entire administration, McNamara insisted on the centrality of economic growth (Kapur, Lewis, and Webb 1997, 217).

Launched in the first five-year period of his presidency (1968–73), the directive to reduce poverty actually followed suit with changes in the sectorial portfolio of the Bank initiated during the Bank presidency of George Woods (1963–68), only now at a much greater scale and on a new basis. McNamara announced that agriculture would experience the greatest expansion among sectors in the portfolio, arguing that it constituted "the critical aspect on which economic growth must be based in most developing countries" (World Bank 1968, 11–12). He also announced the elevation of "social" projects as a Bank priority. Traditionally considered nonproductive expenditures due to a lack of direct economic return, from then on such areas as education, potable water, sewage and sanitation, nutrition, primary health care, urban housing, and family planning received competitive levels of attention from the Bank.

Beyond changes in sectorial allocations, McNamara determined that there would also be changes in loan destinations. Loans to Asia should be intensified, he directed, especially with the return of Indonesia as a Bank client after a military coup backed by the United States brought General Suharto to power (Toussaint 2006, 110–11). But the priority "targets" for investment were Africa and Latin America.

In the name of an "assault on poverty," loans for the first five-year plan period overtook the outlay for the entire twenty-year history of the Bank. And for each client state the Bank established annual lending goals and determined that performance of staff would thereafter be evaluated by the volume of resources involved in the projects under his or her responsibility (Rich 1994, 82–83; Kapur, Lewis, and Webb 1997, 220). The imperative to "move money" at any cost became, in this way, one of the most marked traces of the organizational culture of the Bank. To create demand for its financing, the Bank sent its technicians to the field to sell financeable projects to the governments of client states (George and Sabelli 1996, 57–58). From the perspective of the clients, access to World Bank funds served as a catalyst to borrowing from public and private external sources.

In 1969, as part of this expansive movement and the growing emphasis on the rural sector, the Bank collaborated with the Ford and Rockefeller foundations to create an international network of agricultural research centers to stimulate the worldwide diffusion of the technological modernization packet known as the Green Revolution. The initiative culminated in 1971 with the creation of the Consultative Group on International Agricultural Research (CGIAR) (Mason and Asher 1973, 574). Almost immediately, the new system gained strong public and private support, and in the first ten years the number of donors (governments, multilateral agencies, and foundations) grew from sixteen to thirty-three. Two led the list: (1) the US Agency for International Development (USAID), which contributed 25 percent of the group's resources, and (2) the World Bank, responsible for 10 percent of its resources (Kapur, Lewis, and Webb 1997, 399–401).

From the beginning of the 1970s, CGIAR produced seminal studies on the first generation of varietal wheat and rice with a high level of resistance to pesticides and fertilizers produced in Mexico and the Philippines. The exceptional results of some harvests and a forceful propaganda campaign reinforced the idea that investing in CGIAR was highly profitable (Kapur, Lewis, and Webb 1997, 401). Articulated between the Bank and its bilateral partners, loans and technical assistance projects prompted client states to establish centers of agricultural research. The network of institutions linked to CGIAR rapidly grew and extended its tentacles to the sciences, public bilateral and multilateral assistance agencies, and private agroindustrial firms, giving origins to a power complex based on a specific type of knowledge production rooted in the need to validate and enrich the great corporations of the sector—like Monsanto—and respond to the political demands of the Cold War to promote a "green" revolution in order to combat a "red" one (Goldman 2005). Thousands of technicians and scientists were educated by the CGIAR system, and many of them would later come to occupy positions of influence in government ministries and the boards of control of research centers and multinational corporations.

Construction of the "Assault on Poverty" Concept

Establishing a structure for research at the World Bank gained decisive support at the beginning of the 1970s with the creation of a chief economist position.

Hollis Chenery, a former USAID official and economics professor at Stanford and Harvard, was the first to fill the post. The new department also received ample funding for equipment, the contracting of researchers, travel, and publication of their studies. Its mission was to develop a solid base of data and concepts for the formulation of broad economic policy and programs, providing support for the expanding financial operations of the Bank. The department's duties also included coordinating efforts to find means for making the Bank's "social" projects work that could be replicated in diverse settings.

During the first five years of McNamara's reign, the Bank shifted strategies among a variety of preferential instruments for carrying forward its "crusade against poverty" (Finnemore 1997, 214–16). Projects for family planning, nutrition, health, education, slum urbanization, and agriculture were some of the initiatives that took the lead during the period, but no single one filled the role of the Bank's main tool for "combating poverty."

It's interesting to note that, from the theoretical point of view, the academic literature of the time tended to treat poverty only marginally if not pejoratively, frequently associating it with charitable activities and social services (Finnemore 1997, 207; Kapur, Lewis, and Webb 1997, 247). Before McNamara arrived, the word itself was not yet part of the Bank staff's vocabulary. During the 1950s, the subject of poverty had not been the object of a single declaration by the Bank or its staff, and during the majority of the 1960s, the term made only a few timid appearances in Bank discourse (Kapur, Lewis, and Webb 1997, 130).

With roots in Cold War injunctions and inserted in the Bank's agenda by Washington insiders, the "war on poverty" initially suffered the lack of two basic elements: (1) a rational focus to create structure and support and (2) an operational tool that would permit the reproduction of poverty reduction projects on a large scale. Both internally and externally, the Bank lacked a coherent approach that could orient the projects the institution supported in agriculture, education, and urban development. In addition, the Bank did not have a preferred tool for implementing its "crusade against poverty" that was sufficiently reproducible and statistically reliable enough to evaluate its results. In other words, there was neither adequate theory nor means.

Both revealed themselves during 1973–74 when "absolute rural poverty" was defined as the principal target of the Bank's intervention via new projects of "integrated rural development" and with the publication of *Redistribution with Growth*, a book edited by chief economist Chenery et al. (1974). At that point, the "assault on poverty" directive was born as the driving force of the Bank. To better understand this process, it helps to consider three factors.

In the first place, the stage was set by the macropolitics of the Cold War. In addition to the US loss of the Vietnam War, other events occurred during the 1968 to 1973 period that pushed Washington and its closest allies to search for new "hearts and minds" strategies of action, pressing organizations integrated in its network of external power, such as the World Bank, to do the same. The list is long: the election, government, and ouster of the Chilean president Salvador Allende; Indira Ghandi's election in India; the war between India and Pakistan and the birth of Bangladesh; and the nationalization of oil reserves and implementation of agrarian reform in Peru, among many other developments viewed as disturbing by Washington. In all cases, characterized by nationalism, distributive and redistributive policies proved to have strong popular appeal, and in the assessment of the American establishment, the peasantry served as both judge and jury (Huntington 1975, 302). Gaining the support of this sector or, in the very least, deactivating it suddenly seemed strategically crucial (Goldman 2005, 68–69).

In the second place, the consolidation of a focus on poverty would be unthinkable without questioning the conventional wisdom on the "trickle-down effect" (Finnemore 1997, 208–209). The expression "unseating of the GNP"—pronounced in 1970 by the general director of the International Labour Organization (ILO) to define lost confidence in economic growth as sufficient means to reduce poverty—rapidly gained success during the period as a pointed challenge of the trickle-down effect. The Bank had to contribute to this debate.

In the third place, the construction of the poverty-oriented approach was directly linked to changes in American foreign aid policy. Academics and development insiders vehemently criticized the failings of US foreign assistance, adding to the general pressure generated by the political exhaustion that built each day the Vietnam War continued to be waged. Thus, in 1973, Congress approved new legislation, widely known as the New Directions initiative, to reorient bilateral foreign aid. Posturing itself as a way to attend "basic human needs," the new directive focused on the reduction of "extreme poverty" by extending production credits to "small farmers" (Ayres 1983; Lancaster 2007). Note that the policy was not new but rather the reiteration, in new clothing, of initiatives put in place by Washington since the 1950s and into the 1960s as Community Development and Alliance for Progress programs. At any rate, the New Directions initiative influenced the McNamara administration to establish greater coherence between the Bank's pro-poor discourse and its financing of projects.

Internally, a critical step in consolidating the focus on poverty was that of defining "absolute poverty" as a unit of analysis and an operational criteria (Kapur, Lewis, and Webb 1997, 217). Movement in this direction was perceptible from 1972 on, as evidenced by McNamara's address to the board of governors at the Bank's headquarters in Washington, DC, that September:

> When the highly privileged are few and the desperately poor are many—and when the gap between them is worsening rather than improving—it is only a question of time before a decisive choice must be made between the political costs of reform and the political risks of rebellion. That is why policies specifically designed to reduce the deprivation among the poorest 40 percent in developing countries are prescriptions not only of principle but of prudence. Social justice is not merely a moral imperative. It is a political imperative as well. (McNamara 1981, 223)

The speech recalls the earlier arguments McNamara made connecting poverty reduction to security and, for the first time, hints at the size of the problem he wanted the Bank to address in its new research and development mission.

In 1973 McNamara made another important speech to the Bank board, this time in Nairobi, Kenya. He reiterated concerns about the poorest 40 percent. In fact, the new speech was codified by a concept of poverty stratification that divided the condition into two categories, relative and absolute. By dividing the poor into two groups, he created an identity that broke down the new task of the Bank into what he argued to be more manageable bits. To "attack absolute poverty" was doable. Since "the bulk of the poor today are in the rural areas," according to McNamara, it was up to the Bank to help client states create "rural development" projects to reduce rural poverty. With "absolute poverty" concentrated in rural areas, the Bank could pinpoint the problem and promote surgical solutions such as land reform, credit for smallholders, rural education, irrigation projects, and rural health care as specific means to gradually reduce poverty. Agricultural modernization was seen as complementary rather than contradictory, with the Bank prepared to help "small family farmers" buy the technological packages of new agricultural methods, such as agrochemicals, genetically manipulated seed, and other productivity devices (McNamara 1973). What, in fact, seems to have been presented, argued the renowned rural economist Ernest Feder, was the notion of implementing a "small green revolution" on peasant parcels (Feder 1976, 293–94; George 1978, 238–39). McNamara also proposed a program of rural public works of small and medium scale to generate temporary employment in the countryside for a growing contingent of landless rural workers.

The rural development projects proposed presupposed acceptance of current agrarian structures. Land concentration in the countryside—a fundamental factor in the determination of poverty and social inequality—was taken as a given to be accommodated rather than resisted (Ayres 1983, 104). Despite lip service in favor of land reform, the agenda proposed by McNamara constituted a conservative alternative to redistributive agrarian reform policies.

Published a year later, *Redistribution with Growth* lent academic weight and detail to McNamara's Nairobi speech and gave the Bank a theoretical center to use in order to sell with greater efficacy its new product—integrated rural development—in the international marketplace of ideas, establishing "absolute poverty" and "target groups" such as "small farmers" as legitimate operational categories for public policy (Ayres 1983, 19; Chenery et al. 1974).

Organized by Chenery, the book includes articles by researchers of the Bank's Development Research Center who took as their point of departure the distinction between relative and absolute poverty and focused their attention on raising incomes as the key to reducing poverty's most dire effects. The essential thesis is that economic growth is compatible with poverty reduction. How, then, could the income of "the poor" be raised? Chenery and this team outlined four distinct strategies:

1. maximize GDP growth through increased savings and improved resource allocation in order to benefit all social groups;
2. redirect funds toward the targeted absolute poverty groups through investments in education, accessible credit, and public works;
3. redistribute income or consumption to the target groups through the fiscal system or the direct transfer of consumer goods; and
4. redistribute existing funds to the poorer segments through policies such as agrarian reform.

Thus, in terms of public policy remedies, the book's central proposal was to concentrate public investment on increasing productive capacity and the income of the poor. In the end, Chenery's center recommended the second strategy at the cost of the others: the first was discarded because it was thought to reinforce income concentration, the third for consuming too many resources in nonproductive ways, and the fourth because of its probable impact on the social and political order of client states and presumed inapplicability on a large scale (Chenery et al. 1974).

At best, Chenery's book recommended an incremental wealth distribution strategy to the extent that it was limited to circulating part of the income and new funds generated by economic growth in the form of projects and programs financed through tax revenue and foreign debt. In theory, these investments would augment the "productivity of the poorest" in such a way as to elevate their income through their participation in the market. The World Bank's idea was to share a piece of the raised cake and not the cake itself (Assmann 1980, 11).

The book's title evoked a concept that was negated by its contents at both the governmental and the social levels: the idea of redistribution. In the case of the government, the proposal made public investment in the poor, conditional on elevated state receipts generated by an increase in economic productivity and growth indexes—in other words, the accumulation of capital. Given these conditions, the scheme would permit an increase in expenditures "to combat poverty," and yet it was proposed to alter the share of this expense relative to the overall government budget. As for its impact on society, the proposal left completely untouched accumulated wealth, as well as the entire judicial and institutional structure—that is, the rules of the game that had generated poverty and maintained inequality were to remain in place. Moreover, the scheme proposed by Chenery—heir to a wealthy thoroughbred horse racing family (owners of the famed Triple Crown winner Secretariat)—would preserve the property regime and the structure of productive relations.

Despite criticisms of the trickle-down effect, McNamara and his team never even tried to overcome the dominant paradigm but rather they sought to make it work by accommodating the current economic model and capitalist (liberal) ideology (Ayres 1983, 90). For that matter, since *Redistribution with Growth* disregarded even minimal sacrifices on the part of the predominant sectors, its gradualist strategy of wealth distribution suffered the absence of a political theory. Thus, the coalition building seen as necessary to push forward the Bank's proposal takes the form of a tacit understanding, as if the logic of McNamara's argument were so clear, naturally the elite of the developing world would automatically embrace it. This explains, perhaps, the repeated exhortations found in McNamara's addresses to the board, which represented the world community as manifest in the membership of the United Nations. His speeches as Bank president are riddled with such value-laden terms as "political will," "immense courage," "moral obligation," and "responsibility" (McNamara 1981, passim).

At any rate, the Chenery book served to bolster up the imposition of poverty as a unit of analysis, legitimate parameters, and create an obligatory focus for any and all development initiatives. From the 1970s on, the institutionalization of poverty reduction as part of the international agenda was directly linked to the ever-growing involvement of the Bank in research, especially analyses of input-output relationships and cost-benefit ratios, and the production, compilation, and dissemination of data. The Bank also came to finance local research and train professionals worldwide to produce data and compose projects linked to the theme (Goldman 2005, 77–81; Finnemore 1997, 208). Thus, the Bank not only established a way of interpreting and categorizing social reality (the social question) but also developed poverty science and policy administration methods through its role as a creditor, different from previous and ongoing philanthropic interventions in the area.

The idea that absolute rural and urban poverty could be overcome by increasing "the productivity of the poor" had as its premise the notion that those who were poor lived in such conditions because they were not adequately inserted in activities considered both productive and profitable. Such a proposition depended on three postulates: (1) that the poor had no function in a capitalist system, ignoring the unequal and combined character of the forms of capitalist exploitation; (2) that poverty was isolated from larger social relations, as if it were a phenomenon in a world to itself; and (3) that poverty was a condition of exclusion from the system rather than a product of it, reifying the predatory nature of capitalist development (Assmann 1980, 47; Payer 1980, 140). These postulates enabled the Bank to politically fortify the assault on poverty directive, making it seem self-evident and legitimate in its own right. They also allowed the Bank to evade questions about low salaries and the necessity to create new jobs as it shifted the focus of analysis from the system as a whole to the quality of insertion of independent individuals in the market.

In the same period that the rural development projects were unveiled and implemented, the Bank sought a similar instrument for the urban milieu. It sought a type of project that would target the urban poor, that would serve as a vehicle for investments considered productive rather than philanthropic, and that could rapidly be reproduced on a grand scale (Ayres 1983, 154; Kapur, Lewis, and Webb 1997, 263). The theme was the object of McNamara's 1975 address to the Bank's governors, a speech that once again explicitly revealed the speaker's political outlook:

> Historically, violence and civil upheaval are more common in cities
> than in the countryside. Frustrations that fester among the urban
> poor are readily exploited by political extremists. If cities do not

begin to deal more constructively with poverty, poverty may well begin to deal more destructively with cities. It is not a problem that favors political delay. (McNamara 1981, 316)

The message of urgency was clear, if only implied. If the rich nations delayed in helping to redress the problems of absolute poverty in the cities of poor nations, rebellion if not revolution would reign, and damaging destruction would ensue.

The various sectors of the Bank published numerous documents between 1974 and 1976, and the Bank created a working group to guarantee the realization of the new demand to find a means to lessen absolute urban poverty. "Focus" and "productivity" were key words. In 1972, the Bank authorized some housing projects around the theme "sites and services" that had the objective of creating reproducible approaches to poverty with maximum cost recovery and minimal public expenditure. In other words, the main objective was to demonstrate financial and political viability of pilot projects in low-cost urban housing that could replace conventional schemes of public provision of shelter for the poor. The basic procedure consisted of limiting public expenditures on land purchases and basic construction infrastructure, passing along to future residents the bulk of the responsibility and costs of building their own houses. The experiment had first been put into practice by the Inter-American Development Bank (IADB) and USAID in the early 1960s, and it proved an attractive mechanism for exploiting unpaid labor, for lowering the cost of reproducing the labor supply, and for encouraging social conformity and thus disinterest in communist ideology by means of making property owners out of some underprivileged segments of the population. Beyond the legal difficulties related to buying lots, the "sites and services" strategy proved difficult to reproduce because the quality of the land purchased and services provided tended to be so low and inadequate that the newly created landlord-consumers needed additional subsidies to preserve their new communities (Kapur, Lewis, and Webb 1997, 317–18).

To advance with the goal set by McNamara, the Bank developed a new instrument to expand the coverage, accelerate implementation, and lower costs of the urban poverty initiative that it called "slum upgrading." The new emphasis demanded minimum physical demolition and resettlement and had the advantage of serving to ideologically canonize or legitimate slum housing with the discourse of "helping the poor to help themselves" and the empowerment illusion of the "build it yourself" motto (Davis 2006, 80–81). In the meantime, this approach soon showed itself to have failed at reaching the poorest of the poor, principally because the Bank refused to forgive fees on the paperwork required to emit subsidies.

As an urban housing strategy of low standards, the slum-upgrading project ran contrary to legal housing standards in most of the borrowing countries. For this reason, the Bank had to create diverse autonomous national and local agencies and authorities to take responsibility for the housing policy. Frequently, these entities served to disguise key decisions about urban policy, to thwart efforts to monitor fiscal accountability, and to influence electoral politics. In general, the Bank supported urban development projects for the poor that sought to minimize the role of the state in resolving housing inadequacies (Davis 2006, 76–81).

Between 1976 and 1979, the World Bank also got involved in debates about "basic needs." The discussion was initiated by the ILO as a way of redefining the focus in relation to poverty by adding weight to the concept of "basic needs" as criteria for deciding how to limit projects and allocate resources. Once again, the Bank reacted to ILO initiative (Kapur, Lewis, and Webb 1997, 265–67). All the same, the idea of socially required necessities, unlike poverty, had been part of the World Bank's vocabulary since its inception at Breton Woods. Moreover, with the New Directions reform of 1973, the concept of basic necessities formally oriented US foreign development aid calculations.

The new focus rivaled that produced by Chenery and his team without, however, supplanting it. Over the course of the next five years, the McNamara administration debated just exactly what was possible and desirable as "basic necessities," how to justify them in terms of costs and benefits, and what form they should take so as not to prejudice growth (Ayres 1983, 85–89). After all, one of the pillars of McNamara's discourse was the idea of no trade-offs between economic growth and poverty reduction (or, in any event, the meeting of basic needs). Regardless, the debate failed to reach a satisfactory conclusion, and few projects or related components materialized.

Negating the trickle-down effect was not an objective of the McNamara directives (Streeten 1986, 95–105). Toward the end of his tenure at the Bank, McNamara commented on the "major qualitative change in the Bank's lending and in its development policies. The change arose out of the understanding that if the absolute poor had to wait for the benefits of overall economic growth to trickle down to them, their incomes and welfare would inch forward at an intolerably slow pace" (McNamara 1981, 641). He saw the Bank's role as one of anticipating the inevitable process of capitalist wealth distribution. In other words, the Bank's activities complemented market forces because the natural trickle-down effect of the system occurred at a speed that was unacceptably slow from the political and security perspectives. The meeting of basic needs was also taken as an isolated object in the mix of social relations and political economy, setting aside the need to consider such factors as unemployment and declining wages (Assmann 1980, 49–50).

The discussions surrounding basic necessities did consecrate primary health care and education as sectors ripe for productive investment in peripheral countries. The Bank followed this line, highlighting such projects as policy imperatives for alleviating absolute poverty and reformulating, as well as reducing public expenditures on social policy. At the end of 1979, McNamara created the Population, Health and Nutrition Department within the Bank, which had the exclusive responsibility for approving loans for health care programs, an institutional framework that would stimulate enormous growth in the sector (health had earlier been dealt with as part of broader rural and urban development projects, as well as family planning initiatives). Also that year, the award of the Nobel Prize in Economics to Theodor Schultz served to enthrone the human capital concept in the Bank's education agenda. On the Bank's council of governors, the US and UK representatives enthusiastically supported the Bank's emphasis on basic education. In 1980, the most important of the Bank's publications, the *World Development Report* (WDR), certified the two newest arrows in the social area quiver: health and education. At that moment, the report essentially announced the birth of the principal priorities of the social policy model—centered on human capital development—that was to become hegemonic in the decade to come.

Despite all the exhortations in support of the "fight against poverty," Bank loans for projects even partially oriented toward poverty reduction did not add up to more than one-third of those made during the McNamara years. Even this total is overestimated, as the staff tended to exaggerate the coverage of social projects, inflating the number of beneficiaries considered poor because the advancement of their careers at the Bank depended on the loan volumes under their supervision (Kapur, Lewis, and Webb 1997, 339).

In fact, when compared to the magnitude of the public investment made by client states, the Bank's loans always represented a negligible quantity. McNamara soon discovered this when he joined the Bank. After all, as US Secretary of Defense, he commonly counted on an annual budget of $70 billion. When he became president of the Bank in 1968, however, his budget totaled little more than $1 billion (Caufield 1996, 97–98). For McNamara, it was clear that the Bank would only have influence in the formation of ideas and technical assistance. Thus, World Bank financing served mainly as a vehicle to provoke a reorientation in public spending and government policy (Kapur, Lewis, and Webb 1997, 271).

Since the loans for poverty reduction represented no more than one-third of total Bank financing, one can assume that the direct impact of such policies was not very significant. However, indirect impacts warrant further study. In the countryside and in cities, Bank projects induced changes in the composition and destination of public spending. For every World Bank–arranged loan, client state governments had to provide matching funds in amounts generally much larger than the Bank's share. Later, governments needed to pay back the Bank, which insisted on being the preferential creditor that had to be paid in dollars. Beyond that, Bank-financed projects prescribed certain parameters and conditions that required borrowing nations to redefine sectorial and social policy. In many cases, the Bank loans, technical assistance, and rules made it necessary for client governments to create new public administration agencies to be responsible for the regulation of whole new sectors of the economy. In the rural and urban development areas, for example, it was common for the duplication of the projects to be guaranteed only by the client state's incorporation of models and procedures produced and propagated by the World Bank. In practice, these new entities ended up serving as loan processing centers for the Bank. Often, this scenario had reactionary political implications, as the Bank and its conservative policies helped governments—many of which were dictatorial regimes—to evade popular pressure in support of social democratic reforms, such as agrarian reform. Thus, a vast list of projects financed or support by the Bank provoked highly negative impacts from political, social, and environmental points of view (Rich 1994; Brown 1995; George and Sabelli 1996; Caufield 1996; Sanahuja 2001).

The Bank's messages about poverty and basic needs peaked in the 1972–74 and 1977–78 periods, when the tone of McNamara's customary messianic exhortations about the necessity of increasing foreign aid went up, as did the Bank's investments in social projects. In both of these periods, the Bank took the initiative in presenting the "poverty reduction" theme to countries with historically high wealth concentration. However, such initiatives were especially targeted and regularly set aside in the context of supposed political and/ or financial emergencies, which demanded, according to the Bank, that focus be maintained on political dialogue about macroeconomic problems and the continuity of an ascending pattern of borrowing (Kapur, Lewis, and Webb 1997, 321–39).

From the political point of view, Cold War détente played an important role in declining loans to the social area (Kapur, Lewis, and Webb 1997, 321). Begun by the first Nixon administration, détente relaxed tensions between the superpowers and opened socialist bloc countries to private European and North American capital flow. Moreover, the strategy progressively normalized diplomatic relations between the United States and China.

All the same, given the contradictory meanings the United States and the Soviet Union attributed to détente, the international political scene remained volatile during the 1973–1978 period. Military coups and massacres exploded in Chile, Argentina, and Uganda; a war of succession broke out in Pakistan, and the Khmer Rouge came to power in Cambodia, instituting a policy of mass murder of nonconformists. Portugal (Carnation Revolution), Spain (Franco), and Greece saw the end of dictatorships. The Yom Kippur War broke out in the Middle East. Civil wars tore apart Lebanon, Angola, Zaire, and Ethiopia (some with the United States and USSR militarily supporting opposing sides). The withdrawal of the United States from Vietnam and the Watergate scandal and subsequent resignation of Nixon raised significant doubts regarding America's role in the world (Kapur, Lewis, and Webb 1997, 273; Velasco e Cruz 2007, 378–80).

International economic instability accompanied the political instability. On the one hand, since the end of the 1960s, tensions in the international monetary system turned the increasingly difficult task of maintaining the convertibility of the dollar based on the gold standard. Eventually, the United States under Nixon unilaterally broke with the Breton Woods monetary regime by instituting measures that contradicted the post-WWII accord (Tabb 2004, 82–83; Brenner 2003, 67–73; Velasco e Cruz 2007, 364–65). This move was part of a strategy to destroy the rules that had limited US dominance over international monetary policies, by transforming the monetary regime from one based on a gold-dollar standard to one exclusively based on the dollar standard (Gowan 2003, 45–50; Serrano 2004, 190–204). The central countries suffered a combination of inflation, slow growth, and rising unemployment, especially after the first oil price shock at the end of 1973. They responded to the difficult situation by adopting defensive commercial and monetary policies. On the other hand, a few countries on the periphery—such as Brazil, Mexico, South Korea, and Taiwan—experienced high rates of growth for the entire decade, at the cost of increasing their external indebtedness at a fast pace, enticed by low cost and abundant credit offered by private multinational Banks anxious to recycle oil income. While this was going on, the great majority of nonpetroleumexporting nations on the periphery of the world system got poorer or had low growth rates.

Structural Adjustment and Social Policy Reform (1980–90)

After 1979, the World Bank's social projects, which had come to represent but a minor fraction of the portfolio, came to represent even less of the Bank's loan budget, and the "assault on poverty" motto gradually shifted to the margins of the institution's public discourse. Toward the end of that year, the second oil shock and a dramatic rise in US interest rates caused the Bank to concentrate its portfolio even more on projects that allowed for larger loans, directly supported the balance of payments, and served to obtain foreign exchange and thus made possible the rollover of debts and maintenance of a spiral of indebtedness (Kapur, Lewis, and Webb 1997, 324). Guided by these new priorities, the amounts loaned by the Bank doubled between fiscal years 1978 and 1981, concentrating the borrowing among a few preferred clients—especially Mexico, Brazil, Argentina, India, Pakistan, Indonesia, and Turkey, all of them highly indebted (World Bank 1981, 156–57).

In May 1979, McNamara announced the creation of a new financial tool, the structural adjustment loan (Kapur, Lewis, and Webb 1997, 1227). Such loans were quickly extended and oriented toward programs rather than projects with the objective of preventing a deficit in the balance of payments, above all in countries dependent on imported oil. Authorization for this type of loan was conditioned on the borrower nation's capacity to put in place a stabilization program previously negotiated with the IMF and a package of macroeconomic policy reforms, both oriented toward gearing the domestic economy to accommodate the new external economic environment and maintaining service payments on external debt.

In the two-year period from 1980 to 1981, the Bank operated in such a way as to affirm "structural adjustment" as a necessary means to mold and discipline indebted countries to the new conditions of the international economy. According to the World Bank, these conditions included a new international division of labor that strictly divided the economy between the "state" and the "market," a vision that arose from tandem processes: on the one hand, neoliberal pressure orchestrated by the Thatcher and Reagan governments in England and the United States, respectively, and, on the other hand, a more general change in the correlation of forces between capital and labor. It was not accidental that since 1978 the Bank had been outlining the general contours of the neoclassical critique of capitalist development based on import substitution, and all the prescribed policies to reduce the public deficit attacked, first and foremost, social and worker rights that until then had come to produce a certain power balance between capital and labor.

In March 1980, the World Bank issued the first structural adjustment loan. It went to Turkey, which was characterized as a prototype for future loans (Kapur, Lewis, and Webb 1997, 548). In macroeconomic policy circles, the adjustment measures that were considered preconditions for such loans consisted of (1) trade liberalization, with included price alignment with the international market and lowered tariff barriers; (2) currency devaluation; (3) measures to attract foreign investment; and (4) efforts to promote specialization and expand exports, especially agricultural commodities. In social policy and public administration circles, the adjustments had as their central goal the reduction of the public deficit, especially through means such as (1) cuts in spending for personnel and administration, (2) drastic reductions if not outright elimination of consumer subsidies, (3) savings in the per capita cost of programs in order to expand coverage, and (4) reorientation of the social policy to focus expenditures on primary health care and basic education toward populations in conditions of "absolute poverty." From 1978 to 1982, all of these measures figured as sectorial or economic policy recommendations in the Bank's most important reports.

In August 1982, the Mexican government declared a moratorium, and an external debt crisis broke out among Latin American nations. The monetary authorities of the United States and England, the IMF and the Bank for International Settlements, respectively, met to map out a strategy for administrating the debt (Toussaint 2006, 193–94). They diagnosed the crisis as a problem of liquidity and not of solvency and indicated that an exit strategy lay in paying the loan service. How could the resources for this strategy be generated? The answer proposed was that of reorienting production toward exportable goods by reducing and redirecting public expenditures (Stern and Ferreira 1997, 560). The IMF would have the task of preparing emergency aid packages in exchange for the implantation of short-term stabilization programs and the state's assumption of private debts. The hope was that in three to five years, the measures would reactivate growth and sustain payment of the debt service.

The World Bank soon conjoined this strategy as an auxiliary force of the IMF. The Bank's existing structural adjustment programs—or SAPs, as they came to be called—were then converted to serve as tools to square up the political economies of the debtor nations with the demands of international creditors. Neither the Bank nor the IMF considered special mechanisms to protect or compensate, even partially, the most vulnerable social groups.

Responding to the external environment and to internal changes, the World Bank's research activities suffered a significant change of course at the end of McNamara's tenure in 1981. In the name of economic efficiency and market liberalization, the idea of "combating poverty" was unjustifiably dismantled as the department's organizing principle (George and Sabelli 1996, 163–75; Stern and Ferreira 1997, 545; Kapur, Lewis, and Webb 1997, 338–39).

To the extent that the monetary stabilization plans provoked recession in Brazil, Argentina, and other countries, it became clear to public and private creditors that this was not merely a crisis of liquidity. Thus there emerged a preoccupation with the very sustainability of the adjustment policy. Until then, the official discourse had simply been one of claiming the adjustments were "good for the poor" as they would "directly benefit"—not *indirectly* benefit, as had been claimed in the case of the trickle-down effect (Kapur, Lewis, and Webb 1997, 353). This argument changed toward the middle of 1980 when the Bank started to admit the occurrence of certain "social costs." From then on, the adjustment policy was seen to require the creation of palliative programs of social compensation to alleviate, in a selective manner and on a short-term basis, the regressive impact on the most afflicted populations or those most likely to support the opposition. Often, such programs were organized as "safety nets" through the use of emergency aid financing.

In December 1986, the first operation of this sort was experimented in Bolivia. According to the World Bank's political calculations, a "highly visible" government response was needed to disrupt social protest, in hopes of guaranteeing the sustainability of a coalition government committed to implementing an ambitious SAP (Kapur, Lewis, and Webb 1997, 365).

Since then, the Bank promoted the creation of social funds in dozens of countries in Africa, Asia, Eastern Europe, and, above all, Latin America, through means of loan and technical assistance. The funds functioned as multisectoral mechanisms with the capacity to finance programs and projects through an ample variety of activities, from the creation of temporary jobs and the provision of subsidized food to local organizations of impoverished populations in a project referred to as "community strengthening" by the Bank. Established to function as transitory, short-term tools of action, in just a few years they became permanent vehicles of a new social policy model that inevitably imposed conformity (Stahl 1994, 56–58; Sanahuja 2001, 131–33).

The basic innovation of the new model was the principle of a "demand-driven approach" to the universal supply of goods and public services. In other words, the social funds were focused on target groups, selected in accordance with their vulnerability in the face of the structural adjustments imposed by international financiers. The Bank distributed the responsibility for indicating and administrating new projects under the program to NGOs, grassroots groups, municipal governments, private businesses, and consortiums of any or all of these entities. In general, the agencies created to administer the funds operated with significant autonomy in their area of responsibility, despite formal links to hierarchies such as to specific federal government ministries. Utilized as showcases, they tended to seek high public visibility and normally enjoyed strong political support, directly linked to the upper echelons of the government. Beyond national budget resources, they generally counted on extraordinary sources of financial support from bilateral foreign aid agencies and multilateral banks.

While the World Bank aggravated the precarious status of social policy in the developing world through the creation of these externally driven "social funds" programs, its loans for basic education and primary health care increased during the 1987–89 fiscal period (World Bank 1993, 39). This emphasis contributed to legitimate them as priorities, in detriment to other segments of the education and health care areas.

Soon after establishing the pilot program in Bolivia, criticisms of the monetary and fiscal austerity measures demanded by the SAPs began to be heard from within the UN system. A 1987 UNICEF report had almost immediate repercussions (Cornia et al. 1987). The report criticized the SAPs not on their merits but rather for their form of execution and some aspects of their content. For example, the authors criticized the fact that the program introduced and implemented only Band-Aid-like social policies a posteriori in a classic case of too little, too late. World Bank economists rebutted the UNICEF report, alleging the need to distinguish between the social costs that could be blamed on the SAPs' "corrective" measures from those generated by the initial macroeconomic imbalance itself. Nevertheless, after publication of the report, Bank managers no longer claimed—in public at any rate—that the adjustments were "good for the poor" (Kapur, Lewis, and Webb 1997, 353).

At the end of 1989, with George H. W. Bush as president of the United States, the leading advocates of neoliberal capitalist restructuring held a meeting to evaluate their work in Washington, DC. Among participants were members of Congress and representatives from the US Department of the Treasury, World Bank, IMF, IDB, USAID, and the principal US think tanks. At the conclusion of the conference, they endorsed the broad array of political and economic reforms then being implemented in practically all the countries of Latin America and the Caribbean and agreed on the need to accelerate the process and extend the same package of reforms to other nations and world regions. The resulting accord took the form of the Ten Commandments, and the event, as well as its list of policy prescriptions, came to be known as the "Washington Consensus" (Williamson 1990).

Developed in the aftermath of the fall of the Berlin wall and wrapped in the imagery of the so-called "end of history," the commandments quickly gained status as the unique paradigm of triumphant capitalism, serving as a means to line up peripheral country governments behind the banner of a liberal political program whose main pillars included opening the world economy to the flow of goods, services, and capital and recasting the state as the guarantor of security and profitability of private business interests (Wade 1997, 353). In this context, the consensus signaled the end of Washington's tolerance for economic nationalism and unequivocal support for capital's assault on the post–World War II pact of social and labor rights. The logical incoherence of the "ten commandments" (Gore 2000) caused the consensus's powerful supporters little pause as they set about imposing this normative pact.

Latin America quickly internalized the new policy platform. That is to say that the leading political forces and practically all political parties and ideological currents lined themselves up behind the idea that there was but one solitary objective to be sought, that of constructing an economy free and open to capital. Moreover, it was nearly uniformly agreed that this could be achieved in but one way: through destroying national sovereignty in all matters political and economic while annihilating any and all social and labor "costs" that might impinge on the profitability of capital. In the region's principal countries, new political coalitions committed to the Washington Consensus took power in a series of presidential elections in the late 1980s and early 1990s. During the same period, negotiations with international creditors came to a conclusion, and the financial system reopened, now via financial globalization, a pumped-up form of direct foreign capital investment. It did not take long to weave new alliances and access a great wave of international liquidity that turned viable the political conditions necessary to generate the new type of monetary stabilization plans strictly linked to the neoliberal economic restructuring process (Batista 1996).

In the *World Development Report 1990*, the World Bank presented a step-by-step model for poverty alleviation, linked to state and social policy neoliberalization that would be consolidated as a reference point for clients interested in compensating the "losers" of structural adjustment programs. The report had as its premise the division of social and economic policy. Anchored to the absolute poverty category, it sidelined the question of income and wealth concentration and proposed a two-pronged strategy that mixed poverty alleviation with an emphasis on supporting programs and projects that might renew the redemptive virtues of economic growth with its implications for producing a trickle-down effect. The report conceded that the adjustment might generate certain "social costs," suggesting the necessity of focused interventions (supposedly) compensatory that would promote access to basic social services (above all, primary health care and education) in the form of safety nets and "human resource" development programs. According to the report, the creation of job opportunities that would truly elevate the earnings of the poorest people depended on economic growth, which, in its turn, depended on the implementation of structural adjustment policies.

The SAPs were said to be the only policies capable of "ensuring productive use of the poor's most abundant asset—labor" (World Bank 1990, iii). In other words, the report prescribed a combination of policies directed at liberalizing national economies and intensifying the exploitation of their labor forces (Burkett 1990; Cammack 2002a). Conveniently, the question of conflicts over production and wealth appropriation simply did not appear in the report, allowing the Bank to present poverty alleviation as something that depended only on the distribution of new investments and not on the redistribution of a client's patrimony. To be exact, the only significant innovation in relation to the postulates advanced by the Bank since the 1970s was the program of radical liberalization and privatization. As for the rest, much the same discourse was followed, including renewed confidence in the trickle-down effect.

During those years, with the deregulation of the economy, asymmetric market opening, financial deregulation, and the dismantling of a large part of the public sector, as the Argentine sociologist Carlos Vilas has argued, client states, particularly those in Latin America, abandoned in practice their political commitment to regional integration and social mobility for their entire populations (Vilas 1997a, 1997b). To institutionalize the power relations that commanded both the internal and the external adjustments, the state was directed to indicate new winners and losers. Through the manipulation of currency exchange rates, interest rates, and tax policies, state actions pumped more and more income into capital's coffer, especially that of the financial sector. Subordinated to macroeconomic adjustments, the recasting of social policy gained support centered on three significant changes. First, social policy ceased to be thought of as an input necessary for private investment, as a structural dimension of capitalist accumulation, and came to be seen as an expense. In consequence, the concept of "social integration" gave way to "social compensation." Second, instead of seeking to incorporate the poorest stratum of the population in minimally satisfactory conditions of employment and income, the new social policy tried to impede further deterioration of their living conditions by assuming a supplemental assistance form. Third, social policy was redefined as transitory, whether it was the supposition that macroeconomic adjustments would inevitably produce growth without inflation and sprinkle wealth from the more dynamic to the more stagnant sectors—thus, becoming unnecessary to maintain certain social programs—or whether it was due to conceiving of social policy as an "exit door" from poverty because of its capacity to periodically renovate its clientele. Subordinated to the necessity to guarantee the governability of the adjustment, social policy increasingly assumed a "pumping" function, acting in situations that could explode into political tension or create insecurity for the free flow of capital and merchandise.

During the same period, the neoliberalization of social policy walked side by side with the institutionalization of the thesis that public administration depended on a partnership between state agencies and social organizations (World Bank 1989, 1991). The participation of "civil society" in public policy administration has since become axiomatic. All the same, civil society was then taken as synonymous with voluntary associations and NGOs. Classical social movement entities, such as labor unions, popular movements, and peasant and indigenous organizations, were kept at arms length while the Bank sustained the discourse of "participation" with the regular operational involvement of the private sector (industries, agribusiness, contractors, and consulting firms).

The integration of voluntary associations and NGOs in the design, implementation, and, most important, administration of Bank-financed projects continually grew during the 1980s, accompanying the escalating neoliberalization of the south. From 1980 to 1994, the number of projects that counted on NGO cooperation increased from 6 percent to 50 percent of the total (Covey 1998, 83). In part, this increase responded to pressure by international NGOs as they witnessed the negative social and environment impacts of Bank-financed projects. To great extent, this expressed the growing permeability between NGOs and the network of both public and private international assistance entities. In 1970, the financial contribution of NGOs toward the development of peripheral countries was less than $9 million, while some nineteen years later the contribution reached $6.4 billion, including $2.2 billion in official funds, corresponding to 12 percent of total international assistance, public (bilateral and multilateral) and private (philanthropic) (Barros 2005, 138).

To the extent that institutionalization and professionalization were imposed as forms of surviving an ever-sharpening competition for funding and turf, numerous NGOs adopted at an increasing rate business and multilateral institution administration practices such as their office culture, their organizational structure, and their operating methods—even without necessarily sharing the same objectives (Kruijt 1992; Sogge 1998, 2002; Dezalay and Garth 2005). At the same time, to the extent that neoliberal capitalist restructuring advanced in the south and, after the 1989–91 period, in the east, a huge field of operation opened for those NGOs prepared to fulfill the functions uprooted from state agencies, including among them the administration of poverty assistance, in super-specialized forms and under condition of being a third-party contractor (Davis 2006, 83–84).

Conclusion

Historically, the loan portfolio of the World Bank worked as an instrument to facilitate the circulation, internalization, and institutionalization of the Bank's leading product: economic ideas and policy prescriptions about what to do, who to do it for, and how in matters of capitalist development in its most varied dimensions. The political and intellectual construction of the "assault on poverty" was part of this trajectory from the end of the 1960s. For two decades, this idea fed on loans, technical assistance to governments, collaborations with other development agencies, and thousands of publications financed by the Bank. During this process, the poverty-oriented approach to development contributed to impose on the international scene, in the heart of the structural adjustment programs coming into vogue, a very specific manner to think about and make social policy, one based on the theoretical separation of poverty and wealth production and the notion of minimal social needs. One cannot comprehend how such a twisted political and intellectual transformation could have come about without taking into account the role of the World Bank.

Author's Note

The author is a professor of history at the Rural Federal University of Rio de Janeiro. He earned his doctorate from the Fluminense Federal University in Niteroi, Brazil.

Note

1. One of the principal intellectual orientations that guided the Bank was the idea that income distribution was concentrated in the initial stages of economic cycles and dispersed in later stages, such that after a sustained phase of economic growth, "trickle down" was bound to happen, essentially like rainfall, with the clouds absorbing water and naturally shedding it, such that the lower stratums of the social structure would inevitably benefit from economic growth. Given belief in this notion, debates circled around supposedly secondary questions, such as how long the process might take, how intensive might it be, and how far and wide would the wealth be spread.

3

Pathways out of Poverty

The World Bank on Agriculture for Development

Henry Veltmeyer

The World Bank's *World Development Report 2008: Agriculture for Development* (WDR-08) is an important signature study of a critically important issue: "agriculture for development"—the role of agriculture in the development process as one of three pathways out of rural poverty. The report is presented in the midst of an apparent sea change in the structure of international North–South relations in the organization of global production, to which agriculture, despite the epoch-defining changes in this organization, still makes a substantive contribution. Agriculture, according to the report, also provides the only or principal source of livelihood for a large part of the world's population, particularly in the countries that it classifies as "agriculture based" (mostly in sub-Saharan Africa but also in parts of Asia and Central America), where on average agriculture accounts for over 20 percent of national production, at least 65 percent of employment, and more than 50 percent of the population living and working in conditions of poverty. Agriculture, however, like industry and services, is not static: it is at the base of a long-term and large-scale process of capitalist development and structural transformation resulting in what the report describes as the "three worlds of development"—rural-agrarian (agriculture based), in transition ("transforming"), and urban-industrial (urbanized). This categorization of three worlds provides the context for the report's analysis of what we might term the "rural poverty problematic." The central concern of the WDR-08 is to conceptualize the pathways out of poverty available in each of these worlds, the contribution and role of agriculture in the process, and the possible agencies for change and development.

There is nothing new in this studied concern, except perhaps the opportunity to respond to it under conditions of change in the political economy of global development in the new millennium—and within the framework (and with the lens) of the "new paradigm" in development theory and the recently achieved post-Washington Consensus (PWC) on appropriate policy. But this is precisely what makes the WDR-08 so disappointing: its failure to break out of the old development paradigm of modernization theory or to critically examine the development dynamics of the PWC on the need for a more inclusive form of neoliberalism and a more participatory and equitable form of development. As a result, the WDR is unable to overcome the deficit in development thinking based on belief in the magic of a market freed from the regulatory constraints of the development state—the central proposition and staple diet of the faith-based economics that has dominated development thinking and policymaking over the past two decades. The argument of this chapter is that the WDR fails to break out of the box—to reenvision the role of agriculture in the development process and provide the theoretical and policy tools for addressing and dealing with the rural poverty problematic.

The WDR-08 is the latest of diverse efforts over the past decade in the search for a pathway out of rural poverty. Another such study was commissioned and published by the Inter-American Development Bank (IDB) in 1998, more than a decade ago. This report also sought to square the circle, as it were, to advance a way out of the crisis of rural development without abandoning the system or turning away from the neoliberal policies that by many diverse accounts are very much part of the problem. The IDB report prefaces its account of "the path out of poverty"—its "approach to reducing poverty"—with the twofold observation that (1) the economies in the region were on the way to recovery, being much "stronger as the result of structural reform,"[1] and (2) the failure to redress the "unacceptably high levels of poverty," which, the report's preface continues, are "founded, in large measure, on an unequal distribution of income and assets" (IDB 1998c, 3). But what the report fails to note and certainly to analyze—a failure also of the World Bank's 2008 report a decade on—is that these inequalities not only have deep historical roots but are undoubtedly connected to and exacerbated by the very reforms that they so assiduously espouse and on which they have pinned their hopes and belief. This is symptomatic of a major blind spot, one of several that we point out, that prevents these economists from understanding and coming to terms with the rural poverty problematic.

This chapter argues that the WDR-08 in its ideological concerns and blinders fails to explain or even identify the fundamental dynamics of rural poverty. Because of this, the economists associated with the WDR-08 fail to see the connection of poverty to the neoliberal policies of the Washington or Davos Consensus—or to the PWC reached over the past decade—and even to consider let alone evaluate the abundant analysis contrary to their fundamental domain assumptions or to listen to the voices of the poor that were raised against these policies. This failure and refusal by itself is clear evidence of the working of paradigmatic assumptions that are rooted in a modernization theory of economic development and structural transformation that has guided development thinking and policy for close to sixty years. There has been much talk and writing over the past decade about the need for a new paradigm—a new way of thinking about development, of conceiving and redressing the poverty problematic. However, it is evident—and this chapter argues—that the WDR-08 is not in this mold and that it fails to break out of the mental box that has confined the thinking and policy advice of the World Bank throughout its four-decade war on poverty.

To this end this chapter identifies a number of blind spots in the analysis and conclusions presented in the report. These blind spots, it is suggested, vitiate an otherwise valuable and commendable effort to analyze at length and in detail the global dynamics of rural poverty and the role of agriculture as a pathway out of poverty. Unfortunately, the report's commitment to ideology over science has rendered it incapable of grasping and explaining the fundamental dynamics of rural poverty, agriculture, and development. For example, it is evident that in abandoning farming and migrating to the cities, many of the rural poor have substituted one form of poverty for another. The failure of the WDR-08 to appreciate the negative impact of neoliberal "pro-growth" policies on small-scale production and peasant farming, or to grasp the policy dynamics of rural and urban poverty, leads the authors to support, if not prescribe, policies that narrow the options available to the rural poor rather than create opportunities.

Pathways out of Poverty in the Era of Neoliberal Globalization

The World Bank in its WDR-08 conceives of three pathways out of poverty—labor, migration, and farming. But it is evident although not precisely stated that the authors of the report, like World Bank economists generally, continue to assume that the most practical and advisable solution to the problem of rural poverty is for the poor to abandon farming and exit the countryside.

As De Janvry, one of the WDR-08's leading authors, and Sadoulet (2000) noted in an earlier study on this issue set in Latin America, to that date the exodus of the poor to the cities was the primary form of poverty reduction, explaining virtually all of the advances made on the rural front of the global war on poverty. "Reduction in the number of rural relative to urban poor," De Janvry and Sadoulet (2000, 389) argue in this connection, "has been mainly the outcome of migration, not of successful rural development."[2]

At the time De Janvry and Sadoulet conceived of four "exit paths" available to the rural poor: exiting (outmigration), agriculture (farming), assistance (essentially in support of farming), and "pluriactive," with reference to the livelihood strategy pursued in practice by many if not most of the rural poor, which is to combine farming with off-farm wage labor. In effect, then as now (at least in Latin America) most of the rural poor are poor not because of the low productivity of agricultural activity or their regressive worldview but because they had been rendered landless or near landless in a process of "primitive accumulation" of capital. Dispossessed of their means of social production, they had little choice but to turn from direct production to labor in one form or the other, working the land owned by others, or, more often, to search for nonfarm employment in the countryside or in the cities. In effect, most of the rural poor had no option but to turn from farming to migration and labor, often both.

The workings of this assumption—that the forces of social change dictate the poor exit agriculture and rural society—on World Bank thinking about development are reflected, first of all, in the relative lack of concern for and attention to agriculture in the Bank's annual review of critical development issues. As noted by Akram-Lodhi (2008) in his critical review of the WDR-08, the first and last report on agriculture before the 2008 report was written in 1982.

Another manifestation of the assumption that labor and migration constitute the most effective pathways out of rural poverty is the belief, deeply embedded in the modernization theory that dominated analysis and practice in the 1950s and the 1960s and evidently shared by World Bank economists even today, is that

1. the dominant form of agricultural production, the small-scale agricultural producer or peasant farmer, is economically backward, marginal, and unproductive;
2. the peasant economy of small-scale localized production is a drag on development;

3. capital invested in urban-based industry has a considerably greater return, with much greater multiplier effects on production and employment, than a comparable investment in agriculture would have;

4. development requires, and is predicated on, a modernization process of structural transformation—of agriculture into industry and the peasantry into a working class;

5. rural society and agriculture in this process serves development as a reservoir of labor surplus to the requirements of capitalist development and modernization;

6. farming opportunities for the rural poor, most of whom are engaged in relatively unproductive economic activities and are either landless or near landless, are scarce and restricted either because the limits of land reform have been reached or because of the requirements of capitalist modernization (large or increased-scale production, capital-intensive technology, external inputs, etc.);

7. many of the rural poor who retain some access to land are compelled to turn toward wage labor as a source of livelihood and household income; and

8. because of the economic and social structure of agricultural production, there are simply too many people in rural society chasing too few opportunities for productive economic activity. Thus, farming provides few "opportunities" for the rural poor to change and improve their situation—to escape or alleviate their poverty. Labor migration is the solution.

The combination of these ideas has led many economists and sociologists—including, as it happens, the lead authors of the WDR-08—to view the peasantry by and large as an anachronism, seeking to defend a way of life and an economy that is inherently nonviable, entrenching most in a poverty trap. The best, if not precisely the only, pathway out of this poverty is to abandon farming and migrate in the search of wage labor employment opportunities and inclusion in government services, also more accessible in the cities and urban centers.

These ideas have tended to inform and orient both theory and practice in the development mainstream. Thus, in 1995, a full decade into the era of neoliberal globalization and a market-assisted approach to agrarian modernization and reform, Mitchell Seligson argued in the specific but not atypical case of El Salvador that farming was not a pathway out of rural poverty, that limits of land reform had been reached, and that the efforts of the Democratic Peasant Federation, the largest and most representative confederation of peasant organizations in the country, and the peasant social movement to stay on the land and pursue farming as a way of life was misplaced and bound to fail. The demand of peasant farmers for land and land reform, debt relief, and facilitated access to new technology and credit, he further argued, did not warrant the support of the development community because it runs counter to an irresistible trend toward agricultural modernization. The rural poor would be better off to search for paid employment opportunities, and the development community would be better off to support the efforts of the poor in this direction—to capacitate them to take advantage of existing opportunities for self- or paid employment in the urban centers.[3]

This analysis is symptomatic of the approach taken by most agricultural and development economists over the years and to this date. It also explains, at least in part, the trend noted in the WDR-08 that "the share of agriculture in official development assistance declined sharply over the past two decades," and, as the Bank admitted, "the . . . bigger decline was from the multilateral financial institutions, especially the World Bank" (World Bank 2008, 41).

Given the thinking of World Bank economists, this trend is hardly surprising. It reflects assumptions shared by most scholars and practitioners in the context of the then (and it seems still) dominant orthodox paradigm. Notwithstanding the World Bank's declared commitment to "evidence-based development policies," its approach to thinking and practice in the area of agriculture clearly reflects the working of these assumptions. Even so, more often than not the working of these assumptions is not clear or transparent because they are not normally specified, and often the relevant evidence is "constructed" to suit. Thus, to determine the relative weight of the evidence and fundamental belief (paradigmatic assumptions) is not easy. It requires a careful deconstruction of the discourse in which these assumptions, that delimit or structure both development thinking and practice, are embedded—to expose them and trace their effect on the Bank's and analysis and policy prescriptions. The World Bank's 2008 report, and its forty-two background papers, provides a useful means to this end.

Deconstructing the WDR-08

To deconstruct the text of the WDR-08, it is important, first of all, to identify its authors, whose assumptions in research and analysis inform and "structure" the ideas presented. Of course, it is not easy to sort out the precise contributions of so many authors and consultants, particularly in the case of this report, which, Akram-Lodhi (2008) points out, manifest a surprising "pervasive heterogeneity" of ideas. Given that several scholars associated with the writing of the report, even one of the leading authors in the report team, have been critical of the Bank's interventions in regard to rural economies, the problem of sorting out the World Bank's thinking and its policy position is even more difficult. What it requires is a sorting out of the basic underlying domain assumptions, which presumably do not exhibit the same degree of heterogeneity as the presented ideas. In fact, it is likely—and this is *our* working assumption—that as we deeply probe the text of the report, an underlying unity of thought will appear. Differences in interpretation, even conflicting ideas, may materialize, but often these differences—this heterogeneity—mask an underlying agreement on fundamental principle, a small set of shared beliefs and common assumptions. Thus, the question in regard to the WDR-08 is whether such an underlying unity can be identified in the mix of ideas and the research findings advanced.

Of course, the existence of an underlying agreement and shared domain assumptions does not obviate the utility of specific ideas or take them out of context, particularly because, as Akram-Lodhi notes, "there is a lot in the report with which many people [presumably Akram-Lodhi himself and fellow researchers] would agree" (2008, 1146). In other words, ideas can be detached not only from the context that gave rise to them but from the discourse in which they are embedded and from which we propose to excavate them (Sachs 1999). The problem is to determine the relation that these ideas have to the assumptions underlying them and the empirical evidence adduced in support of a belief in, and use of, these ideas. Nevertheless, as in any archaeological dig—to extend Wolfgang Sachs's metaphorical Foucauldian representation of discourse analysis—this discourse excavation and deconstruction requires that the outcome products (discovered ideas) be carefully cataloged and contextualized. Often it also means the reconstruction of elements that are missing or absent but even so connected to the phenomena explained by reference to the excavated ideas.

This operation in discourse analysis has three basic dimensions. First is inferential logic (piecing together the whole from existing parts) rather than empirical correlation—associating observed patterns to conditions that are objective in their effects (related to these patterns). Second, it means identifying silences or patterns of absence in phenomena (interpretative ideas) that are conspicuous by their very absence, that is, the empirical data presented in the text suggest or point to interpretative ideas that are not given. And third, a critical discourse analysis requires digging beneath the ideas advanced in the text (the WDR-08) to the socioeconomic interests that they reflect, connecting them not so much to the adduced empirical evidence but to the unstated and perhaps barely conscious interests of the authors—to the social group or class with which they identify; in other words, not to view these ideas in terms of a presumed or identified operative scientific theory but to view them as part of an ideology, designed to obfuscate or mask reality rather than explain it. In this connection, it is safe—or almost so—to assume that any text has within it elements of both science and ideology, the first in the interest of advancing knowledge, and the latter in the interests of a group or class with which the author knowingly or unknowingly identifies. The problem, and task, is to sort out the workings and weight of science and ideology relative to the relevant objectively given or constructed "facts."

Appearances and Reality: Stated Aims and Operating Assumptions

The first point made by Akram-Lodhi in his critical analysis of the WDR-08 is that there is a difference between what the report in fact provides and its stated aim: to provide a fresh vision of the agriculture-development relation—in Akram-Lodhi's words, "a paradigm-shifting reimagining of the policy and practice of rural development" (2008, 1147). As Akram-Lodhi notes in his dissection of the report's contents, it falls far short of this aspiration. Rather than a new vision and imagining, or a simple interpretation of the facts, it is, rather, "an intervention that is the logical culmination of prior rural policy and practice at the World Bank" (2008, 1147). In other words, the report in general hews close to the analysis of related developments in earlier and different contexts, staying very close to the assumptions of the old and still dominant paradigm, assumptions shared by all of the economists and practitioners at the Bank regardless of a professed concern for establishing a "new paradigm" and regardless of the apparent heterogeneity in their ideas. These assumptions lead the authors of the WDR-08 to arrive at predetermined conclusions and to prescribe policies that reflect the dominant paradigm, some facts, and many ideas to the contrary. For one thing, neither in the report itself nor in any of the forty-two background papers prepared for it is there any consideration of ideas that reflect a different viewpoint or conflicting assumptions. These assumptions, and the large body of studies that reflects or advances them in their research and analysis, are studiously or consciously ignored—a "fact" that can be ascertained by a reading of the text and by a simple perusal of the studies consulted and the report's list of academic references. On this issue Akram-

Lodhi (2008, 1147) notes, "The Report's recommendations would consolidate the corporate food regime that emerged in the last decade of the 20th century and which now dominates global agriculture." The point is that the viewpoint and ideas of organizations such as *Vía Campesina* and the large volume of academic studies that are critical of this regime are conspicuous by their absence.

The Notion of "Three Worlds of Development"

The WDR-08 distinguishes three broad groups of developing and transition countries, based on the contribution of agriculture to economic growth and the share of rural poverty in total poverty. These three worlds are composed of (1) *agriculture-based* countries, in which agriculture's share of production is greater than 20 percent and the rural poor constitute at least 50 percent of all the poor; (2) *transforming* countries, in which the contribution of agriculture to growth is less than 25 percent and the rural poor are at least 60 percent of all the poor; and (3) *urbanized* countries, in which the contribution of agriculture is less than 20 percent and the rural poor are less than 60 percent of the total.

Both categories (worlds of development, poverty) as defined or measured betray long-held assumptions more than they represent "facts." Behind the notion of three worlds is the clear albeit unstated assumption of a long historical process of productive (and social) transformation—the "great transformation" in the conception of Karl Polanyi, which in the mainstream of development thinking among sociologists and economists over many years, over a century (the twentieth) in fact, has three critical dimensions, each manifest in a metatheory or overarching explanatory framework: (1) *modernization*—the transition and transformation of a traditional-type society based on a traditional communalist culture into one modern society based on a modern individualist culture of achievement orientation in which each individual rationally calculates and pursues a path of self-interest, taking advantage of available opportunities; (2) *industrialization*—the transformation of a preindustrial agrarian society into a modern industrial form of society (a transformative change in the basic structure of production); and (3) *capitalist development* or *proletarianization*—the transformation of a society of small-scale peasant agricultural producers into a proletariat, a class of individuals dispossessed of the land and compelled to exchange their labor power for a living wage.

There is considerable historical evidence of a long-term trend that can be theorized in these terms. On this there is little to no dispute. Where there is considerable dispute and ongoing social-scientific debate—although there is no trace of it in the WDR-08, which is not surprising, or in any of the background papers, which is more surprising—is in regard to the assumption that there is an immutable historic process, that the forces of social change and structural transformation released in this process are irresistible, and that the only possible response to these forces is to adjust to them and to do so in one of just three ways.

Conceiving of Change: Pathways out of Rural Poverty

The central idea advanced by the WDR-08 is that the rural poor have available to them three pathways out of poverty, each a possible response to the forces of change: capitalist development, industrialization, and modernization. Interestingly, although with reference to its paradigmatic assumptions not surprising, the report assumes—there is, in fact, no systematic analysis or theory constructed to the purpose of explaining rural poverty, a major lacuna in the report—that the fundamental source of rural poverty is the economic and social structure of the rural economy rather than the forces of change that surround and beset this "agrarian structure." In this, they differ from, and totally ignore, the analysis provided by scholars with a divergent political economy approach to analysis and a critical theory as to the operation of these forces. Within the theoretical and analytical framework used by the economists at and with the World Bank and, it seems, shared by all the authors who contributed to the WDR-08, small-scale agricultural producers—the "peasants" as self-defined and academically conceived by many—are viewed as having a traditional cultural orientation (toward communalism) and an unproductive economic practice that marginalizes them from the process of productive transformation and the opportunities for self-advancement and improvement that this process generates. In this conception the only way out of poverty is for the poor to participate in the opportunity structure of modern industrial capitalist society, and the best policy advice that can be given to them is to adjust to and not resist the forces of change. "Development" in this context implies intervention in the form of helping the poor make this adjustment—to capacitate them to do so and to see and take advantage of the opportunities open or made available to them, a policy matter of "equity," "inclusion," "participation," and "good governance" (Bebbington, Hickey, and Mitlin 2008; Potter 2000; UNDP 2006; World Bank 1994a).[4]

As for the pathway that the poor might or should take, the report sees the greatest opportunities to be in migration and labor, notwithstanding a professed concern for the significant development contributions that agriculture can make. But this in no way derived from a careful analysis of un- or deconstructed facts or of the thinking and struggles of the rural poor themselves. At the turn into the new millennium, the World Bank collected the voices of more than 60,000 poor women and men from sixty countries, in an unprecedented effort to understand poverty from the perspective of the poor themselves (Narayan et al. 2000). They even consulted with representative organizations of the rural poor such as *Vía Campesina* and the global coalitions that have raised the voice of the rural poor in the struggle for inclusion in the process of change and development and in resistance against the forces of capitalist development under conditions of neoliberal globalization. But none of the voices appear within or can be found behind the text of the WDR-08.

The concepts used to categorize information and research (worlds of agriculture and development, pathways out of poverty) are descriptive rather than analytical. As for the dynamics of change and development associated with these categories, the Bank's focus is entirely on three types of adjustments made by the poor to the forces operating on them, their economies, their communities, and their societies. There is a total absence of any reference to, let alone analysis of, the response to these forces in the form of resistance. And resistance to these forces in different contexts (especially in Latin America) has taken diverse and virulent forms (see, for example, Petras and Veltmeyer 2005). By definition or analytical fiat, to resist is viewed as regressive, a failure to appreciate the insistent and—in the long term—unavoidable dynamics of change. As the authors of the report view it, the only way out of poverty is for the poor to adjust to the requirements of the new world order in which the forces of freedom (the private sector, the market) are liberated from the restrictions of the development state and to take advantage of the opportunities made available in the process.

Farming Versus Migration and Labor

The Bank's differentiation of three worlds is based on a somewhat arbitrary line drawn across two points of agricultural employment as an average share of the labor force: 65 percent, 57 percent, and 18 percent, respectively. There is, in fact, little reasoning provided in support of this categorization that point to substantive differences in the three worlds of development. Why not two or four? Presumably there are dynamics and shared conditions associated with this typology of worlds, which denotes different stages in a development that all countries, it is anticipated and theorized, will undergo. Thus, the category of "urbanized" is a reconceptualization of "modern" and thus "developed" and "industrialized" in the heavily criticized theory that dominated the 1950s and 1960s (criticized precisely for its assumption of universality and immanence). By the same token, the category "agricultural" is a proxy of "traditional" in this theory, associated with "undeveloped" and economical backwardness. As for "transforming," it represents an intermediate stage of development in the direction of modernization and capitalist industrialization in an inevitable and unstoppable process of productive and social transformation.

Several comments are in order here. First, the notion of "three worlds" is not only a descriptive rather than an analytical category but a bad one at that: it does not correspond to reality. Second, it reflects a return to the modernization theory of the 1950s and 1960s—hardly the imagining of a new vision and certainly no paradigmatic shift. It ignores entirely the real possibility in the world today for the rural poor to pursue their own path or to imagine and create their own future along a different trajectory from this preconceived path. It also ignores the possibility for the rural poor, small-scale landholders, and agricultural producers to resist rather than adjust to these forces of change and, under certain conditions, to defend and preserve a society and economy of small-scale producers (Desmarais 2007).

The problem is to determine what might be these conditions, but in several blind spots of the report's analysis, and the inability of its authors to think outside the box (the orthodox paradigm), there is no interest in exploring dynamics of change that run counter to their preconceived notions and the ideology associated with them. The peasantry in this context represents a backward social and economic category that has a declining numerical and political significance as a spent force railing against irresistible force with no potential for constructing their own future along their self-chosen path, which by the report's definition is a poverty trap.

Productive and Social Transformation

A domain assumption of modernization theory is that "development," understood as incremental improvements made in the direction of economic growth, is based on transformative change in the structures of economic production, culture, and society. Ironically, this assumption, explicit in both the 1982 and 2008 WDRs on agriculture, is shared by Marxist political economists and sociologists who have a decidedly different perspective on the process of capitalist development but nevertheless share with orthodox development economists the view of development as a process of structural transformation surrounding the expansion of a "capitalist nucleus" (Hunt 1989).

There is in fact a lot of evidence and argumentation in support of this metatheory of social change (see, for example, McMichael 2003). It is evident that large numbers of the rural poor since the 1960s, particularly in Latin America, have taken the road of least resistance, adjusting to the forces of change by abandoning agriculture along the pathways of labor and migration—

often in the combined form of labor migration. The dynamics of this process are reflected in the statistics on national poverty rates, particularly in regard to the urban-rural distribution of these rates, as well as the substantive evidence of a process of rapid urbanization: in the 1960s most countries would have been categorized by the WDR as "agricultural," but by 2005, after two decades of neoliberal reforms that by many accounts have worked to accelerate the process, every country had completed the transition and transformation into the modern world of agrarian capitalist development and urbanization. Even Bolivia and Paraguay exceeded the urbanization threshold as defined by the report.

There is little dispute over a long trend in this direction. But where there is considerable dispute is in how to understand the dynamics of the process, particularly in regard to the depoliticized nature of the World Bank's understanding of these dynamics. First, there is no awareness in the WDR-08 of the dynamics at work in the process of capitalist development of agriculture. This development is predicated on a process of "primitive accumulation"—dispossession of the direct producers from the land, which, as it happens, not only induces a process of social transformation (conversion of peasants into workers) but is the basic structural—and political!—source of poverty in rural society: landlessness or near landlessness (on the regional dynamics of this process, see the various studies in Moyo and Yeros 2005).

This condition is not the inevitable consequence of an unstoppable process. More often than not it is a political condition rooted in a historic process of expropriation or dispossession by violence and legislation. It is, in the unformulated modernization theory behind the WDR-08, the source of backwardness and poverty: the traditional communalist (as opposed to individualist) culture of peasant society leads to unproductive practices—the failure to invest productively in new technology and superior forms of organization and in taking advantage of the opportunities presented by the forces of change.

Rather than resisting these forces, the landless or semiproletarianized peasant of today—over 50 percent of all—are expected if not required to adjust to change. What about farming as an option—as a pathway out of poverty? For most peasants it is not an option. They simply do not have the wherewithal—first of all land, and then the technology and capital, and then the capacity to exploit these resources productively and effectively. One of the report's ideas that Akram-Lodhi (2008) thinks that we can agree with is that some peasants could indeed adjust to the forces of agrarian capitalism and agricultural modernization and be capacitated to pursue farming as a pathway out of poverty. This is one difference from the 1982 WDR and economists at the Bank over the years. They had always worked with the assumption that the key to agricultural productivity is capitalist development, which specifically excluded the peasant producers who dominated agricultural production in the global South.

The problem is that this policy comes up against another blind spot in the WDR-08. The first blind spot relates to the dynamics of primitive accumulation as the source of poverty. The second concerns the actual dynamics of productive and social transformation associated with the process of capitalist development. In the Latin American context, the rural poor include a large number of landless or near landless peasants but most, over 50 percent in many cases, are semiproletarianized, that is, they have to combine agricultural production or tenant farming with wage labor. In theory, the labor released from the land would be absorbed by urban industry, incorporated into the labor markets of the growing urban centers. But reality has not confirmed this theory. In practice what has occurred is a process of partial or semiproletarianization. Rather than being converted into a modern urban-centered working class, the vast majority of the rural poor, dispossessed of the land, have been converted into a rural semiproletariat, retaining access to some land but increasingly reliant on wage labor as a means of livelihood and household income, and an urban semiproletariat of informal workers, working "on their own account" on the streets rather than exchanging their labor power against capital. Over 50 percent of the rural poor in Latin America can be categorized as semiproletarianized in these terms, with substantial evidence to suggest that they will never complete the theorized transition—the process of social transformation into a modern waged working class. And most of the urban poor are similarly unable and unlikely to complete the process, compelled or led in numerous cases to look further, to migrate overseas in the search of greater "opportunity."

At a macro-level, the problem with the implicit thinking behind the WDR-08 is that the level of urbanization cannot, as in prior theory, be used as a proxy for structural transformation and thus the level of development. In this theory, to which it seems many economists today still subscribe, development is defined in conditional terms as economic growth, measured as an annual increase in the GDP, and at the structural level as industrialization, which tends to be urban-based and -centered, thus leading to a convergence between urbanization and industrialization-modernization, capitalist development-proletarianization and economic development. However, in Latin America there has not been such a convergence: urbanization, over the course of the past three decades, has increased at twice the rate of industrialization and has not correlated well with the degree of economic and social development. Most countries in the region today, after two decades of neoliberal globalization and associated "development," can be placed in the middle-income category, but so could many of them in the 1970s, in a process of transition. As for the "transforming countries," most of which are located in Asia, they currently exhibit the most dynamic forces of economic growth and structural transformation in the world but at a lower rate of urbanization than in Latin America where the forces of adjustment and resistance are more dynamic than the rate of economic growth.

The fact is neither rural nor urban society under given conditions today have an opportunity structure, impeding the efforts of the World Bank and the development community to induce a process of "productive transformation with equity" (ECLAC 1990) and so expand the opportunities available to the rural poor, capacitating them to take advantage of these opportunities—the fundamental policy of the World Bank in its war on global poverty.

A third blind spot in the analysis of the economists at the World Bank and associated with the WDR-08 is their failure to recognize what the urban and rural poor understand all too well—that the very "pro-growth" policies that the Bank prescribes for both urban and rural development are designed to close the poverty trap in which the poor are enmeshed. These policies have in fact been redesigned under the terms of the PWC, but by many accounts they have had but a marginal impact, if any, on the state or rate of rural poverty.

The question is, is there a substantive difference between the policies of the Washington Consensus (the lauded but heavily criticized "structural adjustment program") and the PWC on correct policy? More to the point, what does this policy—and paradigmatic shift—mean for the rural poor? Does it have any bearing on the structure of opportunity available to them in agriculture or the labor market or on the forces of change generated in the ongoing capitalist development process of productive and social transformation? Does it have any bearing on the pathways out of rural poverty in removing existing obstacles? And more to the point, does it have any bearing on the struggle of peasants to take the path of resistance rather than adjustment and on their efforts to construct a different regime, a viable peasant economy of small-scale agricultural production within an alternative paradigm?

Pathways out of Poverty: Sins of Commission and Omission

The WDR-08, like the WDR-82, despite the recognition of diverse patterns and heterogeneity, clearly expects that the "great transformation" from a traditional, precapitalist, and agrarian society to a modern industrial capitalist system will necessarily proceed by degrees through definite, if not predetermined, stages: in the WDR's conception from "agriculture based" to "transforming" and then to "urbanized." Thus the key to this analysis—the implicit theory of development behind the report—is the dynamic of "transformation." But what characterizes this dynamic and releases the forces of change and development? The driving forces? Obstacles? The agency of change?

Presumably the major obstacles to change are rooted in the structure of the agriculture-based societies, most of which today are found in sub-Saharan Africa. Typically, most of the transforming countries are found in Asia—earlier in Japan and southeast Asia and today in China, India, Indonesia, and so on. As for the impediments to growth and transformation, they are undoubtedly rooted in the internal structure of these societies—although the authors betray no analysis or the least understanding of these structures, focusing as they do on an apparent heterogeneity of economic practice in agriculture and a general orientation toward cash crop production and resource extraction within the international division of labor. However, the report also notes common characteristics, which presumably should be factored into any analysis for the failure or slowness of these countries to proceed along the evolutionary path of progress. They include (no analysis is actually made) the fact that they tend to be small in population size or with low population-land densities, are often landlocked, and are commonly emerging from conflict, which means that the trade, infrastructure, and services necessary for markets to work well are weak or sparse. Moreover, agriculture-based countries seem to be particularly susceptible to climatic shock in their reliance on rain-fed water supplies.

As for the transition from agriculture to the first step toward transformation, in the case of agriculture-based countries, and the second set of steps that the rural poor need to take in the context of transformation, the critical issues have to do with the dynamics of a rural-to-urban migration process—relocation of the rural poor to the cities and urban centers where appropriate infrastructure and other requirements for change and development, for equitable social inclusion, as well as its driving forces (capital, technology, trade) and key agents, are based or focused. The point is, it is argued and the report makes clear, many if not most of the rural poor are unable to "farm their way out of poverty" (World Bank 2008, 234), and thus they need to exploit any rural nonfarm opportunities (rural wage labor) and—on a larger scale—opportunities available in the urban centers.

Oddly enough, neither the rural migration nor the labor market dynamics of the urbanization process are presented for analysis. Unlike the structural dynamics of contract farming or the policy dynamics associated with the process of incorporating agricultural production into the global economy, they are taken for granted or perhaps buried in one of the background papers. They are nevertheless taken as key factors in the transformation process, which implies a process of productive transformation (of agriculture into industry) and social transformation (of peasants into wage workers). The focus of the report's limited analysis is on the dynamics of capitalist development of agriculture and the requirements and opportunities provided by these dynamics for farming as a form of livelihood and a pathway out of poverty.

The critical factor regarding the latter is to increase the productivity of agricultural labor (although the report notes that it is already higher in farming than nonfarming, thus providing little constraint). And the key to increased productivity, as the authors of the report see it—again, as in 1982—is improved access to both capital and technology, and to the product and capital markets, more investment in research and extension, and, above all, increasing competitiveness; in other words, market-led development and the agency of the private sector (rather than the state) and capital in this development. Presumably, the state is expected to facilitate and assist this development in the form of providing an appropriate institutional and policy framework, as well as infrastructure, a critical factor in the economic development process and for markets to function properly, and security, a critical factor impeding the development process in the agriculture-based countries of sub-Saharan Africa (Collier 2004).

The key to improving the competitiveness of smallholder farming in agriculture-based countries, and so reducing rural poverty—and again this is the same message of the WDR-82—is to make markets work better in the production of traditional staples and nontraditional agricultural (and resource-based commodity) exports and in higher value crop, livestock, and horticultural products and by integrating smallholders into global agri-food commodity chains, deepening and broadening the export orientation of agricultural production.

The problem—from this perspective—is that the small-scale agricultural producers or peasants are, or appear to be (hence the need for education and training), relatively resistant to this development—in many cases and for the most part unable or unwilling to adapt to the requirements of modern farming and at the same time unwilling to take the migration route out of poverty. Whether this is the result of factors internal to the peasant economy and society—a traditional cultural or mind-set—or other conditions that vary by country and between regions of the global South is not clear. Evidently, peasants in sub-Saharan Africa and Asia are less inclined to take the migration pathway out of rural poverty. Also, how well migration and labor have worked as pathways out of poverty is not entirely clear. In Latin America, for example, a process of rapid urbanization both preceded and followed a process of rampant capitalist development and continued apace in the 1980s, barely slowing down in the 1990s when most countries in the region passed the "urban world" threshold. But the dynamics of this process do not correlate with progress made on the rural poverty front, which not only has resisted diverse strategies designed to reduce the incidence of absolute and relative poverty but has maintained its high level—currently at 51 percent across Latin America— despite the exodus of millions in search for better opportunities elsewhere.

In any case, according to the report's authors, the solution to rural poverty in farming-dependent agriculture-based countries lies in the deeper integration of "competitive" smallholders into the global economy through an expansion of nontraditional agricultural exports, expanded opportunities for rural waged labor, and outmigration from the rural economy. So what of the rural poor in the transitional and transforming societies of Asia and the urbanized societies of Latin America?

The Politics of Poverty Reduction

The striking feature—and another blind spot—in the WDR's analysis of the pathways out of rural poverty is that they are conceived of entirely in terms of an economic adjustment to the presumed irresistible forces of agrarian transformation and capitalist development. In these terms opportunities of the rural poor to "farm their way out of poverty" are few, and the majority are expected—and encouraged—to take the pathways of labor and outmigration.

The critical point of this lapse is the struggle of small-scale agricultural producers and other categories of peasants that make up the bulk of the rural poor in each of the three worlds identified in the report. What is surprising—considering the extensive field experience of at least one of the WDR-08's leading authors (De Janvry) in the contentious area of land reform—is how it entirely ignores the political dynamics of social change that arise out of this struggle. In Latin America, for example, the struggle for land and reform has brought the small-scale producers and the mass of landless and near landless workers—generally conceived of as "peasants" in different forms—into a relation of political conflict with the big landlords and rural bourgeoisie, who through different means under diverse conditions in different rural contexts managed to acquire the lion's share of the arable and productive land, and the state, which in this context generally assumed responsibility for mediating this conflict.

Poverty Relief in Agriculture-Based Countries

The solution to rural poverty in agriculture-based countries lies in (1) the deeper integration of competitive smallholders into global agriculture through an expansion of nontraditional agricultural exports, admittedly a small part of the solution, given that most peasants either have little productive capacity or are noncompetitive; (2) expanding opportunities for rural waged labor, a policy endorsed by the report's authors; and (3) outmigration from the rural economy, the most popular pathway out of rural poverty.

And what of the two other categories of countries in which agriculture plays a smaller role, making a relatively limited contribution to the overall production? For one thing, the WDR argues that agricultural productivity is lower in these countries than it is in agriculture-based societies, which is attributed to competitive pressures for scarce resources, particularly land and water, and a decline in farm size, all of which, according to the WDR-08, have generated political pressures in the direction of the subsidization and protection of food prices, electricity, access to water and fertilizers, and so on. These pressures, of course, work against the World Bank's pro-growth policies and thus against the rural poor, who, the report argues (somewhat tortuously, it might be said), do not benefit from a policy of protectionism and subsidies; this policy, it is argued, benefits the rural elite, not the poor.

The one apparent departure from orthodox development theory, articulated most clearly in the Lewis model, presented by the WDR is in regard to income dynamics. While the Lewis model assumed an initial gap between rural and urban incomes that was functional for economic development in causing a shift of labor to the urban centers (by drawing on the surplus labor generated by the income structure of rural labor), the authors of the WDR-08 argue for the utility and benefits of increasing rural incomes—to retain rather than expel labor. The mechanism for increasing rural incomes, the authors add, is to raise the productivity of agricultural labor by promoting the expansion of tradable agricultural staples and by aligning policy and technology so as to promote export growth of these staples, thus taking advantage of the comparative advantage in agricultural production and capitalizing on this production. Of course, this form of agriculture is relatively capital intensive—capital intensity being the normal route to productivity growth. And the theory of comparative advantages in agricultural production for export is a fundamental pillar of orthodox development policy. Where the WDR-08 departs from this orthodoxy is in the belief that a policy of nontraditional agricultural exports can, and should, be combined with a more labor-absorbing production of high value food crops, horticulture, livestock, and aquaculture products, for which there is a growing demand and both a local and an external market. The point made by the report is that both smallholder farming and rural waged labor can be connected in this way to expand production of nontraditional agricultural exports, thus opening up opportunities along the pathways of labor and farming, the only alternatives to rural poverty and outmigration, the third pathway out of rural poverty.

Poverty Relief in Transforming Countries
A key message for stakeholders in rural development within the transforming countries is that agriculture alone cannot relieve rural poverty. Indeed, the authors argue, farming is an option for very few of the rural poor, partly because of the relative lack of opportunity (given the dynamics of structural change) and partly because of the mind-set of most peasant farmers. For a majority of the rural poor, the only way out of poverty is outmigration or rural nonfarm waged labor. But to expand the farming pathway out of poverty, to provide more opportunities for poverty relief via farming, the WDR recommends policies designed to improve productivity through better soil and water management, technological upgrading, and extension interventions and to increase the integration of farmers into the market, capacitating them to do so via trade and price policies. As for policies in this area, the authors recommend unsurprisingly (considering the operating World Bank ideology of neoliberalism) "getting prices right"—to improve thereby the investment climate for agricultural businesses and to facilitate a tighter linking of smallholders to agri-food processors and agri-food retailers—and, more surprisingly, "contract farming" (because it entails higher incomes).

As for rural waged labor or outmigration for those drawn to more remunerative urban employment, clearly the options favored or recommended by the authors of the WDR-08, the best and indeed only policy is skill enhancement and capacitation.

Poverty Relief in the World of Urbanized Countries
Given the light weight of agriculture and its limited contribution to national production in the urbanized countries, as well as the advance of urbanization in the process of structural transformation, the analytical focus and policy emphasis of the report naturally enough falls on the alternative pathways of rural outmigration and labor, the pathway to which—considering the restricted structure of rural wage employment—also requires outmigration.

Notwithstanding the high degree of urbanization, which normally—in theory at least—correlates with other dimensions of structural transformation and associated improvements in the level of development, groups of urbanized countries in the global South also exhibit high rates of inequalities in the distribution of rural incomes and rural poverty. In Latin America, for example, the rate of rural poverty hovers around 50 percent, notwithstanding decades of outmigration and development programming. There is some correlation in that in many cases the higher the rate of urbanization, the lower the rate of rural poverty. This suggests several things. One, that the rural-to-urban migration process in recent years, especially in the decades of the 1970s and 1980s, which witnessed the greatest rural exodus, did have a moderating effect on the rural poverty rate and, it appears, also generated new forms of urban poverty in the process. Second, the problem of landlessness, by most accounts the major source of rural poverty (in addition to the low productivity of agricultural labor pointed to by the authors of the WDR-08), persists, pointing to the absence or lack of any effective land reform process and mounting resistance to policies of neoliberal globalization. Indeed, in many countries landlessness remains a critical livelihood and political problem and a continuing source of class struggle. The market-assisted reform programs of the 1990s, sponsored by the World Bank, were not designed to redress the land question, which is viewed by the Bank as an essentially political rather than a development process. Instead this market-assisted land reform program is designed to assist small-scale rural peasant producers in making the transition to family farming by improving their access to markets and nonland productive resources, especially credit, which is extended in the form of newly created land banks, a policy of the World Bank that has been hotly contested by the rural social movements, especially in Brazil where the policy has had its greatest extension (Mendes Pereira 2010a).

The WDR-08 points to another third notable feature of rural development in the urbanized countries of the global South, namely, the relatively higher weight of nonfarming activities in the structure of production and employment, which the report links to the productivity and income gains of agricultural modernization and commercial agriculture, which has dramatically expanded in recent years in the context of an irresistible and advancing globalization process. In this context, small landholding farmers, according to the report, are disadvantaged, held back by a relative lack of assets and unfavorable terms and conditions for entry into food and agricultural markets. Thus, neither rural nonfarm labor nor small-scale farming provides a viable route out of poverty. The solution—surprise, surprise—is to transform inefficient, low productivity smallholder agriculture into modern efficient commercial agriculture, well connected to the growing global markets for food and agricultural production in which the countries of the global South have a comparative advantage. As for the rural poor, it is clear that most of them will not be able to farm their way out of poverty. The solution or pathway out of poverty is continuing and further outmigration, a process that the development community should assist by capacitating the rural poor for waged or self-employment and by providing or strengthening the skills platform (the health and educational infrastructure) for this process.

This conclusion and policy advice are hardly surprising: both were essentially predetermined by the fundamental and unshakable assumptions shared, it seems, by all economists at the Bank, even the erstwhile critics who have been incorporated into the extended process leading to the production of the WDR-08, which, according to Akram-Lodhi (2008), cost the Bank more than $600,000.

On the basis of this assumption and the unshakable belief in the irresistible force and structural transformation/progressive development of agricultural modernization, the authors of the WDR-08 do not in any way or at any level address the fundamental questions begged by their policy advice: What are the outcomes of the outmigration process? Is outmigration a pathway out of poverty or merely the substitution of one form of poverty (rural) for another (urban)? A recent study of urban development, as global in scale as the WDR-08, by Mike Davis (2006) points to the latter development. Indeed, diverse studies of urban development over the past decade and a half suggest that under widespread social and economic conditions of neoliberal globalization, the so-called and presumed "structural transformation" associated with and responsible for improvements in social economic conditions ("development") is stalled, leading to an exceedingly uneven development process. In effect, the productive transformation of agriculture into industry and the social transformation of peasant farmers into waged-and-salaried workers have not unfolded as they should (according to theory). This observation leads us to suggest and argue that neither the conditions of rural and urban poverty, nor the policy dynamics associated with the diverse efforts to assist the poor, nor the pathways out of poverty available to the rural poor should be disconnected—as they are in the WDR-08.

Conclusion

The WDR-08 identified five different categories of rural livelihood strategy pursued by the rural poor along the three pathways available to them: (1) market-oriented farming, where at least 50 percent of agricultural production is sold in markets and 75 percent of total income derives from farming; (2) subsistence production, where less than 50 percent of agricultural production is market oriented and 75 percent of total income derives from farming; (3) the combination of farming with wage labor, pursued on a casual or seasonal basis; (4) migration-oriented livelihoods, where over 75 percent of total income is derived from remittances; and (5) diversified livelihoods, where labor or migration income sources contribute over 75 percent of total income.

However, what is striking about the report's categorization of rural livelihood strategies across the three worlds of global agriculture is that, as noted by Akram-Lodhi (2008), they result in a remarkably uniform triad of pathways out of rural poverty: commercially oriented entrepreneurial smallholder farming; rural nonfarm enterprise development and, more particularly, rural nonfarm waged labor; or outmigration. These pathways can be complementary and mutually reinforcing. Indeed, in the report's typology of livelihood strategies, it is outmigration and rural income diversification—that is, mutually reinforcing multiple pathways—that are usually found to be the normal route out of rural poverty in the evidence that is presented. Thus, as Akram-Lodhi points out, "An analytical perspective predicated upon pervasive heterogeneity gives way to a standardized and homogenous set of paths out of rural poverty across the three worlds of global agriculture" (2008, 1153). In this sense, then, the WDR-08, in Akram-Lodhi's words, "offers a dose of agro-pessimism that reflects a unilinear, path-dependent vision of the future of food and agriculture" (2008, 1153). We might add, and we conclude, that the Bank's "agro-pessimism" also reflects the power of an unstated unifying ideology. The analysis provided by the report is more reflective of this ideology than the ostensibly social scientific research provided in the more than forty background papers on which the report's authors have drawn. This is one conclusion that can be drawn from a review and critical analysis of the WDR-08.

A second conclusion that we, together with Akram-Lodhi and others, can draw from a critical review of the WDR-08 is that it is both analytically and theoretically deficient, ignoring critical dimensions of the rural poverty problematic. Four of these deficiencies are identified by Akram-Lodhi (2008).

First is a problematic analytical framework vis-à-vis the relationship between the contribution of agriculture to GNP growth and the ratio of rural to total poverty within the agrarian structure.

Second is the notion of an inverse relationship between farm size and farm productivity, which departs from the orthodox theory regarding economies of scale. The Bank in this connection acknowledges the alternative (heterodox) theory and practice in this regard (neopopulism) but, as might be anticipated, in disregard to substantial evidence to the contrary, falls back on the entrenched notion of an inverse relationship, adducing emerging conditions (new technologies, transaction costs, etc.) that favor land concentration and economies of scale. However, as Akram-Lodhi notes, the empirical basis of this position is weak, reflecting as it does the shared commitment of the report's authors and the Bank's economists to the notion and mental image of the farmer as either a "budding entrepreneur waiting to be unleashed by the power of the market or a worker who would be better off working for the entrepreneur than working their own piece of land" (2008, 1157). As Akram-Lodhi correctly observes, the report withdraws to the familiar albeit heavily criticized modernization theory of the 1950s and 1960s.

Third, behind the Bank's notion of "enabling markets," which underlies the policy prescriptions given in both the 1982 and the 2008 reports on agriculture—a notion that is remarkably (if unsurprisingly) consistent and resistant to empirical analysis of changing conditions—is the apparent view of peasant farmers as potential entrepreneurs, oriented toward commerce and the rational calculus of self-interest, and the unstated need to release the powerful productive force of the market, free from the constraints of the development and welfare state.

Fourth is the failure to grasp, or at least consider and present, the propensity of markets toward monopoly and the obstacles to the small-scale agricultural producer or capitalist farmer provided by the structure and dynamics of corporate power. The only way that peasant farmers in fact (or in the underlying theory of the report's authors) can survive the capitalist development of agriculture is to submit to the forces of this development and undergo a twofold process of conversion into a medium- to large-scale capitalist farmer and then a contractual relationship (as a contract farmer) with the corporations that dominate world trade. But what the authors of the report fail to understand and note is that this trade might be free but it is not fair, and it is anything but competitive: it is in fact geared to the power of monopoly capital rather than the competitive entrepreneurial farmer. The report ignores the actual dynamics of the global market for agricultural and food production, characterized by supermarketization, input agribusiness, and monopoly capital.

Beyond these analytical deficiencies—and there are others—the WDR-08 can be viewed as a powerful if nuanced restatement of a theory that had been all but abandoned by researchers in the field of agrarian transformation and rural development. As it is, the report makes no reference to, or any use of, the large body of work in this unorthodox tradition of alternative development thinking. The authors of the WDR-08 do not acknowledge or critically review and analyze the growing body of ideas and prescriptions for action by activists in a global peasant-based and -led movement committed to the sustainability of small-scale agricultural production and a way of life based on it.

This in itself is hardly surprising, reflecting as it does the presence and workings of various paradigmatic assumptions and an ideology that predisposes analysis toward system-supportive findings and prescriptions and to ignore contrary ideas. But if the economists at the Bank and the authors of the WDR-08 had been able to think outside of the box (the dominant paradigm of modernization theory), they might have been able to conceive of available "pathways out of poverty" in broader terms and not merely in economic adjustment terms. Even without the systematic analysis required and called for by some, it is evident that an active and mobilized resistance provides an alternative pathway toward social change if not out of poverty.

Notes

1. Ironically, this observation, echoed by IMF economists at the time and since, was made precisely at the time of an imminent three-year dramatic downturn of the economy in Latin America, leading ECLAC to foresee another "decade lost to development."

2. De Janvry and Sadoulet (2000, 390) note, "Despite relatively high income levels among developing countries, Latin American countries have high incidences of rural poverty because of the highly unequal distribution of income that characterizes them, both between sectors and within the rural sector." They also note, "Rural poverty is considerably deeper than urban poverty" (2000, 393), rooted as it is in grossly unequal land tenure systems and associated condition of landlessness, land poverty, and near landlessness.

3. This policy advice is the same as that given by De Janvry and Sadoulet in their 2000 study of pathways of rural poverty. "If the exit path is to be promoted as a way of reducing rural poverty [and they do so], the key is to help migrants relocate among the non-poor. . . . Agricultural technology has a clear indirect role here in inducing overall economic growth and thus employment and wages for migrants, but the key for success is education of a type that prepares rural children for non-farm jobs" (2000, 405). As for the "agricultural path . . . that land reform and rural development programmes have most pursued," the authors add, "key aspects of interventions have focused on" (1) "reducing market failures for smallholders"; (2) "constructing agrarian institutions for the delivery of credit, the supply of technical assistance, availability of ex-ante safety nets for the provision of risk-coping instruments and the reduction of transaction costs"; (3) "technology for smallholders [through] the supply of improved crops, farming systems and traits specific to this clientele [and] . . . to identify market opportunities and reduce transactions costs"; (4) "provision of public goods accessible to smallholders and complementary to their particular kind of investments"; and (5) a "macroeconomic and sectoral policy framework that does not discriminate against agriculture and smallholders" (2000, 405). Anything, we might add, but improved access to land and land reform—or the debt relief demanded by the social movements.

4. These conditions are defining principles of the "new paradigm of development thinking and practice" (Atria 2004), as well as the PWC (Craig and Porter 2006). Accordingly, as De Janvry and Sadoulet (2000) note, "New approaches to rural development have stressed 1. Decentralization and improved capacity of local governments, 2. Promotion of grassroots organizations often assisted by non-government organizations, 3. Participation of organized beneficiaries, 4. Devolution to user groups of control over common property resources and local public goods and 5. Collective action for the management of common property resources, the delivery of local public goods and bargaining over policymaking" (2000, 406). Again, anything but land and land reform (on this see Veltmeyer 2007).

4

Fighting Poverty in Mexico

Darcy Tetreault

Over the past two decades, a new paradigm for social policy has emerged in Latin America, one that seeks consistency with the consensus on the need to establish "a better balance between the market and the state," particularly with regard to the war on poverty. Along these lines, pretensions to create a universal welfare state have been largely abandoned in favor of a more cost-effective approach whose centerpiece is conditional cash transfer (CCT) programs that target the extremely poor. These programs transfer income directly to poor families under the condition that they keep their kids in school, visit the local health clinic on a regular basis, and attend workshops. The idea is to break the vicious cycle of intergenerational poverty by helping the poor to develop "human capital," with the hope that young beneficiaries will be able to more effectively insert themselves into labor markets sometime in the future. In Mexico, this program is called *Progresa-Oportunidades* (PROP). It has served as a model for other countries throughout the region, sixteen of which have adopted similar programs (Valencia Lomelí 2008). On the global level, there are now thirty such programs.

PROP has been highly touted by the World Bank and other international development agencies. Empirical evidence suggests that its beneficiaries generally enjoy better health and stay in school longer. The question remains, however, as to whether the program's graduates will be able to find well-paying jobs in the formal economy. Job creation has been mostly left up to the private sector, but under the structural conditions created by the neoliberal reforms implemented during the 1980s and 1990s, there has been no growth in formal sector employment. What is more, in the countryside, where extreme poverty is concentrated, market liberalization has led to oligopolistic conditions that essentially make small-scale farming economically unviable (see chapter 9). In this context, the poor—whether they are better educated and healthier or not—have been forced to migrate to urban centers and eke out a living in the informal sector or to migrate abroad, with a host of implicit dangers and sacrifices.

Originally called the Program for Education, Health and Food (PRO-GRESA, in its Spanish acronym), Mexico's main antipoverty program was launched in August 1997, two and a half years after the so-called "tequila crisis" and just when the Asian financial crisis began to unfold in Thailand, South Korea, Malaysia, and elsewhere. It was in this context, in light of the dangers and instability associated with the unfettered flow of speculative capital and of devastating social consequences that crises have for the poor and the working classes, that the post-Washington Consensus began to take shape. In essence, it was (and is) a reform agenda that does not question the basic tenets of free trade and privatization but argues for the need to "bring the state back in," not just to guide economic growth and regulate financial flows but also to provide quality basic services and investments in social and human capital (Stiglitz 2002). In the sphere of social policy, this mind-set has manifested in what Anthony Giddens (1998) calls "The Third Way," which includes calls for fiscal discipline and decentralization and for the participation of beneficiaries, civil society, and the private sector in the financing, design, and execution of social programs. The Latin American expression of this paradigm underscores these principles and places targeted antipoverty programs at the center of a strategy that seeks to overcome poverty in the long run through human capital formation (Duhau 2000). This is the "new social policy" paradigm that is summarized in table 4.1 at the end of this chapter.

This chapter examines the effectiveness of Mexico's social policy in combating poverty. The analysis proceeds as follows. First, we trace out the evolution of mainstream social policy thinking in the Mexican context. Six phases are identified, starting with the post–World War II period and ending with the consolidation of the new social policy paradigm during the first decade of the new millennium. This sets the stage for a critical analysis of PROP by providing a means for understanding why the program was created in the first place, not just with regard to its stated objectives but also to its function in providing political legitimacy to neoliberal governments and its relationship to the accumulation process. From there, the design and operational characteristics of the program are sketched out, and a brief review is provided of the empirical evidence regarding the program's results. As we shall see, *Oportunidades* is a two-sided coin; while short-term results include healthier infants and youth with higher levels of education, deficiencies in the provision of basic health and educational services, especially in rural areas, combined with faltering labor markets, tend to undermine the program's underlying goal of eradicating poverty. I argue that these shortcomings are not so much a consequence of imperfections in the program's design or implementation but rather symptomatic of deeper structural problems associated with the neoliberal model. The final section seeks to draw out the theoretical and political implications of the Mexican experience with "new social policy."

The Universal Welfare State *a la Mexicana*

The Post–World War II Period (1945–70)

During the post–World War II period, Mexico, like most other Latin American countries, pursued an import-substituting-industrialization (ISI) development strategy, with strong state intervention in all facets of the economy. In this scheme, heavily influenced by Keynesian economics, social policy was linked to economic development through job creation in the formal sector; workers were protected by progressive labor laws (enshrined in the 1917 constitution) and provided with minimum wages, social security, and housing. In accordance with the modernization paradigm, as the urban industrial sector expanded, it was expected to absorb the traditional and backward sectors of society, raising material living standards in the process. In this way, subsistence farming was doomed to extinction, implying the assimilation of indigenous groups. Land redistribution was gradually extended and served as a mechanism for shoring up political legitimacy. Public resources in the agricultural sector were channeled primarily to large-scale farmers and, to a lesser extent, to peasants with commercial potential, who benefited from irrigation projects, subsidized credit, green-revolution technologies, and marketing support. Price controls on basic foodstuffs served as a de facto subsidy for the urban population and as a means for transferring surplus from the countryside to the city. Primary education was the one area where universal coverage was vigorously pursued, even in rural areas. Otherwise, aspirations to construct a universal welfare state in the image of the more developed countries remained an elusive goal (Ordóñez 2002).

In this way, a dual and segmented social structure emerged during the ISI period. On the one hand, unionized industrial workers, public servants, and military personnel enjoyed many of the same social benefits as their counterparts in Europe and North America, with the notable exception of (un)employment insurance. For these sectors of the population, a number of interlocking social institutions were constructed, most important being the Mexican Social Security Institute (IMSS in its Spanish abbreviation), created in 1943, and its equivalent for public sector workers, the State's Employees' Social Security and Social Services Institute (ISSSTE), established in 1959. On the other hand, large segments of the population were excluded from most social policies, namely, the urban poor, informal workers, peasants, and especially indigenous peasants. These groups had to rely on their own social networks of reciprocity, on the charity of the church, or on the paltry services provided for uninsured workers through the Ministry of Health and Assistance (SSA). As several Mexican experts on social policy have suggested (for example, Barba Solano 2006; Boltvinik 2004; Valencia Lomelí 2003), from the optic of Esping-Andersen's classical tripartite typology, this dual system can be seen as a mix between the "corporatist" and the "residual" models.[1]

In the 1940s and 1950s, poverty in Mexico was associated with "marginalization"; the poor were those who were excluded from social benefits linked to the modern, urban industrial sector (Valencia Lomelí and Aguirre-Reveles 2001). Accordingly, the strategy for overcoming poverty was predominantly indirect, centered on economic growth and on the gradual expansion of the "universal" welfare state. The only direct measures took the form of minimum wage legislation or subsidies meant to increase the income of the working class.

Economic growth rates were indeed high: between 1940 and 1970, the GDP grew at an average annual rate of 6 percent, accompanied by a population explosion and a rapid process of urbanization.[2] During the same time period, the middle class grew, and social security benefits were extended to over 25 percent of the population (Ordóñez 2002). What is more, in a region characterized by recurrent military coups, the country enjoyed relative political stability, albeit at the cost of authoritarianism, electoral fraud, and selective repression (Cornelius and Craig 1988). All of this began to crumble, though, in the late 1960s, as the world economy began to stagnate and the ISI strategy became exhausted. The agricultural sector had been neglected, the baby boomers could not find jobs, the escape valve to the United States was tightened with the cancelation of the *Braceros* program, and the informal sector began to mushroom. Excluded segments of Mexican society clamored for a piece of the pie, students mobilized, and the government responded with the 1968 Tlatelolco massacre.

The Basic-Needs Approach (1970–82)

When Luis Echeverría became president in 1970, he was faced with the difficult task of regaining political legitimacy, reinitiating the economic growth process, and confronting problems of widespread social unrest, inequality, and marginalization. His response was a development strategy dubbed "shared development" (*desarrollo compartido*), which entailed a dramatic increase in public spending, financed not through progressive taxation and other redistributive measures but rather through increased borrowing from international banks, which at the time were offering loans at negative real interest rates in their effort to recycle petrodollars. In this manner, not only were conventional social policies expanded in the areas of health, education, housing, social security, and food subsidies, but new somewhat "targeted" programs were also introduced, aimed at the hitherto excluded social groups, particularly the rural poor. The most important of these was the Investment Program for Rural Development (PIDER), which reflected the World Bank's basic-needs approach (Streeten 1981), including a focus on marginalized rural areas, where it sought to raise living standards and agricultural productivity.

The expansion of social policies continued throughout Lopez Portillo's presidential term (1976–82), especially after large oil reserves were discovered in Mexico's territory, lessening the pressure for fiscal discipline. In this context, two more rural development programs were introduced: the National Plan for Depressed Areas and Marginalized Groups (COPLAMAR) and the Mexican Food System (SAM). In the official discourse associated with the first, poverty was understood to be primarily a rural phenomenon, to a large extent synonymous with "marginalization" and seen as "a result of the imbalances generated by the economic policies applied between 1940 and 1970" (Ordóñez 2002, 172). Accordingly, COPLAMAR also adopted the World Bank's basic-needs approach, providing basic public services and infrastructure to marginalized rural areas. For its part, SAM used price controls and general supply-side subsidies to stimulate agricultural production in an effort to achieve food self-sufficiency on the national level. Although these three programs would later be jettisoned in the wake of the 1982 debt crisis, their experience served as an important antecedent to the targeted antipoverty programs that emerged in the late 1980s and 1990s.

In general, the social policies implemented during the ISI period led to significant improvements in living standards for large sectors of the Mexican population (Ordóñez 2002). According to Hernández-Laos and Velázquez-Roa (2003), the incidence of income poverty on the national level dropped from 73 percent in 1964 to 42 percent in 1977.[3] By the end of this period, a fragmented welfare system had been constructed, with food subsidies for almost the entire population, tendencies toward universalism in the areas of basic health and education, and housing subsidies and pensions for unionized workers, civil servants, and the military (Valencia Lomelí 2003). Peasants and especially indigenous peasants continued to represent the most marginalized sectors of the population, and there were (and still are) enormous regional disparities, as well as inequalities, along gender lines.

Betting on the Market: The Reorientation of Mexican Social Policy

The Washington Consensus (1982–88)

At the beginning of the 1980s, a number of factors coincided to set the stage for a neoliberal advance. In Mexico, an $82 billion debt had accumulated over the previous decade, and the Lopez Portillo administration continued to run a high public deficit. Government spending represented 27 percent of the GDP, corruption ran rampant, and capital was fleeing the country at an unprecedented rate. On the international scene, right-wing political parties had gained control of the state apparatus in the United States and Great Britain, and international financial institutions (IFIs) were reoriented accordingly. An oil glut on the world market sent the price of petroleum plummeting (drastically reducing Mexico's foreign revenue), and when the United States hiked up its interest rates, the Mexican government was forced to declare a ninety-day moratorium on its debt payments, triggering a worldwide debt crisis.

For decades ultraorthodox neoliberal economists, lead by Milton Friedman and his colleagues at the Chicago School, had been building an arsenal of criticisms of state-led development and protectionism, pointing toward inefficiencies, price distortions, and rent seeking. The solution, according to these ideologues, was a return to laissez-faire economics. By rolling back the state and freeing the forces of the market, the economy would grow in leaps and bounds, creating wealth and prosperity for all, including the poor, who would not only benefit from job creation but also no longer be seduced by the negative work incentives created by the welfare state. From this perspective, even health and education services could be better provided by the private sector (Friedman 2002). While not all economists associated with IFIs adhere to such radical formulations of neoliberalism, an ideological shift in this direction resulted in what John Williamson (1990) would later coin as the Washington Consensus: a ten-point agenda for reshaping Latin American economies.[4]

During the 1980s, in the context of the debt crisis, the Mexican government adopted this agenda in the form of IMF-designed structural adjustment programs, including far-reaching cuts to social policy. Thus, during President Miguel de la Madrid's term (1982–88), social spending decreased from 9.2 percent of the GDP to just 6.1 percent. Cuts in the areas of health and education were particularly extreme: 77 percent and 71 percent, respectively (Ordóñez 2002). Surprisingly, service provision continued to expand in these areas during the same period, suggesting a strong compromise with regard to quality and underlying the severity of the wage cuts leveled against teachers, doctors, and health care workers. At the same time, in accordance with the Washington Consensus, Mexico began to decentralize health and education toward state-level governments, in an effort to achieve higher levels of administrative efficiency.

Macroeconomic instability ensued until the end of de la Madrid's term, with inflation reaching over 150 percent and almost no economic growth during the entire period. The real value of workers' wages fell by over 40 percent, the incidence of poverty increased to comprise more than 60 percent of the population, and the Gini coefficient increased from 0.501 to 0.549 (Hernández-Laos and Velázquez-Roa 2003). There was recognition among the general public that the working class had borne the brunt of the adjustment process, leading to social unrest and widespread repudiation of the neoliberal agenda. Nevertheless, when Carlos Salinas de Gortari came to power in 1988, through elections stained by blatant fraud, he was bent on deepening this reform process. Faced with a legitimacy crisis and a fragile economy, he set forth on his mission with an innovative social-policy initiative in mind: the National Solidarity Program (PRONASOL), a multifaceted antipoverty program that sought to foster the participation of its beneficiaries.

Social Liberalism (1988–94)

PRONASOL was targeted toward the poor (41 million, according to the program's official documentation) and especially the extremely poor (17 million), in both rural and urban areas. It also recognized a number of "vulnerable groups," including indigenous people, peasants, agricultural workers, slum dwellers, youth, women, and children. Funds were distributed at the discretion of the federal government, with no transparency, leading several critics to point toward a hidden electoral agenda (see, for example, Bruhn 1996; Molinar and Weldon 1994). Indeed, a massive media campaign was orchestrated to connect the program directly to the president himself. In addition, during the first two years that the program operated, state- and municipal-level governments were completely bypassed so that funds could be channeled directly to "solidarity committees," created for the sole purpose of carrying out small-scale community development projects. Even though certain administrative responsibilities were decentralized to the lower two levels of government as the program evolved, it remained highly centralized in the hands of the federal government (Bailey 1994).[5]

Over its lifespan, PRONASOL mushroomed into a complex array of subprograms, grouped together under three main headings: Social Welfare, Production, and Regional Development. The program's budget grew from 1,640 million pesos in 1989 to 9,233 million pesos in 1994, representing 0.65 percent of the country's GDP in its last year (Poder Ejecutivo Federal 1994). Of course, PRONASOL was not the only social expenditure during the Salinas era; social spending rose from 6.1 percent to 9.1 percent of the GDP during his presidential term, with significant increases in the areas of health and education (Ordóñez 2002). Also, the decentralization process was completed for public education, and reforms were undertaken to privatize pension funds, converting them into individual capitalization accounts, managed by private financial institutions.

Salinas called this "social liberalism," a development strategy that adheres to free-market principles but includes government spending for the provision of a minimal level of health and educational services, as well as compensatory programs for the destitute, with mechanisms to foster the creation of "social capital." This strategy reflects what was then an emerging paradigm in social policy throughout Latin America, one that is consistent with the post-Washington Consensus and whose main tenets include targeted antipoverty programs, fiscal discipline (whereby social spending is subordinated to economic policies geared toward maintaining macroeconomic stability), decentralization (that is, the transfer of administrative responsibilities to lower levels of governments), privatization (of pension funds, for example), and participation (for example, of beneficiaries, NGOs, and the private sector) (Duhau 2000).

In the economic realm, Salinas's social liberalism translated into an ambitious program for consolidating the neoliberal-reform process, including the unilateral deepening of trade liberalization (culminating in NAFTA), the extension of market-oriented reforms to the rural sector (see chapter 9), the privatization of profitable state enterprises (for example, TELMEX, which was sold to Carlos Slim with little transparency, leading to accusations of fraud), the (re)privatization of banks,[6] and the liberalization of capital accounts. To facilitate these last two initiatives, in 1990 the government created the Savings Protection Bank Fund (FOBAPROA), ultimately designed to protect the interests of financial capital in the event of an economic crisis.

PROGRESA, Emblematic of an Emerging Paradigm (1997–2000)

The crisis came just after Salinas left office, underscoring the structural instability of his reform agenda and, more generally, of the dangers associated with the free flow of speculative capital.[7] In the first half of 1995, the peso lost 43 percent of its value, inflation rose to over 50 percent, interest rates sky-rocketed, thousands of businesses were forced to close, salaries lost 25 percent of their real value, and two million people lost their jobs (Manning 1996). Incoming president Ernesto Zedillo responded by imposing draconian auster-ity measures, including severe cuts to social spending, and the United States stepped in with a $50 billion bailout package, which effectively protected in-vestors (mostly US) in Mexico's stock market. In addition, FOBAPROA was used to save private banks from insolvency, by issuing promissory notes for liabilities worth 560 billion pesos (approximately equal to $67 billion at the time), which had accumulated at an exorbitant rate in the preceding years, in the context of deregulation. By the end of Zedillo's term, this sum, along with the interest it had generated, would be illegally converted into public debt, effectively transferring billions of dollars from the public purse into the hands of some of the richest families in the nation (Alonso 1998). At the same time, as the government was wont to point out in its expensive media campaign, FOBAPROA also served to protect the bank savings of the middle and work-ing classes.

During the first two years of Zedillo's presidential term, PRONASOL was quietly abandoned; in other words, there was no coherent antipoverty strategy during the crisis. Meanwhile different factions within the Zedillo ad-ministration struggled to impose competing agendas for addressing the pov-erty problematic (Valencia Lomelí 2003). By 1996, the incidence of poverty had increased substantially to over 60 percent of the population, according to Hernández-Laos and Velázquez-Roa (2003), and to almost 70 percent, accord-ing to Székely (2003).[8] It was not until midway through 1997, once macro-economic stability had been restored, that the PROGRESA was introduced, with the primary objective of breaking the vicious cycle of intergenerational poverty by "substantially improving conditions for poor families with regards to education, health and diet" (Poder Ejecutivo Federal 1997).[9]

The principal architect of PROGRESA was Santiago Levy, who acted as deputy finance minister during Zedillo's mandate. In an oft-cited document published in 1994, Levy displayed his arguments and ideas for creating a tar-geted antipoverty program that transfers resources directly to the extremely poor: (1) antipoverty programs should be congruent with neoliberal structural reforms by avoiding supply-side general subsidies and price controls, which in-troduce market distortions; (2) antipoverty programs should take advantage of the mutual reinforcement that exists between nutrition, health, and education; (3) given fiscal constraints, antipoverty programs must focus exclusively on the poor, in the most cost-effective way possible; (4) these programs should distinguish between moderate poverty and extreme poverty; because the extremely poor have to spend most of their income on food, they have less capacity to deal with risk and are therefore unable to integrate themselves effectively into labor markets, to migrate, or to take advantage of educational opportunities like the moderately poor can; and (5) not only is extreme poverty primarily a rural problem, but the poorest of the extremely poor are mostly situated in rural areas (Levy 1994). In accordance with these last three arguments, PRONASOL was replaced by PROGRESA, inter alia, because the former did not focus sufficiently on the extremely poor in the countryside and because it did not have transparent mechanisms for allocating resources. In addition, it was too closely associated with Salinas, who was disgraced by the financial crisis and by corruption scandals shortly after leaving office.

As we shall see in more detail in the following section, during the first four years, PROGRESA was directed only to extremely poor families living in marginalized rural communities. The selection process was based on a highly controversial formula that strove for transparency but excluded 58.5 percent of the extremely poor (12.7 million people), not to mention all of the moderately poor (Boltvinik 2004). In any case, between 1997 and 2000, the number of beneficiaries grew exponentially, from 331,000 families to almost 2.5 million. By the year 2000, PROGRESA had a budget of 9,635 million pesos, equal to just 17 percent of the average annual interest paid on the debt acquired through the FOBAPROA scandal.[10]

Consolidation Behind Smoke and Mirrors (2000–2006)

After Vicente Fox assumed power in late 2000, under the banner of the National Action Party (PAN), there was an intense debate about whether to continue with PROGRESA. While the program had been heavily criticized by some of the country's top social science researchers, many of the same recommended that it be continued, albeit with major changes, not just to the program per se but to Mexico's social policy in general.[11] In the following section we will review these criticisms and summarize the changes made to PROP during the six years that Fox was in power. For now, suffice to say that the program's name was changed to *Oportunidades*; it was extended first to semiurban areas and then to the major cities, and the program was broadened to include new channels for direct cash transfers. By 2004, the number of families incorporated into PROP reached Fox's goal of five million, where it remained until 2009. Between 2000 and 2006, its budget grew from 9,518.2 to 33,532.7 million pesos. Perhaps most important, PROP was encrusted in a broader antipoverty strategy named *Contigo* (meaning "with you"), which was highlighted in an extensive media campaign that sought political legitimacy for the president himself and for the PAN (inter alia, by repeating ad infinitum "Fox is with you"). Aside from this political function, *Contigo* was designed to complement the strategy of combating poverty through CCTs, with three others: the generation of employment opportunities, social protection, and the formation of patrimony in the form of housing and social infrastructure. On the surface, this appeared to address many of the criticisms that had been leveled against Zedillo's antipoverty approach, including the most biting: that it did not include effective mechanisms for generating employment. However, upon closer inspection, it becomes evident that *Contigo*'s sixteen programs and thirty-three subprograms were mostly smoke and mirrors. Indeed, 85 percent of the budget was directed toward just two of these strategies (CCTs and patrimony formation), and within each of these, there was one program that dominated the budget: *Oportunidades* in the first, and the Assistance Fund for Social Infrastructure (FAIS) in the second (Ordóñez and Ortega 2006). Together, these two programs made up over half of the entire federal budget for directly combating extreme poverty, equal to 45,121 million pesos in 2003. In the same year, spending in the area of "employment generation" was just 12.5 percent of *Contigo*'s budget, and this was used primarily for temporary employment programs and microfinancing schemes (Ordóñez and Ortega 2006, 169).

On the institutional level, President Fox created the Technical Committee for Measuring Poverty (CTMP), made up of seven distinguished experts on the poverty problematic, carefully selected and overseen by government representatives. The committee's mandate was to come up with an official poverty-measurement method in order to track the progress made in the war on poverty. Fox, with his businessman mentality, wanted to measure his administration's progress on this increasingly important social indicator. In 2002, the CTMP published its recommendations and its poverty measurements for the year 2000, based on three poverty lines, which would later be baptized "food poverty," "capacities poverty," and "patrimony poverty."[12] On the basis of the patrimony-poverty line, the Fox administration officially recognized that 53.6 percent of Mexico's population was living in poverty in 2000. It also bears mentioning that the Technical Committee underlined the provisional nature of this measurement method, pointing to the imminent need to develop a multidimensional method that goes beyond income poverty. This would be the task of the National Council for the Evaluation of Social Development Policy (CONEVAL), the CTMP's successor, created in 2004, with a mission to "establish norms and coordinate the evaluation of social development programs and policies carried out by governmental agencies, and to establish the guidelines and criteria for the definition, identification and measurement of poverty" (Art. 81, General Law of Social Development [LGDS]).

Another important change in social policy during Fox's time in office was the passing of the LGDS in 2003. The LGDS provided the legal mandate to create CONEVAL. In addition, the LGDS stipulates that social spending must increase every year in at least the same proportion as the anticipated GDP growth and that it cannot be cut in times of crisis. This led to record levels of social spending, equal to 11.1 percent of the GDP in 2006 (CEFP 2009, 9). Moreover, in the context of the current economic crisis (2008 to present), this has served to prevent the government from slashing antipoverty programs, like it has done in the past. On the other hand, as Boltvinik (2006b) points out, in spite of these important achievements, the LGDS is ambiguous insofar as it does not define what "social development" entails and because it conflates three concepts: vulnerability, marginalization, and poverty. More important, the LGDS does not establish any mechanisms for citizens to claim the rights that are at the law's core.

The General Health Law was also modified in 2003, with the intention of universalizing the constitutional right to health protection, which until then was only obligatory under the auspices of formal employment contracts. When Fox took office, 60 percent of the Mexican population was not included in the coverage provided by IMSS and ISSSTE; the vast majority of the excluded were peasants and informal sector workers, highly vulnerable to health-related catastrophes. In this situation, the idea was to provide cost-effective insurance to the poor, reaching universal coverage within a seven-year period. The vehicle for reaching this goal was Public Insurance (*Seguro Popular*; SP), free for the lowest two deciles of income earners and based on voluntary inscription. In quantitative terms, this program has been relatively successful, incorporating 7.8 million households (27.2 million people) by the end of 2008. However, from a more critical view, SP does not effectively protect its beneficiaries from catastrophes, since only 8 percent of its budget is designated for this purpose; the rest is for basic medical attention (Barba Solano 2010a). Furthermore, in Carlos Barba Solano's words, SP "exacerbates the old tendency towards stratifying pluralism and reaffirms the dual character of the Mexican welfare regime" (Barba Solano 2010a, 102). It does this by introducing another layer to an already highly stratified system, with private health care for the rich floating above a four-tier public system for the rest of the population. From best to worst, this system includes IMSS-ISSSTE (for approximately four out of every ten Mexicans), SP (for three), the medical component of *Oportunidades* (for two), and those with no insurance (about one out of every ten citizens). It also bears mentioning that 70 percent of the indigenous population is included in this last group (Barba Solano 2010a).

All in all, the changes made by the Fox administration to Mexico's social policy served to institutionally consolidate and to modestly expand the country's antipoverty strategy, during a period of relative economic stability. How did this correlate with poverty indicators? According to the official poverty line method adopted by CONEVAL, there was a continuous decline in the incidence of all three levels of poverty during Fox's six-year mandate, by as much as 17.9 percent. This, however, has been highly contested. Boltvinik (2006b), for example, argues that it is extremely unlikely that the incidence of poverty declined so abruptly, considering that the GDP per capita grew at about only 1 percent annually between 2000 and 2006. In any case, according to the statistical analysis carried out by Cortés, Banegas, and Solís (2007), insofar that the incidence of poverty was reduced during Fox's term, PROP played an insignificant role. In their words, "The program has not had a significant effect (statistically or substantially) on the reduction of poverty between 2002 and 2005" (2007, 34), which, incidentally, contradicts claims made by Mexico's Ministry of Social Development and the World Bank.

Consolidation Behind Smoke and Mirrors: Part II (2006–Present)

Since Calderón took office in 2006, through highly contested elections once again stained by accusations of fraud, the political legitimizing function of PROP has become even more salient. In this context, the program has been used to lubricate the deepening of unpopular neoliberal reforms. For example, in May 2008, when Calderón announced his strategy to confront the global food crisis, which essentially amounts to further liberalization of trade in the agricultural sector, he included an increase in the food-subsidy component of PROP.

More recently, in 2009, a 1 percent increase in the country's goods-and-sales tax (IVA) was pushed through with the argument that it was needed to maintain and expand PROP. In this case, Calderón's argument was that, in the context of the current economic crisis and in view of depleting oil revenues, alternative sources of public revenue were needed to expand the program. Former presidential candidate Andrés Manuel López Obrador and other critics suggested that, instead of increasing the IVA, the thing to do was to carry out comprehensive fiscal reform that addressed the country's serious problems of inequality and emphasized the imposition of more progressive taxation. Indeed, the Tributary Administration Service reported to Congress in

October 2009 that the four hundred largest companies operating in Mexico pay on average only 1.7 percent of their earnings in income tax. However, when Calderón timidly acknowledged this, declaring that loopholes must be closed and that corporations should pay more taxes, the Mexican business elite sent a clear and strong message that they would not tolerate this sort of discourse from the president. Two days later Calderón adopted a more conciliatory tone.

On a more general level, since 2008, Calderón has cloaked his antipoverty program in a marketing strategy, called *Vivir Mejor* (Live Better; VM), very similar to the one Fox used with *Contigo*. Like its predecessor, VM ostensibly seeks to play a coordinating and integrating role for the various public programs oriented toward combating poverty. This role, however, is purely discursive, since VM does not introduce any coordinating mechanisms per se; rather it acts as an umbrella to promote the image of existing programs, almost all of which were inherited from Fox, with some modifications and expansion. The five objectives of VM can be summarized as follows: (1) to develop and strengthen basic capacities (food, education, health, housing, social infrastructure, law), (2) to help protect the poor from catastrophes (related to health, economic fluctuations, natural disasters, etc.), (3) to promote social cohesion and regionally balanced development, (4) to raise labor productivity, and (5) to incorporate ecological sustainability criteria into social policy. And these objectives are to be accomplished by pursuing three lines of action:

> To continue developing the capacities of Mexicans, especially girls and boys, guaranteeing access to education, health and dignified housing; to provide a Network of Social Protection that avoids catastrophical loss for the poorest families in the event of sickness or loss of employment; to facilitate access to formal employment for all Mexicans, strengthening the coordination between social policy and economic policy. (Poder Ejecutivo Federal 2008)

The first two lines of action are to be carried out through an array of programs, of which the most important are PROP, FAIS, and *Seguro Popular*. Together, these three programs represent over half of the antipoverty budget in 2009 (Poder Ejecutivo Federal 2009). The third line of action is, again, mostly smoke and mirrors, considering that the three main programs for creating employment (the National Micro-business Financing Program, Productive Options, and the Temporary Employment Program) made up only 1.5 percent of the total budget for combating poverty in 2008.[13]

Thus, beyond the rhetoric, the current government has no coherent strategy for creating employment opportunities in the formal sector; rather its strategy amounts to adhering to the principles of deregulation, labor flexibility, and wage suppression, with the hope that this will create the conditions necessary for economic growth and for private sector hiring. Economic growth, however, has been dismal throughout the neoliberal era, averaging only 1.87 percent annually between 1982 and 2009, which means almost zero per capita growth.[14] Likewise, job creation in the formal sector has simply not been able to keep up to the expansion of the labor force, considering that the formal sector represented just 40.1 percent of the economically active population in 1991 and dropped to 39.8 percent in 2006.[15] During the same period, the informal sector grew by almost 50 percent, from 17.32 million to 25.78 million workers,[16] and over 7 million Mexicans migrated to the United States (CONAPO 2008). It also bears mentioning that between 1976 and 2001, the real value of minimum wages dropped by a shocking 77.0 percent (Arroyo-Picard 2003). Average wages increased by a modest 3.2 percent during Fox's term but then dropped again by 2.2 percent during the first two years of Calderón's presidency. What is more, Mexico has been the Latin American country hardest hit by the latest economic crisis, with a 6.5 percent contraction in its GDP in 2009. The incidence of patrimonial poverty increased by 4.8 percent in 2008, reaching 47.4 percent of the population, and this was before the worst of the crisis (CONEVAL 2009). Finally, an estimated 429,000 formal sector jobs were lost in 2009, according to the president of the Bank of Mexico.

All things considered, neoliberalism has had devastating social consequences for Mexico. And this points to the Achilles' heel of Mexico's antipoverty strategy, to wit, it is separate from, and subordinate to, the country's economic policy, which in turn is fixated on maintaining macroeconomic stability at all cost (social and environmental), failing miserably even in this regard. We will reflect on the theoretical and political implications in the final section of this chapter. For now, let us turn our attention to a more detailed analysis of PROP, the centerpiece of Mexico's antipoverty strategy and the darling of the IFIs in Washington.

Progresa-Oportunidades: A Two-Sided Coin

As earlier mentioned, *Progresa* was introduced in 1997, with the primary objective of breaking the intergenerational transmission of poverty. Originally, it operated only in rural zones with high or very high levels of marginalization, according to CONAPO's measurement, which was based on data collected in 1995 by the National Institute of Statistics, Geography and Informatics of Mexico. Only localities with basic health and education services were considered eligible (or those within a five-kilometer radius of existing facilities), thus eliminating many of the poorest of the poor right off the bat. Next, information was gathered door-to-door to determine which families were destitute enough to qualify, based on their belongings, income, and number of dependents. In the last stage of the selection process, the female heads of household from selected families were invited to participate in a local meeting to learn how the program was to operate and to select a representative among themselves (Poder Ejecutivo Federal 1997). Known as *promotora*, this representative was given the responsibility to disseminate information, to help organize meetings, and generally to serve as a link between the community and the program's field-level administrators, without monetary compensation.

The program's interventions and subsidies were (and continue to be) aligned with three mutually reinforcing lines of human capital formation: education, health, and nutrition. Of these, education was considered from the beginning to be "the strategic factor" in breaking the vicious circle of poverty. By providing incentives for extremely poor families to keep their kids in school longer, the architects of *Progresa* hoped that this would translate into higher productivity and better paying jobs in the future. Furthermore, the effectiveness of higher educational achievements among the extremely poor were expected "to get a boost when accompanied with attention for the other two fundamental basic needs: food and health" (Poder Ejecutivo Federal 1997, 5). Thus, when the program was launched, scholarships were made available for families with children in elementary school (*primaria*) and junior high school (*secundaria*), from grade three onward, with increasing monetary values for each successive grade and with girls receiving more than boys in an effort to help close the gender gap. At first, schoolchildren were provided with utensils, but this practice was soon abandoned in favor of an additional cash transfer, paid once a year on the elementary level and at the beginning of each semester for higher grades. Moreover, in an effort to change individual- and family-level conduct in the areas of health and nutrition, beneficiaries received a fixed bimonthly cash transfer that was supposed to be spent on basic food items. Finally, nutritional supplements were provided to families with children between six months and two years of age, other children younger than five years old with symptoms of malnutrition, and women in the stages of breastfeeding and pregnancy.

In exchange for all of this, the beneficiaries of the program were expected to comply with a number of "coresponsibilities," most important being that children had to attend school regularly, and the entire family had to visit the local health clinic for scheduled checkups. The female head of household had to accompany her children during these checkups, and she was expected to attend monthly workshops, designed to promote good hygiene, a balanced diet, and healthy living habits. Failing to meet these coresponsibilities meant that cash transfers would be curtailed and that persistent offenders would be dropped from the program. Moreover, in many rural communities, adult women beneficiaries were expected to perform collective work projects, such as garbage collection. Although these projects were not officially part of the program's coresponsibilities, the organizers (teachers, health workers, and *promotoras/vocales*) sometimes threatened to drop nonparticipants from PROP (González de la Rocha 2006).

Finally, one of the innovative design features of PROP was its commitment to a permanent process of publicly financed evaluation. As stated in the original documentation,

> Evaluation is a fundamental part of Progresa, since it not only allows for the measurement of the Program's impacts, but also for the proposal of corrective measures, the reorientation of actions, better functioning processes and, in general, more effectiveness and efficiency in the use of the resources assigned to reach the stated objectives. (Poder Ejecutivo Federal 1997, 64)

Along these lines, in 2000, the International Food Policy Research Institute (IFPRI) released its finding based on studies carried out since 1998, highlighting *Progresa*'s short-term achievements and setting off a wave of enthusiasm for conditional cash transfer programs in the World Bank and in other international development agencies (Valencia Lomelí 2008). According to the IFPRI,

> After just three years, Mexican children with scarce resources who live in the rural zones where Progresa operates have a greater probability of attending school, they have more balanced diets, they receive medical attention more frequently, and they are learning that the future can be different from the past. (2000, 3)

This optimistic endorsement was only partially offset by suggestions that increased school attendance was not being accompanied with more time spent doing homework and that many community members harbored resentment and misunderstandings vis-à-vis the selection process (IFPRI 2000). The Center for Research and Higher Studies in Social Anthropology is another institute that has been commissioned to carry out evaluations since the late 1990s. Early on, it found evidence that corroborated with IFPRI's positive findings, as well as more critical observations regarding *Progresa*'s selection process, deficient health and educational services, and overworked *promotoras* (Escobar and González de la Rocha 2006). These and other concerns were highlighted in a series of independent studies and critical analyses brought together by Valencia Lomelí, Gendreau, and Tepichín (2000).

The social scientists who contributed to this book offered the following criticisms:

1. *Progresa* does not address the issue of job creation; it assumes that its "graduates" will be able to effectively insert themselves in an hospitable labor market sometime in the future, and it assumes that higher levels of schooling will automatically translate into higher incomes. In the absence of a concerted effort to create formal sector jobs, this is very unlikely.

2. It excludes large segments of the extremely poor, particularly those living in remote rural areas or in urban centers, and it excludes all families living in "moderate" poverty.

3. The program is likely to create intracommunity divisions between beneficiaries and nonbeneficiaries, damaging the social networks that the poor rely on to survive, and it might even provoke intrafamiliar conflicts due to the favoring of some family members over others.

4. The program is designed to increase the demand for basic health and educational services, but there are no provisions made for upgrading and expanding these services; inevitably this will lead to overcrowded schools and clinics, long waiting lines, superficial attention, and overworked teachers and medical personnel.

5. The program is not participatory (even though *Progresa*'s official documentation suggests that it is); beneficiaries have no say in how it is run, and their participation is largely limited to complying with coresponsibilities, which is an individualistic form of participation.

6. The extremely poor are given only the possibility of receiving benefits, not the right (Valencia Lomelí, Gendreau, and Tepichín 2000).

Since the PAN came to power in 2000, a number of important changes and additions have been made to PROP, some of which seek to address these criticisms. To begin with, in 2001, coverage was extended to marginalized neighborhoods in semiurban areas (towns with fewer than 50,000 inhabitants), and scholarships were offered to high school students. In 2002, the program's name was changed to *Oportunidades*, and its geographical scope was further expanded to include urban centers with fewer than a million inhabitants. In the same year, the figure of *promotora* was replaced by that of the Community Promotion Committee, composed of four local beneficiaries (women over the age of fifteen) known as *vocals*, corresponding to the areas of health, education, monitoring, and nutrition. In 2004, the program was finally made available to extremely poor families living in the country's largest metropolitan areas. In the same year, two new components were added: *Jóvenes en Oportunidades* (Youth With Opportunities), which provides students with a small sum of money upon finishing high school, supposedly to help finance further studies, to start a business, or to invest in patrimony, and *Esquema Diferenciado de Apoyo* (Differed Support Scheme), for families that have made socioeconomic progress, to help wean them off PROP. In 2006, *Apoyo a Adultos Mayores* (Support for Older Adults) was introduced to provide 250 pesos a month for all adult beneficiaries seventy years of age or older. In that same year, a subsidy program to buy minimal social security was introduced, only to be abandoned one year later (Levy 2008). In 2007, in the lead-up to the government's privatizing initiatives in the energy sector, another component was added: *Oportunidades Energético* (Energy Opportunities), which amounts to an additional 50 pesos a month for all families incorporated in the program. Finally, in 2008, *Apoyo Alimentario Vivir Mejor* (Food Help to Live Better) was created to help offset the rising costs of basic foodstuffs in the context of the world food crisis, by adding 120 pesos to the bimonthly food subsidy.

As this brief summary suggests, PROP has grown considerably larger and more complex during the past ten years. It now operates in every municipality in the country, in both urban and rural areas. In 2009, approximately 5.2 million families benefited from the program, for a total of 25 million beneficiaries, which is equivalent to almost a quarter of the national population. These families receive on average a transfer of 696 pesos per month (equal to about 50 dollars) (Poder Ejecutivo Federal 2009). The program's total budget in the same year was 47,402.8 million pesos, equal to just 2.04 percent of Mexico's social spending and 0.38 percent of Mexico's GDP in 2009.[17] In other words, *Oportunidades* is indeed a cost-effective approach to combating extreme poverty. But does it work?

As mentioned previously, PROP has been the subject of an unprecedented process of constant evaluation, resulting in an enormous amount of material, much of which can be found on the program's official website (www .oportunidades.gob.mx). However, the problem with most of these evaluations, as Julio Boltvinik and other critics have stressed, is that by paying external research institutes to carry them out, a clientelistic relationship is established, whereby evaluators stress the good news that the Mexican government and IFIs want to hear and downplay the bad. Moreover, these external evaluations tend to focus on the *means* for combating poverty (school attendance, medical checkups, and food), not the *ends* (better education, health, and nutrition; less income poverty) (Boltvinik 2004). Nevertheless, they are an important source of empirical evidence regarding the program's performance. Furthermore, there are dozens of high-profile independent researchers in Mexico who have produced hundreds of documents to critically analyze PROP's effectiveness in combating poverty.[18] What follows is a synthesis of the program's most outstanding achievements and limitations, based on a selective review of this literature.

First, in the area of education, there is ample empirical evidence to confirm that *Oportunidades* has increased school attendance at the junior and senior high school levels but not at the elementary school level (Parker 2003a; Boltvinik 2004). Kids who receive scholarships from *Oportunidades* extend their years of schooling by between 0.66 year and 1 year in rural areas (Valencia Lomelí 2008). On the other hand, beneficiaries complain about the poor quality of public educational services and facilities, and there appears to be no abatement in child labor, but rather compromises have been made between school and work responsibilities (Escobar and González de la Rocha 2006). More to the point, although there are many nuances, empirical evidence suggests that PROP has had little to no impact on the cognitive development of its beneficiaries (Behrman et al. 2008; Levy and Rodríguez 2005; Parker and Behrman 2008; Mancera, Hernández, and Schubert 2008). Along these lines, Mancera, Hernández, and Schubert (2008) found that 55 percent of the beneficiaries that graduate from junior high school lack basic linguistic abilities and reading comprehension.

In the areas of health and nutrition, the evaluations indicate that beneficiaries visit the doctor more regularly, that diets have improved, and that they generally enjoy somewhat better health. This is reflected in taller and heavier infants, less incidence of illness, and a reduction in infant and maternal mortality rates (Levy and Rodríguez 2005; Valencia Lomelí 2008). From an anthropological perspective, "Children and youth go to school better fed, they get sick less often and they stay awake and alert during the school day"

(González de la Rocha 2006, 102–3). On the other hand, the program seems to have contributed little or nothing to reducing the incidence of malnutrition (INSP, cited in Boltvinik 2004; Behrman et al. 2008; Neufeld et al. 2008). Accordingly, administrators have since reformulated the nutritional supplement, particularly with regard to its iron content. Another problem is that about 10 percent of beneficiaries are being forced to pay for medical checkups (which is illegal), and there are usually long waiting lines at local health clinics, obliging overworked mothers to spend long hours waiting for a service whose ultimate purpose is often just to meet the program's requirements (González de la Rocha 2006). Moreover, from a gender perspective, although PROP seeks to empower women by putting them in charge of cash and in-kind transfers and by providing girls with more monetary incentive than boys to stay in school, the program is predicated on the assumption that women will stay at home and play the traditional role of housewife. Along these lines, González de la Rocha (2006) and others have confirmed through their field research that it is much more difficult for women working outside the home to register for the program and, for those who do manage to get registered, to perform its coresponsibilities.

With regard to poverty, early optimism has given way to skepticism and disillusion. In 2000, the IFPRI triumphantly announced that *Progresa* had reduced the incidence of poverty by 8 percent in the communities it operated in. Several years later, however, Cortés, Banegas, and Solís (2007) used a more sophisticated analysis to demonstrate that PROP was having only a miniscule impact on the incidence of income poverty. They found that between 2002 and 2005, *Oportunidades* reduced the incidence of capacities poverty (the official poverty line used to determine eligibility for the program) by a mere 0.22 percent (Cortés, Banegas, and Solís 2007). The program's effect on the severity of poverty (that is, how far a poor family's income is below the capacities poverty line) was found to be somewhat greater: 11.5 percent in 2002, 9.7 percent in 2004, and 12.1 percent in 2005. But this only confirms the obvious: that the money delivered to extremely poor families has actually slightly increased their incomes, bringing them up closer to the poverty line. In any case, the overriding objective of *Progresa-Oportunidades* is to break the *intergenerational* transmission of poverty, so the more pertinent question is, to what degree have its first "graduates" been able to effectively insert themselves into labor markets? On this point, the latest round of external evaluations has pointed toward dismal results.[19] On the basis of research carried out in rural communities where the program has operated, Eduardo Rodríguez and Samuel Freije conclude,

[The (ex-)beneficiaries of Progresa-Oportunidades] find themselves in a less favorable position than their cohorts in rural zones in general . . . it cannot be said that there is any type of additional effect by the Program on being employed in the labor market . . . with regards to this generation's improvement over the last, no important effect has been found in terms of better salaries, formal sector employment or better qualified positions. (2008, 20)

Finally, there is evidence that *Oportunidades* is being used for political-electoral purposes. Indeed, during the months leading up the 2006 presidential elections, Fox launched a massive TV media campaign to promote his government's achievements in expanding the program.[20] More recently, Foust Rodríguez (2010) discovered that twenty-three of the thirty-two state-level coordinators for *Oportunidades* were registered members of the PAN. In other words, the administrative apparatus of PROP is becoming increasingly infiltrated by public servants openly affiliated with the ruling party. In this context, it is disturbing to see that the only democratic element of PROP—the election of *vocales* on the local level—was canceled in late 2008,[21] leading one expert to observe diplomatically, "The risks are greater [now, for clientelism and political electoral manipulation] and, therefore, the need for autonomous observation and citizenship is more urgent than ever in the history of Oportunidades" (Valencia Lomelí 2010, 30).

Conclusion

PROP is emblematic of the new social policy that has emerged in Latin America during the neoliberal era. It is considered to be a pioneer for nationwide CCT programs, which have proliferated throughout the region during the first decade of the twenty-first century. The Mexican federal government, IFIs, and contracted evaluators have been quick to draw triumphant conclusions regarding the program's short-term positive impacts and its potential for eradicating extreme poverty in the long run. There were political reasons for this. More careful and balanced evaluations (for example, Valencia Lomelí 2008) reveal nuances and shortcomings. For example, while there is no doubt that the program has led to more years of schooling and better health, it appears to have contributed little or nothing to reducing malnutrition, to improving the cognitive ability of student beneficiaries, and to reducing the incidence of income poverty in the short and medium term. Poor quality and overcrowded basic health and educational services, especially in rural areas, tend to undermine some of these broader goals. Moreover, the program imposes a traditional role on women, it burdens them with extra time commitments, and it is difficult to access for women working outside the home. The beneficiaries' participation is limited to complying with preestablished coresponsibilities, there are still many errors of inclusion and exclusion, and access to PROP's CCTs is not a redeemable right for families living in poverty. Part of the problem is that beneficiaries are seen as subjects, not actors (Sen 2003), and poverty is mostly conceptualized on the individual or family level, in terms of insufficient income and the absence of "human capital." In this way, social networks, popular organization, and cooperative productive schemes are ignored. Poverty is to be overcome when children who have benefited from the program grow up and insert themselves into the labor market with higher levels of education and better health, resulting in higher productivity and more income.

As many critics have pointed out, the problem with this hypothetical model is that it assumes that higher levels of education will automatically translate into higher wages. While empirical evidence on the international level does indeed point to a strong correlation between these two variables, any macro-causal relation rests on an indispensable condition: massive job creation. As we have seen, in the case of Mexico, formal sector employment has stagnated, and real wages have plummeted during the neoliberal era. Without job opportunities in rural communities, the poor are forced to migrate en masse to urban centers and to the United States. In this way, for the first time since the Revolution, Mexico's rural population began to decline in absolute terms at the turn of the millennium. Inversely, the urban informal sector has burgeoned, constituting a veritable reserve army of cheap industrial and service sector labor. In this context, an average increase in years of schooling allows employers to jack up their entrance requirements (for example, jobs that required a junior high school diploma in the past now require a high school diploma). What is worse, the same job pays less in real terms than it did thirty years ago (Boltvinik 2004). In this way, the new social-policy paradigm promoted by the World Bank and the Inter-American Development Bank (summarized in table 4.1) has led to greater opportunities, not for the poor but rather for Capital, which is able to capture the benefits of any increase in labor productivity. Indeed, during the neoliberal era, what we have seen is an increase in inequality and persistently high levels of poverty and inequality. According to the CONEVAL's Multidimensional Poverty Measurement Method, in 2008 over 80 percent of Mexico's population was living in conditions of poverty or vulnerability, and this was at the beginning of the crisis.

To put it succinctly, neoliberal ideology is bankrupt. So what are the alternatives? Radical and reform-minded experts on social policy in Mexico have made myriad recommendations. In a nonexhaustive literature review, Valencia Lomelí, Foust, and Tetreault (2010) analyzed 277 recommendations in scholarly journals and books that deal with social policy in Mexico. They found many contradictions between authors, which is not surprising since the review sought to represent diverse ideological postures. These differences notwithstanding, it is possible to discern several major themes on which there is broad consensus:

1. *Basic universalism*, which is the need to construct a basic universal welfare system in the areas of health and social security, consolidating existing programs (which together constitute a segmented and stratified system) into one homogenous system that provides quality services to all. Even Santiago Levy (2008) agrees on this point, although he differs with regard to how to finance it. In any case, basic universalism does not preclude targeted programs for the extremely poor and vulnerable groups; rather it advocates constructing them on top of a broader and better universal system.

2. *Fiscal reform*. While Levy (2008) suggests an increase in the country's goods and services tax (which is what Calderón has done), Lomelí-Vanegas (2010) and others propose a new fiscal pact that goes beyond (but includes) closing loopholes and "modernizing" the existing tributary system, a pact that is defined through democratic processes with broad participation, implying more progressive income taxes, "negative" income taxes for the poor, green taxes, inheritance taxes, and increased contributions from large companies and the rich in general.

3. *Social rights*, which are rights legally enforced in practice. In other words, these include guaranteed access to quality public services in the areas of health, nutrition, social security, and education, including a minimum pension for seniors and the establishment of an emergency fund for times of crisis. This goes hand in hand with the normative vision of basic universalism. Boltvinik (2010) even goes so far as to suggest a Sufficient and Unconditional Universal Food Income for all Citizens, in order to "demercantilize" food. Others stress the need to honor the San Andrés Accords regarding the rights of indigenous peoples.

All of this is echoed in the International Covenant for Economic, Social, and Cultural Rights.

4. *Labor policy*. Reformist proposals converge, first, on the need for massive job creation programs and easily accessible and affordable financing for small businesses, the need to strengthen independent labor unions and to reincorporate their demands into official labor policy, and the need to recuperate the purchasing power of wages and, second, on the need to stop using wage suppression as a tool for combating inflation and attracting foreign investment.

5. *Integrated rural development and food sovereignty*, including protection from unfair competition, credit, subsidies and extension services for small-scale farmers (especially organic farmers), marketing support, and infrastructure. See chapters 9 and 10 for a more detailed summary of the demands that have come from independent peasant and indigenous organizations.

6. *The reconceptualization of poverty*. Poverty is a multidimensional phenomenon that must be conceptualized and measured in complex terms. There is large body of literature on this debate, with diverse proposals that go beyond the scope of this chapter. Suffice to say that CONEVAL's Multidimensional Poverty Measurement Method represents a major advance. However, as the proponents of "basic universalism" point out, inequality must also be recognized, as both a cause of poverty and a problem in itself, one that undermines social cohesion, solidarity, and institution building.

Finally, on a more general level, there is wide consensus on the need to reorient the country's overall development strategy, giving overriding priority to the eradication of poverty, basic universal welfare, less inequality, job creation, and ecological sustainability. How to do this depends on one's ideological posture: while reform-minded analysts suggest the need to form broad-based social democratic coalitions that can impose greater regulatory control on capital and establish more effective redistribution mechanisms, Marxists and social activists associated with radical movements call for the mobilization of the masses in order to put an end to capitalism in its current form and to build some sort of socialist alternative, either state led (like in Venezuela) or decentralized along the lines of classical anarchism, with the Zapatista's *caracoles* serving as a contemporary example.

Table 4.1
The New Paradigm for Social Policy Promoted by the World Bank
and the Inter-American Development Bank in Latin America and Elsewhere

Theoretical and ideological framework	Classical and neoclassical economic theory, public-choice theory, neoliberalism, and free-market fundamentalism, corresponding with the "liberal" or "residual" model in Esping-Andersen's typology.
Guiding principles	Fiscal discipline, prioritization of social spending based on cost-benefit analysis, targeted antipoverty programs geared toward human capital formation, demand-side interventions that minimize market distortions, decentralization in the areas of health and education, privatization (especially in the areas of social security, housing, waste management, and other basic services), and participation in the form of "coresponsibility."
Main objectives	To alleviate extreme poverty, to develop human capital (in order to feed the accumulation process), and to provide political legitimacy.
Role of state	Guarantee macroeconomic stability by steering the neoliberal course, decentralize social policy functions (financing, implementation, and evaluation) to the private sector and to civil society, implement targeted antipoverty programs, provide universal basic education and health services, improve infrastructure in marginalized areas, and provide microfinancing and temporary employment programs.
Role of private sector	Drive economic growth, create jobs, determine prices (including wages and of natural resources), provide elite social services, and participate in the financing and administration of state-led services.
Role of civil society	Participate through official channels in the implementation and evaluation of social policies and hold the government accountable by denouncing irregularities.
Conceptualization of poverty	Lack of individual and family-level capabilities, vulnerability, and insufficient income to meet basic needs, with a distinction between extreme and moderate poverty.
Causes of poverty	Crisis of ISI model, SAPs, macroeconomic instability, slow economic growth, and individual exclusion from labor markets.

(continues)

Table 4.1 (*continued*)

Relation to economic policy	Social policy is subordinated to economic policy, which is oriented toward maintaining macroeconomic stability through fiscal discipline, free trade, export-oriented growth, free flow of capital, privatization, deregulation, labor "flexibility," and "competitive" wages.
Centerpiece: targeted antipoverty programs	CCT programs that target the extremely poor, based on a rigorous and transparent selection process. These programs seek to minimize errors of inclusion; to foster human capital formation through mutually reinforcing interventions in education, health, and nutrition; to close the gender gap by delivering cash transfers directly to female heads of household and by providing additional monetary incentive for keeping girls in school longer; to increase (in the short term) poor families' income, consumption of food and nutritional supplements, and demand for basic health and education services; to break the intergenerational transmission of poverty in the long run through higher levels of formal education, which supposedly translate into higher levels of productivity; and to carry out a constant, rigorous, and multidimensional evaluation process that provides the feedback necessary to continually fine-tune the program.
Fragmented universalism	Limited to the provision of basic health, education, and social security, with a focus on improving quantitative indicators, especially with regard to coverage. In practice this translates into a highly fragmented and stratified social welfare system with poor quality service (or none at all) for marginalized sectors.

Source. Ideas borrowed from Barba Solano (2006), Duhua (2000), and Valencia Lomelí (2003).

Notes

1. Esping-Andersen (1990) constructs a typology of prototypical welfare-state regimes that emerged after World War II in the industrialized countries. Three models are presented: liberal, conservative, and social-democratic. The "liberal" or "residual" model relies heavily on the market and provides only minimal, often means-tested, assistance to individuals and families that are unable to meet their basic needs; in the "conservative" or "corporatist" model, social security is strongly linked to formal sector employment and distributed through traditional family structures; and in the "social-democratic" model, the state strives to provide a minimal and

acceptable standard of living for all, irrespective of one's employment status or prior earnings. The first model finds its reflection in the United States, Canada, and Australia; the second, in Western European countries such as Germany, Italy, and France; and the third, in the Scandinavian countries.

2. In 1940, Mexico had a population of 20 million people, 35 percent of which lived in cities; by 1970, the population had grown to 48 million people, with almost 60 percent living in urban centers. In addition, in the context of the *Braceros* program (1942–64), an estimated 5 million Mexicans workers migrated to the United States legally, accompanied by approximately the same number of illegal immigrants (Durand and Massey 2003, 58).

3. Hernández-Laos and Velázquez-Roa (2003) use the Normative Basket of Essential Satisfiers (CNSE in its Spanish abbreviation) to calculate a poverty line equal to 32.83 pesos (equivalent to 4.20 dollars) per day per person in both rural and urban areas, using August 1996 prices.

4. Briefly, the ten points included in the Washington Consensus are fiscal discipline, prioritized public spending in areas with high economic return, tax reform, financial liberalization, competitive currency-exchange rates, commercial liberalization, removal of obstacles to foreign direct investment, privatization, deregulation, and strengthening of property rights (Williamson 1990).

5. Bailey (1994) criticizes PRONASOL for centralizing power in the hands of the federal government.

6. Mexican banks were nationalized in 1982 in a vain attempt to stop the hemorrhage of capital flight and restore macroeconomic stability.

7. For a detailed analysis of the immediate causes of the 1994–95 crisis, see, for example, González-Gómez (1999), Griffith-Jones (1996), and Lustig (2002).

8. See Tetreault (2006) for a detailed comparison of the poverty line methods used in these two studies, as well as a third used by CEPAL.

9. More thoroughly, PROGRESA's original objectives were "to substantially improve the education, health and food conditions for poor families, particularly for boys, girls and their mothers, providing them with sufficient educational services and quality health care, as well as food support; To integrate these actions so that the educational benefits are not affected by children and youth's lack of health or malnutrition, nor because of work that makes it difficult for them to attend school; To make sure that households have sufficient means and resources so that their children complete basic education; To induce parents and all members of the family to be responsible and to actively participate in bringing about the benefits associated with children and youth having better education, health and food; To promote community support and participation in PROGRESA's actions so that health and educational services benefit all families that live in the localities where it operates, as well as to unite community efforts and initiatives in similar actions or ones that complement the program" (Poder Ejecutivo Federal 1997, 39).

10. Between 1995 and 2001, the Mexican government paid 338 billion pesos in interest alone for FOBAPROA (Castellanos and González Amador 2002), equivalent to an average of 56.5 billion pesos annually.

11. Valencia Lomelí, Foust, and Tetreault (2010) provide an in-depth study of recommendations made by Mexican social scientists over the past twenty years, with regard to the poverty problematic.

12. Originally, the CTMP (2002) came up with the following three poverty lines: PL1, equal to 30.32 and 21.73 pesos per day per person in urban and rural areas, respectively; PL2, equal to 41.82 pesos in urban areas and 28.12 pesos in the countryside; and PL3, equal to 52.17 and 34.91 pesos, respectively. Boltvinik and Damián (2003) argue that if the PL3 had been calculated correctly, it would have been equal to 77.40 pesos in urban areas and 41.82 pesos in rural ones. In any case, the government rejected PL3 (presumably because it would have indicated too dire a situation of widespread poverty) and inserted a line between PL1 and PL2, resulting in the three official lines used today: "food poverty" (equal to PL1), "capacities poverty" (invented by the government), and "patrimonial poverty" (equal to PL2). Between 2006 and 2008, in the context of the global food crisis, the cost of the basket of essential goods in Mexico rose by 18 percent (CONEVAL 2008), resulting in an increase in the three official poverty lines. Thus, in 2008, the food poverty line was equal to 31.63 pesos in urban areas and 23.57 pesos in rural ones, and the patrimonial poverty line was equal to 63.50 and 42.73 pesos in urban and rural areas, respectively (CONEVAL 2009).

13. Calculations are based on data garnered from Poder Ejecutivo Federal (2009).

14. Calculations are based on data provided by the Ministry of Finance (*Secretaría de Hacienda y Crédito Público*; SHCP) (www.shcp.gob.mx). The average annual population growth rate between 1980 and 2010 is calculated to be 1.64 percent, based on official statistics provided by National Population Council (CONAPO) (www.conapo.gob.mx).

15. Calculations are based on data included in Levy (2008, 90–91).

16. Calculations are based on data included in Levy (2008, 90–91).

17. Calculations are based on budget data retrieved from the CEFP (2009) and INEGI (www.inegi.org.mx).

18. In a nonexhaustive review of Mexican journals and books, Valencia Lomelí, Foust, and Tetreault (2010) examined 162 publications, written by 168 academics, to identify 277 recommendations regarding Mexico's social policy geared toward fighting poverty.

19. These evaluations and past ones are available online at the following website: http://evaluacion.oportunidades.gob.mx.

20. During the lead-up to the 2006 presidential elections, President Fox used public funds to promote his successor, Felipe Calderón, inter alia, through a TV campaign titled "The Government's Achievements and Actions 2006: Oportunidades," aired between February 22 and 24, March 14 and April 17, and April 19 and May 14, 2006 (Valencia Lomelí 2010). This was only one of several factors that helped swing voters away from the heavily favored PRD candidate, Andrés Manuel López Obrador (AMLO), to Calderón and the PAN, during the narrowly contested presidential elections in July of the same year. Election-day fraud was highlighted in the press, but much of the most blatant rule-breaking was carried out beforehand, with the use of public revenue to indirectly promote the continuity of the PAN, as well as a smear campaign launched by the private sector against AMLO, portraying him as an authoritarian radical similar to Hugo Chavez in Venezuela, a danger to the country's macroeconomic stability, and a threat to its fledgling democracy. It also bears mentioning that electoral support for the PRD was weakened to some extent by divisions in the so-called "Left"; while urban-based social movements enthusiastically supported AMLO's candidacy, the Zapatistas kept their distance and focused on "The Other Campaign" (*La Otra Campaña*).

21. Until 2009, the four *vocales* that make up the Community Promotion Committees (CPCs) were elected in a popular assembly made up of local women head-of-household benefiaries. Official documentation stressed the importance of this democratic process, suggesting that it was representative of the participatory nature of PROP itself, which sought transparency and political-electoral neutrality. Along these lines, the main message from the evaluations carried out in 2004 was the need to make the CPCs more autonomous vis-à-vis the state and even to foster their participation in the constant redesigning of *Oportunidades*. However, in a surprising move in late 2009, the program's Technical Committee—led by the national coordinator, Salvador Escobedo—gave state-level coordinators (72 percent of whom are PAN militants) the power to designate *vocales* on the local level (Valencia Lomelí 2010).

Part II

Deconstructing the Poverty Reduction Strategy

5

Poverty Reduction Programs and Rural Poverty

Anthony O'Malley

Poverty reduction is directly or indirectly a central theme for most development research and policy. Ranging from numerous NGO local initiatives to copiously documented World Bank conditionalities on development assistance, poverty reduction has always been front and center as *the* problem of development. Part of the centrality of the poverty problematic has been the fact that it is, to judge by past and current data, the most intractable problem of development. The record for poverty reduction since the Second World War is absolutely dismal, and it's enough to cause even the most optimistic development thinkers and practitioners to despair of any permanent solution to global poverty beyond periodic, ad hoc interventions that nudge lines on graphs or bars on histograms tentatively up or down but basically leave the aggregate situation more or less unaltered. The various so-called "pathways out of poverty" have seemed more like labyrinths and mazes rather than any reasonably negotiable, albeit tortuous, routes.

Our research program on poverty reduction in Latin America has not focused on any particular poverty reduction initiatives but concerned itself with what might be called the *generic question*: the causes, the why, and the wherefore of the empirically substantiated intractability of poverty reduction. By implication, this has caused our research to be focused on poverty reduction initiatives in Latin America, especially those of multilateral agencies and the government policies influenced by them, along with independently formulated national initiatives.

We have been especially interested in rural poverty and the poverty reduction programs (PRPs) associated with it. Many, if not most, rural PRPs are an extension of national PRPs. And so our research approach has been two-pronged, one of assessing both national PRPs and the component of the PRP aimed at rural poverty reduction.

Statistics on rural poverty are of deep concern, even within the context of very large national poverty percentages and well-documented urban poverty (urban and periurban slums). For example, in Latin America between 1990 and 2008—during which the overall poverty rate, using standard measures, dropped from 48 percent to 33 percent—urban poverty fell from 42 percent to 33 percent, while the rural poverty rate lagged well behind this urban decline, falling from 66 percent to 61 percent. During this same eighteen-year period, the urban absolute poverty (indigence) rate declined from 15 percent to 11 percent, while the rural absolute poverty rate barely moved from 40 percent to 38 percent (CEPAL 2009).

Most aggregate national poverty rates seriously lag behind GDP upward trends—that is, contractions in GDP per capita have immediate deep inverse effects on poverty rates, which persist for long periods, even after GDP per capita has recovered to previous levels or has even surpassed them. For example, in 1980 the overall poverty rate in Latin America was 40 percent. GDP per capita declined to a moderately lower level, but the poverty rate increased dramatically to 49 percent. But as GDP per capita increased considerably and steadily in the period 1990–2004, the poverty rate remained well above 43 percent, declining very slowly to arrive once again at 40 percent in 2004, even though GDP per capita had been increasing throughout the entire period (CEPAL 2009). Disaggregated figures show that rural poverty rates respond to contractions even more sharply, with steeper increases, and lag well behind urban poverty rates, with long-term decreases during recoveries.

Rural poverty has special characteristics such as being bound up with the dynamics of a finite asset, land; being bound up with a dispersed population whose demographics present serious challenges for national, regional, and municipal social service delivery; and being bound up with a social dynamic, these days increasingly one of serious conflict, that remains remote from the public eye and the accountability of local authorities and economic interests.

As preparatory research for our principal focus on rural PRPs, we are attempting to formulate a conceptual and analytical foundation for understanding PRPs in general, which we can then use to further our understanding of rural poverty in particular. We reviewed official governmental and allied multilateral agency PRPs in Latin America, including national initiatives falling into the PRP group of so-called "noncontributory conditional cash transfers" (CCTs) such as Honduras's Family Allowance program, Chile's Social

Protection Grant, Colombia's Families in Action, Ecuador's Human Development Grant, and Mexico's Opportunities program, among others. Although researchers have measured comparative increases in economic participation by the poor—as defined by the standard World Bank poverty line of $1.25/day— during the life of CCT programs in Latin America, the measures themselves, not to mention the arbitrary poverty line that serves to establish the division between the poor and the nonpoor (and that crucially leaves out those borderline nonpoor precariously vulnerable to poverty), call into question the validity of these putatively positive economic effects. This is especially true since the positive trends are, once again, typically fragile and susceptible to GDP contractions, and all measures make no reference whatsoever to tackling the complex sources of poverty (Espina 2008). Our research has attempted to provide an analysis that could address the fundamental causes of poverty and thus provide a conceptual foundation for formulating long-term solutions to this central development problematic.

Perspectives on PRPs

There are many types of PRPs that vary according to institutional emphases, national government priorities, and ideological orientations. Although they are all worthy of empirical and analytical research in themselves, we have evaluated them as types of initiatives and found that they can be conveniently divided into four perspectives on PRP justification, formulation, and implementation:

- *Reductionist*—The PRP is fed by one-dimensional "poverty line" data based on money (income/consumption). Emphasis is on PRP increasing incomes/consumption per household through growth (for example, World Bank).
- *Distributionist*—The poverty rate responds both to distribution and to growth. Special policies are needed to distribute growth outcomes to ensure full participation by poor in the economy. Emphasis is on PRP distribution programs, while facilitating growth (for example, CEPAL).
- *Expansionist*—The current definitions of poverty by both reductionists and distributionists fail to capture the true meaning of poverty in its more complete development sense of human development as the deprivation of entitlements and obstacles to capabilities in the realization of greater human freedom; the true goal of development is progress (for example, Amartya Sen).

- *Syncretist*—Only a combination of distributionist and expansionist strategies will create effective PRPs based on the central operational concept of "social exclusion." The reductionists' emphasis on growth is retained but subsumed under the goals of the other two perspectives (for example, UN Department of Economic and Social Affairs).

These perspectives have their advantages and disadvantages, although, as we shall see, they share a common oversight regarding the origins of poverty. We provide here a brief summary of the strong and weak points of each perspective.

Reductionism

This PRP perspective has the attraction of being simple and straightforward. A poverty line of some specific amount—currently $1.25/day—is set so that the cohort of "the poor" can be measured. It also focuses national efforts on the single dynamic of GDP growth in which, it is said, lies the foundation for the eradication of poverty. PRPs are necessary as bridge policies, but of themselves they will not contribute to the alleviation of poverty. Another attraction of this approach is that the household indexes used to establish the poverty line allow cross-sectoral national and international comparisons. All in all, this perspective harmonizes nicely with the current default neoliberal, or kinder postneoliberal, thinking on macroeconomic policies and development.

The disadvantages of this perspective have been the subject of much research and criticism (O'Malley and Veltmeyer 2006). The principal problems are that it is primitive in the sense that modern persons are poor in much more complicated ways than the simple "caveman" satisfactions catered to by growth:

> The sort of society implied by a *poverty line* approach is like a primitive society before the discovery of fire, whose persons had to find caves for shelter and have a club for hunting and getting sufficient protein. These two items constituted the threshold by which to measure whether cave men had satisfied their basic needs or not. . . . Obviously, these are not the necessities of a modern, complex society in which the requirements are not simply eating and hunting, but rather also include access to energy, transportation, clothing, goods for washing faces and cleaning teeth, cooking food, recreation, and so on. (Claude, quoted in Espina 2008, 21)

In addition, the simplistic poverty line approach it represents—no matter how massive the statistical research that flows from it—misses a great deal of the "near poor" who are vulnerable to poverty, living on $2.00/day, and also misses the employed poor. For example, in nine Latin American countries, 39 percent of employed persons live below the poverty line. It also cannot account for the severity in poverty during periods in which the poverty rate actually falls, nor can it address the important phenomenon of the inverse poverty rate/GDP growth rate lag mentioned previously. It shares the weakness of all approaches whose driving policy orientation is market fundamentalism.

Distributionism

This perspective has the advantage of giving distribution of the economic product, along with the reductionists' income creation, an equal role in decreasing the poverty rate. Both growth and distribution must be the cornerstones of PRPs. More important, the near poor (the vulnerable) and the employed poor must be brought into PRPs, even though they may not fall under the poverty line. A distinct advantage is the turn away from market fundamentalism and the important role given back to the government as a major actor in poverty alleviation and development, especially with regard to the formulation and implementation of distribution programs.

The approach has, however, a number of drawbacks. It is, in the end, critically dependent on current understandings of GDP growth as being the core of development. Market fundamentalism reenters the perspective in interesting ways, not simply by granting the market the status of an independent variable that national economies must adjust to, both internally and externally, but by adopting reductionist understandings of social actors as "human capital formation" whose national improvement allows a better competitive position and insertion into global markets. In the end, the policies of distribution sit uncomfortably with other national growth-oriented policies of creating an FDI-friendly (foreign direct investment) climate and social deference to markets, not to mention the problems associated with concepts such as "national competitiveness" in a world in which the international coordination of PRPs has become increasingly necessary. In addition, like all those with statist perspectives, the distributionists assume that far too much development can be attributed to policy-driven initiatives by government: for example, data show that the poverty rate decline and GDP growth during 1990–2008 was due more to circumstances—a US-led boom, the "demographic dividend" (smaller families, lower economic dependency ratio), high world prices for commodities, and so on—than to successful government interventions.

Expansionism

This perspective greatly expands the range of conditions that define "poverty," especially "relative poverty." This expansion of the definition of "poverty" includes the deprivation of entitlements, the existence of obstacles to exercising capabilities and capacities, a lack of full participation in the socioeconomic enterprise, and the existence of obstacles to personal freedom. It has the advantage of being an antidote to stats-driven reductionism, including the elements of reductionism in the distributionist approach. It has the added attraction of tying international initiatives to poverty reduction into classic notions of development and enlightenment progress. This is especially true of the work of economists such as Amartya Sen who see the poverty problematic as essentially a challenge to our sense of pragmatic justice (Sen 2010).

A disadvantage of this approach is its sheer complexity, and the difficulties in operationalizing its concepts for implementation in PRPs. This is especially true of Sen's most recent work in which poverty is theorized as a form of injustice, even given his interesting pragmatic understanding of justice. Moreover, many capabilities/capacities reflect intrasociety standards, a fact that compromises commensurability with other societies and thus compromises international coordination of PRPs. In the extreme case, this may result in a scarcity of comparative poverty statistics and an inability to address common causes of poverty throughout the developing (and developed) world. Again, in the extreme, this perspective would result in all sorts of people becoming "impoverished" whom we would not immediately think of as importantly poor.

Syncretism

As its name implies, this perspective gathers into itself the first three perspectives, emphasizing features of this perspective or that depending on the issue or dimension of poverty being addressed. In its policy briefs, it emphasizes the ascendancy of social policies (distributionism, expansionism) over mere economic policies (reductionism). It has the advantage of being formulated by large multilateral agencies—especially the United Nations—whose features are tied to definitive resolutions of international summits, whatever the practical worth of the latter. An additional advantage is that it suggests, en passant and gingerly, that there may be structural causes explaining the origins of poverty, especially structures of ownership and assets. The perspective has the virtues of all syncretist approaches, namely, that it can, as the occasion warrants, say the right thing to some people at the right time, which is not an inconsiderable feature in the international context. Also, it has a pivotal concept about which all other aspects of poverty turn, to wit, social exclusion.

If the approach has the virtues of amalgamated perspectives, it also has the vices. It is an overwhelmingly disconnected basis for operationalizing in any PRP in that the parameters—poverty indexes, entitlements, cash transfers—have dimensions that are, in reality, not always consistent with one another. Social exclusion is a diffuse concept—like social capital—that has so many real-world forms and may be manifested in so many ways that it is difficult to conceive a PRP that could address the putative social exclusion problematic in any comprehensive manner. Moreover, there is little attempt to devise a gradient in which the more fundamental forms of exclusion are clearly separated out from more rarefied forms of lack of socioeconomic participation. Like distributionism, at crucial points in its thinking it returns to explanations such as "sustained poverty reduction depends on a fast pace of economic growth" (United Nations 2010, 7) and thus reveals itself to be crucially dependent on growth-oriented approaches as the basic dynamic underlying development.

The Structural Problematic

PRPs have formed part of the general development dynamic since the Second World War, whether subsumed under national general welfare programs or in the form of specific national and international policies directed at ameliorating the conditions of the poor. The "engine" for generating the wealth needed for such programs ideally was, during the first half of this period, industrial capitalist production led by a developmental state.

The engine in the second half of the postwar period, after the ascendancy of neoliberalism and its associated policies beginning in the 1970s, was export-oriented production within a highly competitive global market of free trade, capital mobility, referee national governments, and liberalization and privatization restructuring policies at all levels of government. In the latter part of the postwar period, neoliberal restructuring has been the global structure, and perforce national structure, around which PRPs have been conceived.

Virtually all PRP perspectives—in particular, the four categories of perspectives outlined previously—accept as a default understanding that growth as currently understood, generated by the resident structures of capitalist economic ways and means, is at the core of long-term poverty reduction. That is to say, all PRP perspectives are what might be termed "ameliorated capitalist engendered poverty reduction."

However, data gathered over fifty years of PRP interventions suggest a different understanding than the default understanding described in the previous paragraph. Given that capitalist economic structures have been the core of PRPs, past and present, and given the dismal fact that poverty over the past sixty years in Latin America, no matter what the policies, has fluctuated around the 39 percent rate (almost twice that in rural settings), this suggests to an observant development researcher that perhaps it may be the core (the putative engine) of development that is possibly implicated in the intractable poverty rate over the past half century. It suggests that the default understandings about capitalist structures as the engines of poverty reduction—or indeed, development—may be the "elephant in the room" of the spectacular lack of success of PRPs. CEPAL data (CEPAL 2009) strongly suggest—as its distributionist perspective recognizes uneasily—that recent GDP growth in Latin America has been circumstantial and not policy driven. Rather, it admits, growth has been due principally, as we mentioned previously, to (1) a China- and US-led boom in consumption, (2) high prices for commodities, and (3) a demographic dividend (lower economic dependency ratio). This suggests that all CEPAL's distributionist policies—and the policies of the other perspectives that are crucially dependent on growth—are ultimately hostages to the cycles of global capitalism, which no amount of CCTs will ever remedy or ameliorate since even the government's "cash" is also ultimately dependent on the core development phenomenon of growth.

If this be true—and data suggest that it is—then all the current PRP perspectives outlined previously are really positions in which competitive, market-led capitalism is still the essential engine for poverty reduction, and thus equality and poverty reduction have as inherent structural limitations the need to ensure the preservation of the essential socioeconomic features of the continued healthy functioning of capital, which includes its privileges, elite entrepreneurial status (first right to the socioeconomic product), social deference to its relatively autonomous "mechanisms," and social acceptance of its default positive valuation as a necessary condition for poverty reduction. If, as facts suggest, it is this very structural core that may be the obvious truth with regard to vanquishing poverty in Latin America, then the four PRP perspectives—even the teasingly radical UNDESA syncretist position—will never bring about the ultimate goal, the disappearance of poverty among Latin American nations. This is the perspectives' unfortunate, and in a concrete sense crippling, inner dilemma. And it is this dilemma that calls for a new analytical understanding of the structural causes of poverty on which PRPs with some chance of long-term success may be based.

Pathways out of Rural Poverty

To return to the specific focus of our research, the reorientation to understand poverty is critically relevant to rural poverty given (1) its greater depth and persistence, (2) its proven resistance to PRP interventions, and (3) the special features of its location. An overwhelming body of literature has shown that reductionist interventions in rural settings, such as that described in the *World Development Report 2008*, have produced negligible empirical, that is, measurable, outcomes. But even CCTs—the magic wand of distributionist economic participation—have had little effect on rural poverty, as evidenced by its steady maintenance, even in GDP per capita growth times, above 60 percent. Another considerable body of research has shown that "ameliorated capitalist interventions"—especially of the sort advocated by CEPAL targeting human capital formation for national competitiveness—basically boil down to the transformation of humans into forms of capital that can be more successfully inserted into capitalist market relations. If limitations imposed on nations by capitalist market relations are part of the key to the obstinate persistence of poverty in Latin America, then this may be the wrong pathway out of poverty— and doubly so for rural populations.

Data over a long period suggest that the basis of rural poverty—as with most forms of poverty—is overwhelmingly structural in origin and not circumstantial or inherent in rural idiosyncrasies. The structural core of all PRP perspectives—no matter how embellished with distributionism and expansionism—is capitalist engendered growth. A considerable body of contemporary research in agrarian studies has shown that capitalist-led and -structured interventions in rural settings have had an overwhelmingly deleterious effect on rural populations. What this strongly suggests is that poverty reduction in the countryside will be successful only when it proceeds on the basis of a complete structural transformation of basic economic and social relations regarding ownership of land, deprivileging and decentering of agribusiness, and similar changes that remove, or at least recognize, the "elephant" standing in the PRP room.

Much transformation of the rural poor and PRPs can dead-end in the face of supralocal—particularly national—development agendas. The success of rural structural pathways out of poverty is not just a matter of national organization. Much nationally sponsored/directed transformation can, in turn, dead-end in the face of supranational development realities (for example, Bolivia) and default understandings that remain deeply entrenched as a consequence of the neoliberal revolution of the 1970s (for example, Brazil). The former progressive restrictions on capital mobility—resolutely dismantled over the past forty years—have not been even partially restored. Nations compete with one another, if not in a race to the bottom as an FDI locale then at least as courteous noncooperants in one another's fates, each with an eye to a successful insertion into markets controlled by transnational entities operating according to their own rules of self-preservation.

PRPs, and rural poverty eradication especially, will make significant progress when the structural conditions of perpetuation are transformed and PRPs enjoy the same international coordination that default macroeconomic policies have enjoyed.

6

Microfinance
Crediting the Poor

Henry Veltmeyer

Microfinance is access to financial services and small loans for poor households. As a concept it originated with Muhammad Yunus, the economist who founded the influential Grameen Bank in the 1970s. But in the 1980s it came under increasing attention in the context of both Asia and Latin America until, in the 1990s, it was transformed into a major poverty reduction tool in the arsenal of the international development community in its war waged against global poverty.[1] Over the past decade, the number of microfinance organizations (MFOs) has grown from some 3,000 in 1998, serving 12 million beneficiaries, to 10,000, serving over 150 million clients spread over 85 countries. Although the dynamics of growth are unclear, there is little question that among the main reasons for the later and now enthusiastic support from the international financial institutions in the development community was the discovery that financing the poor was a very profitable business. The initial discovery and then the dawning realization that funding the poor can be profitable can be traced out in the 1990s when NGO after NGO, in many cases with international co-operation, were transformed into a financial institution—an intermediary microfinance institution or a bank. Behind this transformation was the discovery that, via the technique of solidarity lending, the default rate on microfinance loans is surprisingly low, indeed much lower than is commonplace in the commercial bank sector. Clearly, for the poor the issue is not interest rates per se[2] but the lack of access to capital. The poor will save and utilize financial services and pay back loans with interest at rates that owners of small- and medium-sized businesses cannot afford and that large-scale multinational capitalist enterprises do not have to pay.[3]

Armed with the idea that poor people should have access to financial services notwithstanding their difficulty in providing collateral, microfinance arose in response to doubts about state-delivered subsidized credit to poor farmers. From humble beginnings, with the initiation of formalized micro-credit starting from the mid-1970s in Bangladesh and Latin America, the range of services under the umbrella of microfinance has grown to include microsavings and microinsurance. The philosophy of microfinance is "development," emphasizing "teaching people to fish" instead of giving them fish. Therefore, it seeks to enable the poor to engage in productive and self-sustaining activities that lead to "development."

Although it is far from a silver bullet to the problems of poverty, microfinance has nevertheless enjoyed a degree of apparent success in promoting economic development and empowering the poor via supporting entrepreneurship, increasing their income, and facilitating their establishment of viable businesses. With a yet untapped market of 500 million poor workers, the future of microfinance holds much promise as a profit-making if not a development enterprise.

In this chapter, we will explore different aspects of microfinance—its strengths, limitations, past and future possibilities, with a geographical focus on Bolivia, which has what is regarded as the most advanced microfinance sector in Latin America and has been a model worldwide.[4]

The Microfinance Sector in Bolivia

In the mid-1980s, when the international development community turned to Bolivia as a laboratory for the design of a new development model based on the Washington Consensus, both international cooperants/donors and the government realized that efficient public interventions in microfinance might help to improve social welfare. This could happen, or it might be needed, if and as long as "market failure" prevented the legitimate demand of poor households from being matched by a private supply of financial services. In Bolivia, the first attempts to mitigate possible market failure in microfinance with government-owned development finance institutions failed. This, along with the growth of distrust in direct government intervention, made room for a second round of nongovernmental interventions (Monje 1995). By several accounts (see, for example, Gonzalez-Vega et al. 1997) this round of microfinance institutionalization, compared with MFOs worldwide, met with "uncommon success."

According to Navajas and Schreiner (1998, 2), "In terms of outreach, financial performance, cost-effectiveness, and sustainability, the best MFOs in

Bolivia," all of which have received support from both the government and donors, "are also among the best in the world." This is somewhat surprising considering that government and donor microfinance support has in many cases been mediated by "apex organizations," financial intermediaries that, according to the authors, suffer from at least six shortcomings, including (1) "not designed with the strength of the microfinance sector nor the welfare of the poor in mind"; (2) "serv[ing] the needs of donors or government rather than of the microfinance market" ("At times . . . strengthen[ing] microfinance so as to help the poor came just as an afterthought"); (3) "high startup costs in terms of time and effort" because of "squabbles among donors and within government"; and (4) "fail[ing] to emphasize sustainability . . . crowd[ing] out the private-sector apex most focused on sustainability" (Navajas and Schreiner 1998, 3).

In the authors' judgment a nongovernmental apex organization (financial intermediary), such as Funda-Pro, "may be sustainable, since it cannot rely on more and more funds from donors . . . [which] instills [market] discipline. . . . This apex organization may well intermediate funds for the best MFOs for a long time as long as the competition with the government apex organizations does not drive it out of the market" (Navajas and Schreiner 1998, 4). As for the "potential market" for microfinance, the authors note, "It is difficult to know what the *legitimate* demand for microfinance might be in an undeveloped or nonexistent market" (p. 5). However, they add, "Bolivia is the poorest country in South America. The gross domestic product per capita is about US$800 . . . [and] about 70 percent of its 7.4 million people live below the poverty line defined as satisfaction of some basic needs" (p. 5). Thus, "income is low, but economic growth has been steady for the past decade . . . [and] about 2.5 million people are economically active [and] about one million are self-employed or work in family enterprises" (p. 5). Therefore, they conclude, the microfinance market holds considerable potential for the private entrepreneur (financial intermediary, whether nongovernmental or commercial in form). In this regard, they note that "households with *legitimate* demand [that is, unlikely to default on a loan] can pay the costs associated with an efficient, sustainable supply" (p. 5).

Bolivia, Navajas and Schreiner note, "has many poor households who might demand microfinance. For example, the dominance of small-scale farms in the Andean plateau and in the Andean valleys has meant that many rural people are self-employed on farms." Furthermore, "in the 1980s the collapse of the mines as a source of employment forced many households to turn to microenterprises to earn a living. Finally," the authors add, "the flood of cheap imports used to launder dollars has created a big sector in petty trade, and traders on the street corners of urban Bolivia sell anything from boxed breakfast cereal to microwave ovens" (p. 5). With these considerations, the authors suggest, "500,000 may be a useful first guess for the number of creditworthy households in all of Bolivia that might at some time have a legitimate demand for some type of microfinance" (p. 6).

This particular microfinance market assessment was conducted in the late 1990s after twelve years of experimentation with neoliberalism and before the outbreak of organized popular resistance in the social movements sector that would culminate in the ascension to state power of Evo Morales, leader of the *Cocaleros* (the movement of coca-producing indigenous "peasants," many of them former miners made redundant by the closing of mines in the 1980s) and the Movement Towards Socialism (MAS [*Movimiento al Socialismo*]). The question is, how did the private sector, and the NGO-sector of financial intermediaries and microcredit providers, respond to this pent-up demand by the poor for microcredit—for loans repayable at rates of annualized interest up to and even greater than 30 percent?

But of greater import are two questions will be addressed immediately: (1) How did microfinance figure in the arsenal of poverty reduction strategies mobilized by the international development community in the context of the PWC, five years of uprisings and class warfare, and the turn against neoliberalism in the form of the MAS regime of Evo Morales? And (2) what has been the impact of microfinance on the lives of the poor?

Microfinance Comes to Bolivia

In 1999 Bolivia's National Statistics Institute (INE) estimated that close to 1.5 million people out of an "economically active population" of 3.1 million worked in the unstructured and unregulated "informal sector," which constituted around 65 percent of total employment and contributed an estimated 15 percent to 20 percent to the GDP. According to National Chamber of Industry data in 1999, 92 percent of all economic enterprises in the country were small businesses or microenterprises based on family labor. As for financial services provided by the institutions in the traditional banking and financial services sector, they were highly concentrated, totally excluding the microenterprises and most small businesses. At the end of 1999 the banking system had a total of 311,630 registered clients, but 0.5 percent accounted for 51 percent of the loans extended to the private sector. Before the appearance of microfinance, microenterprise owners had very limited access to credit and this in the informal market at usurious rates up to 10 percent a day.[5] Thus the demand for credit was, and remains, very strong, and the potential market is huge.

The first organizational response to this "market opportunity" was made in 1986, barely a year into the first "structural adjustment" loan extended by the World Bank and the IMF to Bolivia. In this year PRODEM (*Promoción de la Microempresa*) was formed with USAID funding and the participation of the private sector, together with several similar but smaller NGOs, in order to service the need of small-income owners of what would be termed "microenterprises" for capital. The response of PRODEM and some of the other NGOs that followed was innovative albeit not new (it had been pioneered by the Grameen Bank). It took the form of a *solidarity group* approach—credit provided to a group of persons, each with low income who in the spirit of solidarity would agree to share responsibility for the loan taken out by any members of the group. And the arrangement of the loan, generally for less than $1,000 and often less than $500, was simplicity itself (effected with the simple presentation of the borrower's ID), and the schedule for repayment was very flexible, adjusted to the circumstances of each borrower and could be made weekly, fortnightly, or monthly. If the individual borrower were unable to meet the terms of the loan on the date due, then the other members of the group would, thus providing a guarantee of loan repayment and, as it turned out, an exceptionally low default rate, making the business of microfinance both a low risk venture and profitable.[6]

By 1991, four years after the founding of PRODEM, the microfinance sector was solidly entrenched in Bolivia, already providing a model for similar developments in other parts of the world. But subsequent years in the decade saw a substantial expansion of microfinance—a period of consolidation (1992–97). Financial NGOs on the model of PRODEM materialized and took form in virtually every country in the region, providing a major impetus to microenterprise development in the informal sector of the expanding urban centers and their economies and societies.

The organizational forms of this microfinance institutionalization were diverse. Lapenu and Zeller (2001), in a global survey and review of MFOs in Africa, Asia, and Latin America, identified in their database 1,500 institutions with 46,000 affiliates and branches and that reach 54 million members and 17 million borrowers worldwide (in 85 countries). These institutions were organized as follows: (1) *cooperatives*—many with 10,000 to 200,000 members; (2) *solidarity groups*—94 percent with fewer than 50,000 members, 37 percent with fewer than 1,000 members; and (3) *village banks and links* (local organizations linked to the formal banking network)—none with more than 30,000 members.

In terms of legal status, these MFOs can be classified into five major types of organizations: NGOs, cooperatives, registered banking institutions, private financial funds, and government organizations and projects. In Latin America, these legally defined MFOs are distributed as follows: most are cooperatives or NGOs, but there has been a trend toward conversion of NGOs into regulated microfinance banks. Overall, 54 percent of all MFO members are women, whereas in Asia and Africa fewer than 50 percent of MFO members are women (Ynaraja Ramírez 2000, 30). As for Bolivia some of the most important international financial institutions that are still or currently operating are as follows:

- Pro Mujer (*Programas para la Mujer*), a "communal bank" formed in 1991 to the purpose of providing microfinance services to low-income women in the periurban areas such as El Alto, today on the highland periphery of La Paz. Pro Mujer pioneered the notion and methodology of communal banks as a means of reaching the poorest of the poor.
- IDEPRO, another communal bank, was founded in 1988 thanks to a private initiative but began operations in 1991 with the aim of promoting the "integral development" of urban microenterprises via a combination of financial and nonfinancial services.
- BancoSol (Banco Solidario S.A.) began its operations in 1992 as Bolivia's first private bank that specializes in microfinance and since 1994 has experienced an annualized increase in its microfinance portfolio of 12 percent on loans averaging $600.
- FADES (*Fundación para Alternativas de Desarrollo*) was formed in 1986 by a consortium of organizations with the purpose of promoting rural development.
- FUNDA-PRO (*Fundación para la Producción*), a "second-tier" NGO, formed as the result of an agreement signed in 1991 by the government of Bolivia and the United States regarding the institutionalization of FOCAS (*Proyecto de Formación de Capital en Areas Secundarias*). It specializes in programs of institutional strengthening, opening new markets, research on microfinance issues, and the provision of financial and educational services.
- PRO-CREDITO began operation in 1991 as a financial NGO but has since participated actively in the creation and shareholding of various private financial funds (*Fondos Financieros Privados*).

- COOPERATIVA Jesús Nazareno is a cooperative based in Santa Cruz that began operations (in the urban areas of Santa Cruz) in 1992, using both a "solidarity group" and an "individual" approach; it extends loans in support of urban microenterprise, with six-month loans averaging $520 in size and offered at a rate of interest that fluctuates from 18 percent to 36 percent a year.

- CRECER (*Credito con Educación Rural*) is an example of "village banking" or, in the Latin American context, a "communal bank." The primary goal of this group is to provide financial and educational services, primarily to women. These services focus on enhancing the food security and well-being of the family. CRECER requires that all clients save 10 percent of the total amount of their loan. Training in microenterprise development, village banking management, health, nutrition, and family planning is required.

- CIPAME (*Corporación de Instituciones Privadas de Apoyo a la Microempresa*) is a private financial corporation formed in 1993 (with legal status in 1994); it has eight affiliates, six of which offer financial microfinance services in the urban areas, and including FIE (*Centro de Fomento a Iniciativas Económicas*), which was founded in 1985 to promote the development of small enterprises and microenterprises that have experienced difficulty in accessing credit and financial services. Other associated organizations, all concerned with economic and social development, include CIDRE (*Centro de Investigación y Desarrollo Regional*), Banco Sol, PROA (*Centro de Servicios Integrados para el Desarrollo Urbano*), CEDLA (*Centro de Estudios para el Desarrollo Laboral y Agrario*), and FUNBODEM (*Fundación Boliviana para el Desarrollo de la Mujer*).

The success of these and other MFOs, particularly in regard to and measured in terms of the delivery of effective and efficient (also profitable) financial services to low-income operators of microenterprises, has been explained with reference to diverse factors, but two stand out: (1) a philosophy and a methodology that are grounded in a culture of both solidarity and entrepreneurship and (2) organizational and procedural flexibility, which allowed the NGOs that operate in the microfinance sector to achieve some economies of scale, to minimize the risk of defaulting on loan repayments, and to improve the quality and the scope of financial services available to the urban poor. Other factors identified by researchers include a competent and highly motivated cadre of professional service providers, financial institutions that were designed for sustainability, and institutional development of the financial market. The combination of these and other factors have allowed the institutions in the microfinance sector to provide a vital service to the poor, converting large numbers of them into productive economic agents and, in the process, contributing to the alleviation of poverty among certain categories and a significant number of urban and rural households.

Most significant perhaps in the evaluation of the "performance" of the MFOs, at least from a neoliberal perspective, is that credit and finance had been extended to the poor, or to a sector of low-income earners, without any subsidies or the participation of the government. In the 1970s, the government had been an important agent of both economic and social development, having assumed responsibility for regulating private economic activity and redistributing, for the sake of equity, some of the market-generated national income to those less well-off or poor. These social and development programs turned out to be so expensive as to push virtually every government, in both the North and the South, into a fiscal crisis, generating conditions for a conservative counterrevolution—and several decades of neoliberalism characterized by the retreat of the state and the strengthening of civil society in the development process. The institutional development of microfinance was a significant if not a dominant feature of this process—the privatization of economic and social development.

The second phase of microfinance development, which analysts have periodized from 1992 to 1997, saw not only the further expansion and extension of microfinance and credit services but its institutionalization—the conversion of relatively informal organizations into formal institutions operating within the framework established by the government for the operation of these institutions in the delivery of these financial services.[7] Some highly profitable financial NGOs such as the Banco Sol were transformed into a regulated microfinance or commercial bank, authorized to access international capital markets. Institutionalization gave the financial NGOs access to other services such as holding deposits of money, which they invested in the international capital markets.[8]

The institutionalization of microfinance as an economic sector and model was made possible by, and required, an intensive process of dialogue and negotiation of "experts" in the sector with local authorities, as well as the support of the donors engaged in "international cooperation." By mid-decade these development associations, and international and regional financial institutions such as the World Bank and the IADB, had become major enthusiasts regarding microfinance, viewing it as a significant factor of economic development and poverty alleviation. Ynaraja Ramírez (2000) sees the support of the development community in this period as "crucial." Without it, he argues, many of the now successful and viable microfinance institutions at work in Bolivia would have found the doors closed against the initiatives and proposals that gave rise to them. The collaboration between the Bolivian government (headed at the time by Gonzalo Sánchez de Lozada, minister of finance under Bolivia's first neoliberal regime, who had led the negotiations with Washington on Bolivia's economic model) and the Washington-based (and -led) international organizations in the field of development was a critical factor of microfinance and microenterprise development in Bolivia and elsewhere. For example, PRODEM, the NGO that pioneered microfinance in Bolivia, was created with the active and financial support of USAID. In office as president, Sánchez de Lozada, who was a major ally of Washington in the neoliberal project of macroeconomic policy reform and a major advocate of NGOs as an agency and agent of international cooperation, created PAM (*Programa de Apoyo al Microcrédito y Financiamiento Rural*), with the aim of providing institutional support to microfinance NGOs.[9]

Microfinance: What Impact on the Lives of the Poor?

"Meet Rosa," writes Kemmis Betty (2010), a UK member of the Democracy Center, "Rosa, who sells fruit in the markets of El Alto . . . [and] travels every fortnight to Alto Beni to buy fruit—mainly bananas—from her vendors, and is able to sell at a price that covers her travel costs and leaves her with a small profit. For many years," Kemmis Betty points out, Rosa has also been a customer at one of Bolivia's many MFOs. "In many ways," he notes, "Rosa is a typical customer [in that] microfinance borrowers mainly live in urban or semi-urban areas and work in the informal economy, buying and selling in Bolivia's sprawling markets or perhaps producing goods in a home workshop. Like many customers," he adds, "Rosa doesn't just have a loan with her MFI [Microfinance Institution, synonomous with MFO], but also a savings account (the MFI requires that she makes deposits along with each loan payment) and a life insurance policy" (Kemmis Betty 2010).

"Rosa," Kemmis Betty explains, "once tried to get a loan from a larger bank, but she . . . couldn't provide proof of income and she didn't possess anything that the bank would accept as collateral." But, "at her MFI, she is a member of a lending group that is bound together by a group guarantee [a solidarity bond]. This means," he adds, "that if one borrower doesn't pay, it falls on the others in the group to cover the difference." The idea "is that social pressure created within the group ensures that everyone will pay if they are able, [thus by] using this method MFOs are able to offer credit to those without paperwork and guarantees."

In Kemmis Betty's account, Rosa recalls that there have been occasions when one member of the group wasn't able to pay, putting additional financial strain on the other members. For this reason, he notes, "Rosa is thinking about taking out an individual loan (now that she has an established credit history). MFOs in Bolivia are increasingly offering individual loans to customers such as Rosa, where the collateral might be a market post, a cow or even a tree."

"To be certain," Kemmis Betty notes, "non-profit microfinance loans do not come cheap in Bolivia." Although Rosa is a customer of a nonprofit MFI, her annualized interest rate is over 30 percent, a figure that makes even credit card rates in the United States or United Kingdom look like a bargain. "Indeed," he adds, "it is often the poorest clients, taking out the smallest loans, who are paying the highest rates of interest." He asks, why so high? And indeed we might also ask. The main reason, he opines, "is that the administrative costs of servicing so many small loans are much higher than for traditional banks making fewer, larger loans. . . . Interest rates also cover the risk that borrowers may not pay back their loans, as well as the cost of borrowing for the institution itself (although most MFOs aim to be fully sustainable)."

Although improving efficiency and bringing down costs is something the industry needs to keep working at, Kemmis Betty argues, "the Bolivian microfinance market still has some of the lowest rates in Latin America." And "while the rates charged are high relative to the traditional banking sector, they tend to be low compared to other informal sources of credit available to the poor, who may charge 10 percent a day." But, he asks himself, "is Rosa actually better off for her MFI loan, given the price she's paying? Has the loan helped her [to] exit poverty?" In answer to this question, Kemmis Betty notes that Rosa's business has grown gradually over the years: "she's been able to buy larger quantities of fruit with the capital from her MFI—and her income has grown as a result. However," he adds, "the impact has hardly been dramatic: Rosa still sells fruit at the same stall, lives in the same house *and is still poor.*"

What does this mean then? What does Rosa's story tell us about microfinance as a poverty reduction tool, a pathway out of poverty? As to this, Kemmis Betty cites a recent review by the World Bank's Consultative Group to Assist the Poor to point out "that we don't really know the impact that microfinance has in terms of poverty alleviation at the aggregate level. The methodology of studies to assess the social impact of microfinance," he notes, "has always been a source of contention, and the few randomized controlled trials have produced inconclusive results."

However, for Kemmis Betty this does mean that the possible value and contribution of microfinance to poverty alleviation should be discounted. "The real value of microfinance might be more subtle"—a matter of "day-to-day cash flow management." In this regard Kemmis Betty cites a "groundbreaking study published in 2009, which put together detailed financial diaries for over 250 families," so as to point out "that for someone such as Rosa, whose income and expenses are not only low but also seasonal and unpredictable, day-to-day cash flow management can be very complex. Rosa," Kemmis Betty adds, "like most people in her economic position, needs to carefully manage her finances to ensure that she has enough to pay for everyday necessities . . . and to cover larger one-time expenses." In this regard, "both savings and loans are important financial tools for poor households to have the money they need in hand when they need it. . . . This is one of the key values of MFI credit."

"In the end," Kemmis Betty asks rhetorically, "is microcredit a magic wand that ends poverty?" Not based on the current evidence, he adjudges. But here—echoing the view of Navajas and Schreiner (1998)—as in most markets, the real test of a product's value is whether there is a demand for it. Despite the high costs, the impoverished themselves clearly see a value in microfinance, as evidenced by strong demand and high repayment rates. That is, the demand by the poor for microfinance is evidence of its value to them (or their need for it?).

"Twenty years of microfinance in Bolivia," Kemmis Betty concludes, "has not eradicated poverty, not by a long shot." But, he adds, "it has provided a large number of the country's poor with access to more reliable, and cheaper credit then they would have been able to obtain otherwise." And as a result, "many people have managed to lift themselves at least a little higher on the economic ladder."

Conclusion

Until the mid-1990s the World Bank, in its leadership role vis-à-vis the fight against global poverty, emphasized the labor pathway out of rural poverty on the belief that urban labor markets provided the most convenient "opportunity structure" for the rural poor in their search for an improvement in their social condition. In fact, "international cooperation" with the effort of governments in the region to facilitate access to these markets was concerned predominantly with "human resource development"—developing the human capital needed to access these markets and take advantage of the opportunities for well-paid jobs and decent work that they provided. In this, expenditures on education and health were seen to be particularly "productive," increasing the productivity of labor and economic activity and enhancing the opportunities available to the poor for social mobility and self-advancement, thereby lifting themselves and their households out of poverty. However, by mid-decade it was evident that the formal labor markets were unceasingly unable to absorb the vast supplies of surplus labor generated by the forces of progressive change and that the new opportunities existed in the burgeoning "informal sector." Hence the renewed interest in, and indeed enthusiastic support for, the microfinance and microcredit approach, even in the absence (at the time) of empirical evidence that it provided as a useful tool in the fight against poverty.[10]

Enthusiasm for the "microfinance revolution" (microfinance and microcredit as pathways out of poverty) reached global proportions in the 1990s and reached a crescendo in certain policymaking (and development) circles in Latin America. However, for the most part the excitement around microfinance has been based so far more on rhetoric than on hard evidence. In fact, one of the most surprising features of the evaluations and assessments that have been conducted over the years is the lack of any substantive evidence that microfinance has contributed significantly to a reduction of poverty at the macro-level. A study conducted for CEDLA (Bebczuk 2008, 20) based on a "brief inspection of flourishing microfinance experiences in Latin America and the Caribbean" is revealing in this regard. Not one of the six criteria used to evaluate these experiences had to do with either the impact of microfinance on the lives of the poor or its actual role in the reduction of poverty in the aggregate. Consequently, it is not easy or possible to draw any "lessons" regarding microfinance as a poverty reduction strategy, either from the ten "experiences" that Bebczuk reviews or from several decades of evaluative studies and assessments of the microfinance approach to poverty reduction. And this is undoubtedly because in Latin America, in the form that the strategy was pioneered in Bolivia, it was viewed more as a business or a potential commercial venture rather than as a poverty reduction tool—hence the predominance of commercial criteria in microfinance evaluations and a trend for the conversion of some financial NGOs into commercial banks and for the traditional banks to get involved in microfinance.[11]

A number of official reports over the past five years have documented a substantive gain in the long war on poverty since 2003. But there is no evidence whatsoever that microcredit has contributed to this "achievement," modest as it is and overstated that it certainly is. For one thing, the minimal evidence that does exist regarding the poverty-microfinance nexus suggests that it is the less worse-off poor, not the destitute or the ultrapoor, who benefit principally from microfinance (World Bank 2000a, 75). In this regard Navajas et al. (2000) report that in the case of Bolivia, for the urban area of La Paz two of the three predominant MFOs disproportionately lend to those above of the poverty line and that the poorest group as the share of borrowers in all three institutions (at 2 percent to 5 percent) was well below its share in the population, reinforcing the perception that MFOs have difficulty in reaching the very poor. In the case of Mexico, recent data suggest that microcredit, whether provisioned privately or publicly, has played a minimal role in securing household income and the poverty reduction strategies pursued by the poor themselves.[12] Not only has the official poverty rate stubbornly stayed at around 50 percent over two decades of antipoverty programming by the government, but it seems that the bulk of the financial resources used to finance their microenterprises was provided by family members and friends. The creation of the microenterprise required financing in 86 percent of cases, according to INEGI, but for most the source of finance was the owner's savings or loans from family and friends; only 0.7 percent received any financing or credit offered by the government, and only 2 percent were financed by microfinance providers (*La Jornada*, December 27, 2009, 18).

There is no doubt that there is some truth to the widespread notion of the relative success of microcredit in Latin America over the past two decades. A substantial number of people in the region have received, if not substantively benefited from, microcredit schemes of financial inclusion of the poor. At the same time, for a difficult-to-measure number of the poor who migrated to the cities and urban centers in the search of greater opportunity and social improvement in their social condition, microcredit or microfinance was undoubtedly a necessity if not a boon. In the absence of microfinance, many poor households might indeed not have been able to survive or lift themselves out of abject poverty. However, one of the reasons for the demand by the poor for microfinance is the all-too-prevalent problem of government neglect or the reliance on the market and the private sector.

In the last few decades of the twentieth century and the first of the twenty-first century, plenty of Latin American (and, for that matter, Middle Eastern, African, and Asian) governments under the sway of neoliberalism did not commit themselves to nurturing the lives of their citizens to the extent that one might expect, given the rhetoric surrounding the new development program of inclusive development and the focus on poverty reduction. In the context of the predominant concern of neoliberal regimes for market-led economic growth and social developments—whether this concern was ideologically motivated or pragmatic—the door was opened wide for the advent of microcredit organizations. The governments in these conditions were more than happy to let the financial NGOs and the private banks do their work. But just because the microcredit organizations and banks, and even the multinational corporations and other capitalist enterprises in the private sector, were invited to participate in the development process (and have subsequently achieved various degrees of success, at least as measured in terms of the number of microcredit beneficiaries) does not mean that credit provision or the responsibility for social development should be turned over to them. Indeed, the lack of any evident positive impact of privately provisioned and administered microfinance on the lives of the poor, and on the rate of poverty, suggests quite the contrary.

Microfinance can well be seen as more of a profitable business, a source of profit than a tool for poverty reduction. Even among the "beneficiaries" of the Grameen Bank, 55 percent of those who have received loans over the years by a number of accounts still cannot meet their most basic nutritional needs. In a study by ACCION International, a US-based apex intermediary organization, of its affiliates in Bolivia, Peru, and Haiti, from 51 percent (Bolivia, Peru) to 63 percent (Haiti) of microfinance loan recipients were non-poor, while 49 percent to 37 percent lived and worked with incomes below the national poverty line (Marulanda and Otero 2005). This analysis of the poverty-microfinance nexus illustrates the complexity of the topic. Do we conclude that microfinance institutions can and do reach the poor—although not the poorest of the poor, since they are found in the rural areas while in Latin America microfinance is concentrated in the urban areas? Or do the statistics, minimal and limited as they are, together with our own review and limited analysis, suggest that microfinance has had a fairly minimal impact on the lives of the poor?

More generally, a "Grameenized private sector"—the privatization of development, or a market-led and -based approach versus state-led development—poses a number of problems. Given a history in which many regimes have neglected the economic and social needs of their citizens, the support for microcredit in many cases has presented an opportunistic escape of their social and governmental responsibilities. By openly shifting responsibility for the well-being of their citizens to private financial institutions like ACCION International or FINCA, governments have been able to elude one of their most important obligations. Although one can make a valid claim that Latin American governments have not always been properly held accountable for their citizens' well-being, we should aspire toward an improved and a somewhat more moral model of government that might on the whole achieve more than what a scattering of microcreditors have achieved.

Notes

1. In 2006, the Nobel Peace Prize was awarded to the Grameen Bank of Bangladesh, founded by Muhammad Yunus, the economist who founded the influential Grameen Bank, putting a global spotlight on the enterprise of providing microcredit for the poor. The Grameen system of putting small bits of capital in the hands of fruit sellers, seamstresses, and other especially small businesses has been repeated all over the world in developing countries. Yunus, the man who started it all, wrote in his book *Banker to the Poor: Micro-Lending and the Battle against World Poverty* (2001, 204), "I believe that 'government,' as we know it today, should pull out of most things except for law enforcement and justice, national defense and foreign policy, and let the private sector, a 'Grameenized private sector,' a social consciousness-driven private sector, take over their other functions."

2. In actual fact, the interest rates associated with microfinance loans are not as favorable as many of the microcreditors make them sound. Over the course of a single year, a loan from ACCION International, an MFO that operates in Peru, can carry as much as a 20 percent interest rate, clearly very high, even though it might be relatively low when compared to the alternative available sources (loan sharks in the past have charged interest rates that were many times higher than those of ACCION International). However, other MFOs can charge as much as 4 percent interest a month, which can become as much as 50 percent after twelve months. And a 20 percent interest rate on a loan given to someone who might barely make a few dollars a day often can be burdensome to pay back.

3. In Bolivia loans on the informal market can be arranged at rates that work out to be 100 percent to 200 percent (even 300 percent), in both the urban and the rural areas (Ynaraja Ramírez 2000).

4. In actual fact, as emphasized by Weiss and Montgomery (2004, 3) in their review of microfinance as a poverty reduction tool, "microfinance developed in Asia and Latin America under very different ideological, political and economic conditions." Hence, they point out, "there are distinctive differences in the microfinance industry in the two regions. A brief look at the history of two of the most famous MFOs (the Grameen Bank in Bangladesh and Banco Sol in Bolivia) gives an informative picture of how the industry in the two regions can be characterized."

5. See note 4.

6. PRODEM, the organization that pioneered microfinance in Bolivia, after five years of operation had a default rate of 0.002 percent (Ynaraja Ramírez 2000).

7. The strong financial performance of larger MFOs in Latin America, compared to those reported in Asia, is linked with a trend toward the commercialization of microfinance in the region. In 1992 Banco Sol became the first example of an NGO transformation to a commercial bank and thus became the first regulated microfinance bank. Banco Sol surpassed other

Bolivian banks in profitability and became the first MFI to access international capital markets. Following this successful example, at least thirty-nine other important NGOs worldwide transformed into commercial banks over the period 1992–2003 (Fernando 2004).

8. Implementation of a new regulatory framework for the financial sector in 1990 resulted in the following system: nine national commercial banks, four foreign commercial banks, thirteen savings and credit mutual funds, six private financial funds, four mixed (private-state) funds, seventeen credit cooperatives, three very big financial NGOs, and another thirty or so smaller ones offering microcredit.

9. By presidential Supreme Decree 24436, PAM was incorporated into the *Fondo de Desarrollo del Sistema Financiero y Apoyo a la Producción* (FONDESIF) in December 13, 1996.

10. The enthusiastic support of the World Bank and the IADB for the idea of another pathway (*el Otro Sendero*) espoused by Hernan de Soto can be dated to this belated "discovery" that in the absence of industry and the public sector cutbacks wage labor had exhausted its capacity to absorb the large volumes of surplus rural labor. In this context, in comparison with Bangladesh, the intervention of Bolivia in the field of microfinance was typically urban rather than rural, less concerned with poverty and more focused on microenterprise. Thus it targeted the "economically active poor"—people with established businesses that needed capital to grow. That is, from the start Bolivian microcredit was itself seen as a business, potentially as a branch of commercial banking (Rutherford 2003).

11. Following the successful example of Banco Sol, at least thirty-nine other important NGOs worldwide were transformed into commercial banks over the period 1992–2003, according to Fernando (2004). In Latin America, Banco Agricola Comercial (El Salvador), Banco del Desarrollo (Chile), Banco Wiese (Peru), and Banco Empresarial (Guatemala) are examples of private commercial banks that are involved in varying degrees with microfinance.

12. In 2009 INEGI, Mexico's official national statistics institute, identified 8,108,955 "microenterprises," 5 million of which operate in streets but have a base in a private home (*domicilio particular*) (*La Reforma*, December 27, 2009, 18). The data collected by INEGI show that 20 percent of these enterprises net an income for the family or household equivalent to one minimum wage ($4.70 a day), another 14 percent generate income equivalent to between one and two minimum wages, and 10 percent derive an income of between two and three minimum wages. With an estimated three minimum wages needed to satisfy an average family's needs—it is estimated that the minimum wage in Mexico, set with a slight variation, for three "economic regions," has lost 80 percent of the purchasing value that it had in 1982—this analysis yields a poverty rate of 44 percent, which is just below the national poverty rate in 2008 (47.4 percent; the urban poverty rate, according to highly questionable official calculations, is closer to 40 percent). In addition, while in the vast majority of microenterprises only the owner works, 31 percent have from one to fifteen employees, but most of these employees, more than half in any case, do not receive any wage at all because they are family members—spouse or partner and kids. Of these "workers" 90 percent were contracted verbally and for an indeterminate period. In addition, 86 percent have little access to medical or health services, an important element of the government's strategy of inclusive development and poverty reduction.

7

The PRSP

Poverty Reduction Through Inclusive Neoliberalism

Anthony O'Malley and Henry Veltmeyer

A **Poverty Reduction Strategy Paper (PRSP)** describes a country's macroeconomic, structural, and social policies and programs designed to promote growth and reduce poverty, together with associated external financing needs. PRSPs are prepared by governments through a participatory process involving civil society and development partners, including the World Bank and the International Monetary Fund (IMF). The PRSP is a policy tool cast within the World Bank's Comprehensive Development Framework (CDF) and designed as a guide for national economic policy and all development assistance. Presented to the World Bank Board of Governors in 1998, the framework spells out four principles, all of which mark significant shifts in thinking about development since the 1990s.

The PRSP entails, as a condition of accessing debt relief or development funding, the requirement of a developing country government, with social participation, to write a long-term, comprehensive, and results-oriented paper that would outline the government's poverty reduction strategy. It was expected that with the PRSP the developing country would take ownership of its own development under conditions of social participation, democratic accountability, partnerships with donors, and ultimately more effective poverty reduction.

The renewed concern with and focus on poverty reduction partly originates from the increasingly destabilizing effects of global neoliberal governance and a growing concern with the potential threats to global order associated with pervasive poverty. The link between security and poverty and social inequality found expression in a number of UN publications (for example, UNDP 1997a) and concern expressed by Ethan Kapstein (1996), vice president of the Council on Foreign Relations and a senior fellow at the Center for a New American Security, regarding the possibility that the social inequalities produced by the neoliberal policies of the Washington Consensus generate conditions of social discontent and the forces of resistance that could well be mobilized against the governments that implemented these policies.

A report published by the UK Ministry of Defence added fuel to this concern by pointing out the profound political implications of the global divide in wealth and development that continues to breed "forces of resistance" and will likely lead to a "resurgence of not only anti-capitalist ideologies . . . but also to populism and the revival of Marxism" (2007, 3). As for the World Bank, it was James Wolfensohn, appointed president of the Bank in 1995, who was responsible for the shift in thinking. Wolfensohn's concern and thinking was evident in his speech to the Security Council of the UN in which he remarked, "If we want to prevent conflict, we need a comprehensive, equitable, and inclusive approach to development" (quoted in Thomas 2001, 160). In this context, poverty reduction, social inclusion, and social cohesion were all understood—and still are—as important preconditions for both governability and global political stability.

The introduction of the CDF and the PRSP approach to the poverty-development-security problematic in 1999 was met with two responses in academe and the development community. On the one hand, supporters of the international financial institutions (IFIs) argue that the PRSP signifies a fundamental rupture in development thinking and a progressive move away from policy conditionality toward country "ownership" and poverty reduction. On the other hand, critics of the development establishment maintain that the PRSP represents not a significant shift away from neoliberal policy practice but rather an attempt to deepen the hegemony of neoliberalism by revising it in the direction of greater social inclusion—to create a more inclusive form of capitalist development on the basis of the post-Washington Consensus (PWC).

From the Washington Consensus to the Post-Washington Consensus: A New Development Model for Latin America

> The poor are the main actors in the fight against poverty. And they must be brought centre stage in designing and monitoring anti-poverty strategies. (World Bank 2001, 12)

Subjected as they were to intense criticism in the 1990s (see chapter 2), the World Bank and the IMF led the effort to consolidate a new consensus around the need for a new development paradigm and economic model to guide development policy. In this consensus (see World Bank 2007a), the Bank and the IMF moved away from structural adjustment conditionality, or rather softened their approach in this regard in moving toward poverty reduction and country ownership of development policies. This reorientation was reflected in the first instance in the design and presentation, in 1990, of the CDF, described by the Bank as an attempt to operationalize a holistic approach to development, integrating the economic and the social and emphasizing the needs and participation of the poor in the development process (Wolfensohn 1999; Pender 2001, 407). As part of this policy shift, the Bank also opened up a theoretical "discussion" about development, which led to the emergence and consolidation of a new consensus that represented a theoretical convergence between (1) the Washington Consensus on neoliberal globalization, (2) a neo-Keynesian paradigm elaborated by Joseph Stiglitz among others, and (3) a new form of Latin American structuralism advanced by Osvaldo Sunkel, José Ocampo, and other theoreticians at ECLAC (Ocampo 2007; Sunkel and Infante 2010).

Articulation of the PWC was accompanied by the elaboration of a new policy tool, the PRSP, which emphasizes country ownership and civil society participation as two of the key principles in development cooperation. According to the World Bank and the IMF, policy changes resulted in the abandonment of structural adjustment lending and the policy conditionality associated with it, in favor of a development approach that emphasizes partnership and cooperation between the IFIs, developing country governments, and civil society organizations. In the process the Bank and the IMF positioned themselves as providers of information and knowledge, while borrowing governments were asked to assume the responsibility for, or ownership of, the development strategy they propose to pursue and the policies that they choose to implement (Stiglitz 1998, 21). As for the poor the objective is to empower them to act for themselves, converting them into the main "actor" on the development stage, supporting their decision as to which pathway to take and capacitating them to act in their own interest in taking advantage of their existing "opportunities." The role of the government is to facilitate the process of self-development by removing any existing impediments and by implementing a policy of social inclusion and economic assistance (social compensation) in the form of conditional cash transfers to the poor.

The PRSP is the most prominent policy tool of the PWC, and it is here that the shift to an inclusive neoliberal development model is most clearly visible. Endorsed in 1999, the PRSP was officially incorporated into all IFI development policies and programs and is the basis of all future IFI concessional lending, as well as debt relief under the HIPC (Heavily Indebted Poor Countries) initiative (Cling, Razafindrakoto, and Roubaud 2003, 1). The national PRSP is the tool through which the goals of a country ownership, civil society participation, and poverty reduction are to be achieved. Each PRSP sets out a comprehensive plan for the country's macroeconomic, structural, and social policies and programs for a period of three years. The policy content of the document is supposed to be formulated by the developing country itself and to reflect the country's individual circumstances and characteristics. Thus, the criticism of the structural adjustment program (SAP), that it was designed as a "one size fits all" approach, would be circumvented.

The principles that underpin the PRSP approach (see Klugman 2002, 3) suggest that development strategies should be

1. country driven and owned, and predicated on a broad participatory process in the formulation, implementation, and outcome-based progress monitoring;
2. results oriented, focusing on outcomes that would benefit the poor;
3. comprehensive in scope, recognizing the multidimensional nature of the causes of poverty and measures to attack it;
4. partnership oriented, providing a basis for the active and coordinated participation of development partners; and
5. based on a medium- and long-term perspective for poverty reduction, recognizing that sustained poverty reduction cannot be achieved overnight.

To successfully implement the PRSP and achieve results, every country is expected to follow five key steps: (1) assess the state and conditions of poverty and its determinants, (2) set targets for poverty reduction, (3) prioritize actions for poverty reduction, (4) establish systematic measures of poverty trends and evaluate the impact of the government's programs and policies, and (5) describe the main aspects of the participatory approach (Klugman 2002, 4).

In addition, the IFIs have identified four priority considerations, considered to be imperative for bringing about economic growth—implementing "pro-growth" policies—and ensuring that the poor benefit from this growth (that "pro-growth" is also "pro-poor"). These include sound macroeconomic and structural reform (that is, neoliberal) policies, such as trade liberalization and banking sector reform, appropriate sectoral policies and programs, good

governance, and realistic costing and appropriate funding for poverty alleviation programs (Klugman 2002, 16). This constitutes the framework for all
discussions and decisions surrounding the PRSP, although the Bank at the
same time insists that the PRSP Sourcebook does not prescribe policies but
rather aims to describe "empirical facts" and "best practices" and to provide
"technical knowledge" and analytical tools for developing countries. And,
notwithstanding the insistence that developing country governments should
"own" their development policies and that they and their partners in civil
society should fully participate in the design of the poverty reduction strategy and policies, the Sourcebook makes it unambiguously clear that the IFIs
ultimately have the final say in either embracing or disproving the national
poverty reduction strategy: "while the shift to country ownership will allow
more leeway in terms of policy design and choice, acceptance by the Bank
and the IMF boards will depend on the current international understanding
of what is effective in lowering poverty" (Klugman 2002, 4). In other words,
the governments are totally free in their decisions and choices as long as they
decide and choose wisely.

The PRSP in Latin America: Nicaragua, Bolivia, and Honduras

The PRSP in Nicaragua: From Structural Adjustment to Poverty Reduction

In 2000, on the eve of its first PRSP-based agreement with the World Bank
and the IMF, the rate of poverty was around 46 percent, according to the
World Bank's income measure, but closer to 72 percent according to calculations made by using the alternative UBN measure preferred by many scholars and development practitioners (Vargas 2001, 164; Castro-Monge 2001,
420). At any rate, it was evident that a decade of neoliberal policies based on
"structural reforms" in macroeconomic policy ("structural adjustment" lending), and a new social policy in the form of the FISE (*Fondo de Inversión Social
de Emergencia*), had resulted in no changes and had yielded no benefits to the
poor, hence, the resort to a new strategy: to abandon or replace a structural
adjustment strategy with a poverty reduction strategy.

After Nicaragua was accepted into the IFI's HIPC initiative for severely
indebted countries in late 1999, the Nicaraguan government began to work on
a PRSP, the first of several and one of the first anywhere. In December 2000,
Nicaragua was approved for $4.5 billion in debt relief under the HIPC initia-
tive on the condition that it would elaborate a national PRSP endorsed by

the IFIs. The responsibility for preparing the PRSP was assumed by SETEC, a government body staffed by many economic "experts" on the payroll of the IDB and other international "cooperants" (Dijkstra 2005, 449), and a direct line to the president of the country. Indeed the World Bank concluded that the PRSP was prepared "in a highly centralized manner" by a group that "enjoyed support at the highest level of government" and, the Bank admitted, with scant or no social participation (World Bank and IMF 2005, 63). In 2001 the government went briefly "off-track" because of "policy slippages in the monetary and fiscal area" but managed to sign an agreement with the IMF in late 2002. This agreement, signed without any tangible evidence of "social participation," a policy pillar and supposed condition of the PRSP, was followed with another agreement that led, in 2005, to Nicaragua's second-generation PRSP, termed the National Development Plan (NDP). The first full PRSP (SGPRS, the Strengthened Growth and Poverty Reduction Strategy) was finished in 2001; the NDP, containing or in the form of the government's second PRSP, was completed in 2005.

A review and analysis of these two PRSPs is most revealing, both of the thinking behind the proposed strategy and prescribed policies and of the pressures on the government to conform to the PWC on how best to fight poverty. First, poverty is attributed not to the structure of social inequality—after a decade of neoliberal policies, Nicaragua had become one of the most unequal societies in the world—but to a number of endogenous factors and "past disastrous economic policies and severe political turbulence" (Government of Nicaragua 2001, 12). As for the disastrous economic policies, they referred not to the policy agenda of the post-Sandinista regimes over the previous decade but to a series of erroneous macroeconomic policies implemented during the 1980s under the Sandinista government (p. 13). Specifically, the government blames the Sandinistas for policies that led to economic collapse and a totally unsustainable level of debt. These policies, the SGPRS asserts, contrast with the "prudent [pro-growth] macroeconomic policies" of the pre-Sandinista regime and the policies of the post-Sandinista governments, which were on the right track but that need to be adjusted and fine-tuned on the basis of a strategy, outlined in the PRSP, that is able to generate both growth and poverty reduction. The key point advanced in the SGPRS is the need for structural reforms, and a mix of macroeconomic and social policies, that will generate the growth of output and incomes. Indeed, it is argued, the failure of the Sandinistas in this regard was that "the social programs [that they] implemented . . . were not accompanied by the necessary structural changes to render them sustainable, based as they were on the redistribution of existing income and property rather than on the growth of output and income" (Government of Nicaragua 2001, 13).

As to the specific form of this strategy, that is, the mix of policies able to generate both growth and poverty reduction, it is outlined in more detail in the 2005 NDP. The thinking and the idea behind this outline is that the most efficient way to address or redress poverty is to combine "sound macroeconomic polices" (read neoliberalism) and a strengthening of human capital of the poor through targeted social investments in the areas of health and education.

This is, of course, the recipe prescribed by the architects of the PWC. But what the SGPRS (PRSP I) and the NDP (PRSP II) add is the notion that the fundamental agency of economic development (growth of output and income) is the private sector freed from the regulatory constraints of the welfare-development state and that the fundamental agency for achieving poverty reduction are the poor themselves, empowered to act in the search of opportunity and improvement. The role of the government, with international cooperation and social participation, is only to establish an appropriate institutional framework and policy agenda designed to facilitate this "development." This means under prevailing conditions a partnership strategy of poverty reduction based on a policy of social inclusion and conditional cash transfers.

The poverty reduction strategy outlined in the PRSP I and PRSP II consists of five pillars: (1) economic growth and structural reform, (2) investment in human capital, (3) better social protection for vulnerable groups, (4) good governance, and (5) institutional development. Reference is also made to the principle of social equity, understood and presented as it is by the economists at the World Bank, not as social justice but as the provision of equal opportunity in closing the welfare gap. However, since "virtually all SGPRS will encourage increased equity [and] better health, nutrition for the poor, as well as improved and stronger control over their reproductive health services, will go far to reduce the gaps in welfare," no specific policy provision is needed to achieve social equity (Government of Nicaragua 2001, 37).

As for the first and strategy-defining pillar, the economic reform strategy outlined in the PRSP I had been widely criticized for being too narrowly focused on macroeconomic policy and not putting enough emphasis on the development of the forces of domestic production. Consequently, for the period 2005–2009 the second-generation PRSP (NDP) placed more emphasis on actions that would enhance the investment climate and promote the productive base of the economy (Government of Nicaragua 2005, 2). However, while the PRSP I largely disregarded the domestic economy and local markets in advancing a strategy of export promotion, the NDP prioritized the attraction of direct foreign investment. This was "because of the positive impact on competiveness, the creation of new and better jobs, the transfer of technology and managerial know-how, and the generation of foreign exchange" (Government of Nicaragua 2005, 35). In addition, the NDP explicitly espoused "free trade" and a market-driven deregulated economy as the best and most efficient means of activating the forces of national production. In effect, the PRSP advanced the belief or argument of the economists at the World Bank that a neoliberal policy framework provides the optimal conditions for economic growth and that economic growth (increased output and income) is an essential precondition for a strategy of poverty reduction and an important means of implementing it.

The thinking and influence of the World Bank in the design of both PRSPs is evident throughout but particularly in the relative neglect of the forces of production in the agricultural sector and rural development. In the World Bank's understanding (see chapter 3), the capitalist development of the forces of production entails a process of structural transformation, which opens up several pathways out of poverty, namely, labor and migration. The purpose of development in this context, the fundamental concern of the development community, according to the World Bank, is to clear these pathways of any obstacles, facilitating thereby the decisions and actions of the poor in search of an improvement in their social condition, capacitating them to act for themselves. This is the reason why the Bank and PRSPs see the solution to poverty in an adaptation by the rural poor to the forces of change rather than in rural development, supporting the poor in their demand for land reform and their efforts to work the land and secure their rural livelihoods.

This policy orientation is reflected in the actual budgetary outlays in the PRSP and the portfolio of programs and projects approved by the World Bank and the IMF. For example, neither the SGPRS nor the NDP made any provisions for land reform or credit for rural smallholders in support of an option to stay on the land to work it productively on the basis of a smallholder model of agricultural development. Both PRSPs relatively neglect the productive capacities of the rural poor in favor of their transformation into capitalist entrepreneurs or facilitating their outmigration in the belief that rural smallholding peasant production is fundamentally unproductive, a poverty trap from which the poor need to be released.

In addition, despite the rhetoric favoring the rural small- and medium-enterprise sector in the total budget for the implementation of the SGPRS, for the first five years only 0.2 percent was allocated in support of the sector (Trócaire 2004a, 8). Instead of supporting local production for local markets, the

SGPRS, and even more so the NDP, allocated the lion's share of fiscal resources to six economic clusters, mostly if not exclusively in the modern capitalist sector, that promised to capture a share of the world market: tourism, coffee, beef and dairy products, shrimp farming, forestry, and light manufacturing (Government of Nicaragua 2005, 6).

As for its strategy of poverty reduction, the NDP points out, "The way to ensure . . . poverty reduction is through the development of private activity and the strengthening of productive and commercial interrelations" (Government of Nicaragua 2005, 6). In this regard the NDP allocates additional resources in infrastructure and human resource development—capacitating the rural poor to take advantage of the wage labor opportunities that await them in the economy as it expands and adjusts to the forces of capitalist development and globalization. The policy of social inclusion and economic assistance (social compensation or conditional cash transfers) in this context can be viewed as supplementary, a complement to the essential economic growth and human capital (education) pathways out of poverty.

The PRSP in Bolivia: The Policy Dynamics of Participation

By 1999, 63 percent of the population (approximately 5.1 million) were still below the poverty line, and 37 percent were living in extreme poverty. In rural areas, more than 80 percent of the population lived in poverty conditions, and approximately 60 percent lived in extreme poverty (Republic of Bolivia 2001). Despite the enthusiasm with which the SAPs had been implemented, the overwhelming consensus was that while GDP had increased, the SAPs had failed to live up to their promises. In 1997 Bolivia became involved in the HIPC initiative, and in order to qualify for debt relief, the government had to go through the PRSP process, which included a participatory national consultation.

The participatory national consultation for the Bolivian Poverty Reduction Strategy Paper (BPRSP) took the form of the National Dialogue 2000. Dialogue 2000 was originally structured on the basis of a social agenda, with the goal of creating a participatory process of defining the mechanisms for allocation and social control of debt-forgiveness resources under the HIPC initiative. But in the context of the national dialogue process, the design of the PRSP, which originally included only social issues, was expanded to include an economic and a political agenda (Eyben 2004). However, the basic structure and the discussion of how to reduce poverty were linked to the question of the scope of the PRSP. Many in power saw the PRSP as an instrument of debt relief and were not at all interested in a PRSP as the overarching framework for all public policies and expenditures. They believed it would be "more than good enough" if the PRSP process were to result in a popular consensus on the transparent and equitable use of the funds from HIPC debt relief. Thus the National Dialogue was designed around the basic but limited question of how to spend the debt relief (Eyben 2004).

Dialogue 2000 is in three parts. The "Social Agenda" involved the identification of priority actions that would reduce poverty through investment in the areas of road infrastructure, production support, education, health, basic sanitation, and land. The participants identified problems impeding poverty reduction and recommended mechanisms and criteria for the allocation of HIPC resources at the municipal level (Republic of Bolivia 2001). For the "Economic Agenda," participants considered a variety of problems and solutions in the productive area. These included productivity, competitiveness, and capacity of the productive apparatus to generate employment. As a result, four areas of action were acknowledged: technological innovation, state reform, promotion of private sector participation, and productive use of HIPC II resources (Republic of Bolivia 2001). The "Political Agenda" process brought together various sectors of civil society, the policy system, and representatives of the state at different levels in an effort to discuss issues surrounding democracy, transparency, participation, and citizenship. The results of the dialogue were important inputs in the process of preparing the BPRSP. A draft version was provided and discussed with civil society, and a roundtable seminar called "The Government Listens" was conducted. This second round of consultations made it possible to introduce changes suggested by various sectors of society.

The Bolivian poverty reduction strategy focused on the idea that a close relationship exists between economic growth and changes in the level of poverty. It suggested that economic policies were dependent on progress in social policy and that achievements in the social area would be determined largely by economic performance (Republic of Bolivia 2001). The main goal of the BPRSP was to reduce poverty and to promote human development, placing emphasis on the most vulnerable members of society through improving access to markets, building capacities through the provision of basic public services, and promoting citizen participation within a context of "growth with equity" (Republic of Bolivia 2001).

The main areas of strategic concern identified in the BPRSP are (1) enhanced employment and income opportunities, (2) the building of productive capacities of the poor, (3) enhanced security and protection, and (4) the promotion of social integration and grassroots participation (Republic of Bolivia 2001).

The BPRSP proposed several strategies and policies in each area. To expand employment and income opportunities, the BPRSP proposed to support the productive capacity of small agricultural producers through microfinancing and technical assistance and to promote rural development through investment in infrastructure, rural electrification, and the delivery of irrigation and microirrigation systems. Emphasis in this area was placed on primary education and health services, the quality of human resources to build on the capacities of the poor, increased coverage of basic sanitation, and improved housing conditions. In the third area of strategic concern—increased safety and protection for the poor—"security" included protection from violence, as well as economic risks and natural disasters. As for social integration and participation, the fourth main area of concern, it would be encouraged through training for civic organizations. The aim was to meet the demands and needs of the poor, particularly in rural communities and among indigenous peoples, and to provide them with increased opportunities to improve their incomes and quality of life and to improve "social control" (Republic of Bolivia 2001).

The BPRSP promised an improvement in GDP growth, an improvement to health and education systems, and better access to improved agriculture production and rural development. As for Dialogue 2000, by some accounts at least, it seems to have produced a level of participative national consensus that found its way into the PRSP. But what were the dynamics and how effective was that participation? What were the consequences in regard to the final outcome of mandating the participation of civil society? Was the PRSP more effective regarding poverty reduction than it would have been without such participation?

Molenaers and Renard (2003) argue that on first reflection the answer to this question is obviously positive. Listening to the poor makes politicians and planners more aware of the real needs and constraints of the poor. By allowing the poor to participate, they are empowered, hopefully resulting in more resources being directed toward them. However, they argue, the condition of "participation" imposed by the World Bank in its PRSP Sourcebook is too vague to be monitored and too ambitious to be workable. For one thing, the Sourcebook does not provide guidelines for distinguishing relevant from nonrelevant actors; the only condition is that special attention should be put on those who represent the poor or groups who are specialized in assessing poverty. However, as Molenaers and Renard found, vagueness produces large margins of freedom. The insistence on broad-based participation by "all" of the listed civil society actors, they conclude, is unrealistic and too demanding, giving governments too much latitude to select participants at their convenience. The government, as it turned out, chose the representatives for the poor—local government representatives and members of certain organizations who were judged appropriate by those in charge of the process. Of course, it would be incredibly difficult for everyone to participate in a meaningful way in the process, but that those who were able to participate were largely selected by the government and those in power speaks volumes about who actually owned the process.

As for "ownership" the concept is poorly defined and difficult to operationalize. Ownership is not just about influence and access. It is more than joint decision making and joint agenda setting. It is about social relations of production—property in the means of production—and these are social relations of power. Ownership of the PRSP then, at best, like property in the means of production, is necessarily or inevitably very unequally distributed (Molenaers and Renard 2003). In this connection, not only did those in charge of the process choose the representatives, but the topics for discussion during the National Dialogue 2000 were also set by the organizers, not by the participants. And of course the agenda was predetermined, structured by the economists at the World Bank and the IMF. Furthermore, the government with scant evident social participation set the focus and scope of the topics, and issues of structural change were not allowed to be part of the discussion.

It is thus not unreasonable to question whether the PRSP process is possibly effective in reducing poverty if the institutionalized practices or structures that produce and reproduce it, or the underlying relations of economic and political power, are not topics for discussion and action. The process ignores existing inequalities and structural divisions, and the idea that harmony, consensus, and, thus, ownership will eventually result from participation, and that synergies between civil society and government are created when they enter into a dialogue, is not very credible, especially in a complex, multiethnic society with deep inequalities and extreme socioeconomic gaps (Molenaers and Renard 2003). The concepts of ownership and participation, it might be argued, mask rather than reveal who has the real power over the PRSP agenda. The power, as with previous structural adjustment policies, rests with the donor community and with the ruling elite.

The PRSP in Honduras: The Policy Dynamics of Inclusive Development

Honduras entered the HIPC initiative in 1999 as the second-poorest country in the Western Hemisphere, with levels of poverty among the highest in the region. To qualify, the government was required to elaborate a PRSP in which it outlines its proposal to deploy relief resources so as to achieve a sustained reduction in the level of poverty from 63.9 percent in 2002 to 40 percent by 2015 (Cuesta 2007, 333). Under normal circumstances Honduras should have reached the completion point of the HIPC initiative in 2002. However, having gone "off-track" in its agreement with the IMF, the PRSP process was slowed down due primarily to a lack of resource flows. Honduras finally graduated to its "completion point" in 2005, five years after the boards of the World Bank and the IMF approved Honduras's PRSP (Ruckert 2010).

In her critical assessment of the Honduras PRSP experience, Ruckert (2010) clearly establishes a fundamental continuity between the conditionalities between the PRSP process and the earlier SAP process. These conditionalities conformed to and were indubitably determined by the IFIs' neoliberal policy agenda of "structural reform" rather than by any popular consultation or through the participation of other stakeholder organizations in civil society. The only elements of the PRSP that could be seen as a departure from the fundamental neoliberal policy recipe were the expansion of a social safety net and the introduction of conditional cash transfers. However, these were also defining features of the other PRSPs, both in Latin America (Bolivia, Nicaragua) and elsewhere. These policy "reforms" in fact were central to the poverty reduction strategy pursued by virtually all governments in the region in the new millennium in response to the challenge of achieving the Millennium Development Goals under the PWC on the need for a more inclusive form of development.

As for the specific strategy outlined for simultaneously achieving economic growth and the reduction of poverty, the twin goals of the new development paradigm, there is nothing particularly noteworthy about the proposed national development path laid out in terms of six strategies. As the government conceived of it in its PRSP, these six strategies were designed to "reduce poverty significantly and sustainably, based on accelerated sustained economic growth whose benefits are distributed more equitably through greater access by poor people to the factors of production, including the development of human capital and social safety nets" (Government of Honduras 2001, iv).

The strategy boiled down to the following elements: (1) productive investment in agriculture and in extractive and other industries to generate increased output and employment; (2) increased investment in economic and social infrastructure, particularly in the areas of education and health care (human resource development); (3) institutional development—strengthening the institutional framework of the market and public administration; (4) credit and technical assistance to the small producer, and specific measures to increase the productivity of small and medium-sized enterprises; (5) social development, facilitating the decisions of the rural poor to migrate in search of better opportunities (jobs, etc.) and expanding the opportunities available to the poor—leveling the playing field and capacitating the poor to take advantage of these opportunities in the interest of "equity"; and (6) inclusion of the poor in government programs of welfare and social security to assist them in the form of a social safety net and conditional cash transfers, to ensure thereby that their basic needs are met, and to increase participation in programs designed to enhance the value of human capital.

As noted there is nothing novel in these policy measures, implemented as part of a strategy designed to achieve economic growth and reduce poverty. The CDF for these policies conformed to the post-Washington policy consensus on the need for inclusive development based on (1) structural reform in macroeconomic policy, (2) a new poverty-targeted social policy and specific measures designed to enhance human capital, and (3) greater social inclusion and a new development paradigm focused on the empowerment of the poor and implemented with a policy of administrative decentralization and social participation.

The specific difference in the design of this policy agenda from the institutional and policy framework of "development," and the agenda that governed the construction of national policy in the 1990s in Honduras and elsewhere in the region, is in the form and quality of "social participation" in the design and implementation of the economic growth/poverty reduction strategy. "Participation" was already seen in the 1980s as a vital component of the development process. Economists at ECLAC (Boisier et al. 1992; ECLAC 1990) had conceptualized it as the "missing link" in a strategy designed to generate "productive transformation with equity" (ECLAC 1990). For others, the secret to inclusive development is social or popular participation, in a development process engineered not just "from above" (the state) and "from the outside" (international cooperation) but "from within" and "from below" (Sunkel 1993; Sunkel and Infante 2010). However, it is evident that notwithstanding the importance of "participation," throughout the 1990s an effective method for achieving participation—creating a participatory form of development—had not been achieved, hence the shift from a clearly nonparticipatory development process assisted, at the level of international cooperation, by a policy of "structural adjustment lending," to a more participatory process impelled by a PRSP approach.

Given its assigned role in the development process, and its centrality in the PRSP (an essential "condition"), it is important and highly relevant to describe the measures proposed, and taken, to ensure not just the inclusion of the poor in the development program designed for the PRSP but also their effective participation in all phases of the development process. In regard to Honduras, Ruckert (2010) concludes that the government undoubtedly made some effort to engage civil society in the PRSP process, even setting up several institutions and a body, the *Foro Democrático*, for the purpose of facilitating state-society interaction. However, she concludes that genuine social participation was not achieved and that there is no evidence of any inclusion of ideas that derive from this sector. As for what these ideas might be, the situation is not as clear in Honduras as it was in Nicaragua. In Nicaragua, civil society was highly polarized between a sector that was disposed to participate—enter into dialogue with the government on the PRSP and so forth—and a sector of organized resistance that ultimately led to the construction of an alternative PRSP, which crystallized and gave form to an alternative economic model for national development. In Nicaragua the situation was very different. Various elements of the SAP and neoliberalism more generally have generated forces of resistance in civil society, but these forces (unions, NGOs, political parties on the political left) have not been effectively organized in the service of an alternative way of understanding and approaching development. At the same time, the government totally ignored the constructive criticisms from the NGO sector and failed to engage the effective participation of civil society. The participation that the government did indeed document was very minimal and inconsequential in terms of impact on the final outcome, the PRSP accepted by the IFIs. Without a doubt the development plan outlined in the PRSP conformed very closely to the guidelines established by the PRSP framework established by the World Bank and was constructed by technicians and consultants connected to the World Bank and the IMF. In this context, Ruckert (2010) concludes, it is not possible to write or talk of participation in any meaningful way. Indeed, she argues, the entire PRSP process can be understood in Gramscian terms as an effort to consolidate "neoliberal hegemony"—to provide a cover of legitimacy to a new modality of neoliberalism, "inclusive development." The PRSP, she argues, is an effective tool fashioned to this purpose—to rescue neoliberalism, or neoliberal globalization, from the legitimacy crisis brought on by the SAP of the World Bank and the IMF.

A Critical Assessment of the PRSP

Unlike Bolivia where the social movements were more powerful, throughout the 1990s in both Nicaragua and Honduras the resistance and the opposition to neoliberalism was led by "civil society," an opposition that prevented the government from following through on its halting commitments to the IFIs regarding the PRSP. In the new millennium, civil society continued to lead the opposition, particularly in regard to the policy of privatization—to privatize what remained in an effort to convert Nicaragua and Honduras into another El Salvador, where the government was thoroughly "on side" with the neoliberal project and with US influence over government policy, what others have termed "US imperialism."

In Nicaragua the contestation of US influence and neoliberal policies derives from the Sandinista era, which provided a base from which organized labor and other organized groups in civil society and the popular sector could mobilize the resistance to neoliberalism (Stahler-Sholk 1997). However, the participation of civil society in the elaboration and implementation of the PRSP, according to Ruckert (2010), remained rather "shallow," possibly because of the residual opposition to neoliberalism and the expectation of the IFIs that the government include neoliberalism in its proposed antipoverty strategy. In any case, it is evident from Ruckert's critical assessment that country ownership "remained largely absent in Nicaragua," as it did in Honduras (2010, 145).

Ruckert's (2010) analysis also revealed a fundamental contradiction or ambiguity with regard to the participation of civil society in the project of international cooperation and the PRSP process. On the one hand, they were contracted by the "community" of "overseas development associations" to mediate between the IFIs (and other donors) and the communities and grassroots organizations of the poor to secure and facilitate their "participation." On the other hand, a number of NGOs, armed with a rather critical view of the neoliberal policy agenda, were clearly concerned that in their participation in the PRSP consultations they would provide legitimacy to the neoliberal policies involved in the PRSP, thus implicating them in the deepening of social inequality and the persistence of widespread poverty. In this concern, a number of NGOs started up a parallel PRSP process and elaborated a parallel document, *La Nicaragua Que Queremos* (Bradshaw and Linneker 2002). The result was that the IFIs failed to achieve the policy consensus that they sought in forcing the government to open up the PRSP process to stakeholder organizations in civil society.

This meant two things. One was that the participation of civil society in the PRSP process in Nicaragua and Honduras was and remains, in Ruckert's words, "shallow." Another was that the entire process was not nearly as participatory as projected by the architects of the PRSP and the inclusive development model. A third outcome was that the Nicaraguan government was rather reluctant to take responsibility for, and failed to accept, "ownership" of the halting and inconsistent efforts to reduce poverty by means of a supposedly more inclusive form of neoliberalism. Predictably the IFIs attributed the lack of success in achieving and an appreciable success in poverty reduction to a failure of the government to secure consensus and a resulting inconsistency in the application of the policy agenda outlined in its PRSP, an agenda that did not differ appreciably from the agenda of previous "structural adjustment" neoliberal regimes contained by the forces of resistance (on this see Ruckert 2010, 147ff).

At the same time, the IFIs were unwilling to derail and disown the PRSP process or to make significant concessions, even when it became evident that large segments of civil society felt and declared publicly that their voices were not included in the national PRSP.

The most striking features of the PRSP in each Latin American case was that it was essentially "negotiated" between the government and the officials of the IMF and World Bank with scant social participation, and how little the agreed-on development program and policy agenda departed in its essentials from the neoliberal agenda of previous regimes. As to the neoliberal character of this regime, we need only look at the policy agenda pursued by the regimes that succeeded the Sandinistas in Nicaragua.

The first salient fact regarding these regimes is the enormous influence and weight of the United States in establishing the fundamental ground rules in the construction of national policy. As documented by William Robinson (1997), US intervention played a fundamental role in the reorganization of the Nicaraguan state and civil society in the wake of the "Nicaraguan Revolution." The USAID program became the largest in the world, and the US Embassy became the most heavily staffed in Central America (Robinson 1997, 31). As Robinson notes, USAID's Strategy Statement in this connection was a "remarkable blueprint of a neoliberal republic," laying out as it did "a comprehensive program of restructuring every aspect of Nicaraguan society on the basis of the economic power of the US and the IFIs would be able to wield over the shattered country" (p. 31). In this period financial aid—and the government was heavily dependent on it—was conditional on satisfactory implementation of the policies set out in the "grand strategy" that the US government elaborated for the country and the numerous agreements signed with the IFIs over the next decade.

However, while the state apparatus was surrendered to the forces of economic freedom and development, the subsequent turn toward neoliberalism, and the capitalist development of the economy according to the rules of the new world order, was highly contested—the second salient fact regarding the policy and political regimes that succeeded the aborted Nicaraguan Revolution.

The correlation of forces between an economic (and political) elite oriented toward and tied to the institutions of global capital and the diverse forces of resistance in the popular movement favored the former. For one thing, the massive debt contracted by the government and the private sector was a powerful lever used by the elite and the government to argue that it had no choice but to toe the IMF and World Bank line on "structural reform." By 1992 Nicaragua's debt stood at $11 billion, one of the highest in the world on a per capita basis. Even so, notwithstanding the powerful lever of this debt, the establishment of local and foreign capital, backed up by the IMF and the World Bank, was unable to consolidate its hegemony over the construction of national policy. Every move toward neoliberalism, every agreement with the IFIs and the international development community, was contested by forces of resistance organized within both the popular sector and a civil society that had been strengthened by the short-lived Nicaraguan Revolution.

Thus it was that the World Bank, under the presidency of James Wolfensohn, finally succumbed to an emerging new consensus on the need for a more inclusive and participatory form of development. As noted at the outset, the result was a new poverty reduction strategy, and a new social policy, constructed within the CDF built to the purpose. The evident aim was to accommodate the forces of resistance and civil society to the new policy agenda, a gentler and less draconian form of structural adjustment. The deal? A reduction of one-half in the rate of extreme poverty and the alleviation of the most severe social conditions of poverty in exchange for, and as a condition of, the engagement of civil society and popular participation in the development process.

A series of evaluative reports and reviews (inter alia Hermele 2005; World Bank and IMF 2005a) tells the story of close to a decade of development geared toward the new poverty reduction strategy implemented within the framework of a new development paradigm and the PRSP as a policy tool. The results can be briefly summarized as a marginal reduction in the rate of extreme poverty.

Conclusion

A critical examination of the PRSP in Bolivia, Honduras, and Nicaragua shows that the IFIs have become increasingly involved in governance in the social sphere, through linking conditionalities to achieve social and poverty reduction outcomes. The result is rather contradictory: the combination of neoliberal "pro-growth" policies of commodification and neoliberal globalization that by diverse accounts exacerbate conditions of social inequality and poverty with policies of social inclusion and assistance designed to alleviate the conditions created by these very policies.

The basic poverty reduction strategy designed and permitted by the PRSP process is economic growth and the adjustment by or adaption of the poor to the requirements of the new world order: neoliberal macroeconomic "reform" and "good governance," the engagement of civil society in the responsibility for social development and the maintenance of "order." As the World Bank argues, in the context of Honduras's PRSP, "economic growth becomes the principal vehicle for raising income per capita, and the latter will have a significant impact in terms of poverty reduction" (Government of Honduras 2000, 36). As for the policies needed to bring about this growth, the World Bank has never wavered: structural adjustment to the requirements of the new world order in which the forces of economic and political freedom are released from the regulatory constraints of the welfare-development state. As for social development the World Bank is just as clear, although indirect and entirely implicit. A policy of asset and income redistribution, requiring fundamental structural change—change in what ECLAC (2010b) conceptualizes as the "structure of inequality"—and a confrontational politics (a confrontation of the relations of economic and political power that sustain this structure), is not required or appropriate (it generates relations of conflict and undermines the major productive force in society). Rather, what is required is social development: investment in human capital or social infrastructure, leveling the playing field for the poor, expanding the choices available to them, and capacitating them to take better advantage of their opportunities. To assist the poor in this process, the governments, with international cooperation and social participation, should undertake to provide an appropriate institutional and policy framework and design and then pursue a poverty reduction strategy aimed at releasing the needed forces of change and development.

Another conclusion is that civil society organizations play a relatively minor role in the implementation, if not the design, of the PRSP. This is in part at least because of the underlying agenda of the IFIs in insisting on the participation of civil society. The aim, it could be concluded, and the unstated or hidden agenda, is not to involve the poor in decisions and policies that affect them in a positive or negative way and to truly empower them (that is, to change the structure of inequality that produces and reprocess the conditions of their poverty). The aim, rather, is to disempower the poor—to prevent them from joining or forming social movements with more confrontational politics, and to weaken these movements, and to disarm the poor, taking from them their one weapon, the power to mobilize the forces of resistance against government policies and dynamics that undermine their livelihoods and keep them in poverty.

It can be concluded that the PRSP is a technocratic, depoliticized mode of development and governance. As noted by Craig and Porter (2006), one an academic and the other an official at the Asian Development Bank, PRSPs tend to ignore power issues and the political economy of poverty and inequality. They are the result of a broad consensus at the international and national levels that combines economic integration, good governance, and investment in human capital, a "third-way" remorphing of neoliberal approaches. Craig and Porter (2006, 1–10) argue that PRSPs are best seen as "inclusive liberal approaches held together and legitimated by . . . apparently apolitical catchwords like participation, partnership, and community." In effect they consider the emerging convergence in policies for poverty reduction as "an attempt to generate a level of global to local integration, discipline and technical management of marginal economies, governance and populations unprecedented since colonial times."

8

Conditional Cash Transfers as Social Policy
Contributions, Limitations, and Illusions

Enrique Valencia Lomelí

In recent years, conditional cash transfer (CCT) programs have emerged as an indispensable component of poverty reduction strategies under the post-Washington Consensus on the need for a more inclusive form of national development. CCTs refer to cash money given to poor parents under the condition that they send their children to school and health visits. As a policy tool for combating poverty, the aim is twofold: ensure quick cash injection into communities to enable vulnerable people to purchase food and ensure that their basic needs are being met (thus reducing poverty in the short term) and, at the same time, generate the social conditions of human development, strengthening the human development of family members to break the intergenerational reproduction of poverty.

As an advance on the Social Investment Funds in the 1990s under the "new social policy," the CCT programs have been hailed as being among the most significant innovations in promoting social development. Nancy Birdsall, president of the Center for Global Development, in this connection was quoted in the *New York Times* of January 3, 2004, as saying, "I think these programs are as close as you can come to a magic bullet in development." They are, she suggested, creating an incentive for families to invest in their own children's futures, an incentive for individual household heads to adjust their behavior toward the social optimum. Subsidies are provided in exchange for specific actions. As such, they act like a price effect on these actions, expected to induce individuals to increase their supply of these actions by raising their price via a CCT. In effect, the underlying assumption is that poverty is not the product of the economic and social system in place—the "structure of inequality" as ECLAC conceives of it—but rather the result of poor decisions made by the heads of poor households, and that the solution therefore is to adjust the behavior of the poor instead of change the system.

CCT programs began to be applied in different parts of Latin America and the Caribbean halfway through the 1990s, and in little more than a decade they spread widely throughout the region and in other parts of the world. Under a CCT program, money is transferred from the state to needy households to help support them—provided they conform to certain conditions regarding schooling, health care, and nutrition deemed to be in the broader public interest. As indicated in table 8.1, at least sixteen countries in the region now have a CCT program in operation. On average, these programs have been operating for four years, though eight of them started in only the past one to two years. Just two have been functioning for a decade or more, and six have been active for periods ranging from three to six years. Over the past decade, CCT programs have expanded significantly, and at one time or another over the past decade, some 113 million people, conservatively estimated, have received CCT support, representing around 19 percent of the population in Latin America and the Caribbean (Cecchini and Madariaga 2011, 7).

The remarkably fast spreading of CCT programs in Latin America and other regions of the world has been labeled the "CCT wave" by a World Bank report (Fiszbein and Schady 2009, 3). Notwithstanding the heterogeneity among political regimes that promote these programs and welfare states that develop them, as well as with regard to the programs themselves (benefits, coverage, and their place in social policy, among other aspects; Cecchini and Madariaga, 2011), all of them share at least one common denominator: cash transfers as an instrument to stimulate household investments in human capital, especially for children and youth.

To be sure, this "CCT wave" was not a spontaneous development but rather pushed forward by local, national, and international actors involved in the design, implementation, evaluation, and promotion of targeted antipoverty programs. Along these lines, a vigorous "epistemic community" (Haas 1992) has emerged,[1] with a common vision regarding poverty and the policies needed to deal with it (Martínez Franzoni and Voorend 2011). This epistemic community promotes the sharing of experiences and evaluations, and it has generated a common vocabulary or code within the context of a policy paradigm based on the need to use public resources "efficiently" via targeting, strategic investment in human capital, and strict evaluation of results.

Table 8.1

Conditional Cash Transfer Programs in Latin America by Year of Initiation, Budget, and Coverage

Country	Program Name/Abbreviation	Year Begun	Budget/GDP	Coverage (1,000s)
Argentina	Plan Jefas y Jefes (PJJ)	2002	0.80% (2003)	1,991 persons
Brazil	Bolsa Escola (BE)	2001	0.41% (2006)	5,600 families
	Bolsa Familia (BF)	2003		11,200 families
Chile	Chile Solidario (CHS)	2002	0.10% (2005)	157 families
Colombia	Familias en Acción (FA)	2001	0.09% (2005)	515 persons
Costa Rica	Progr de Transf Monetarias Condicionadas (PTMC)	2006	0.02% (2002)	12 families
Dominican Republic	Plan de Solidaridad (PS)	2005	0.34% (2006)	230 families
Ecuador	Bono de Desarrollo Humano (BDH)	2004	0.60% (2005)	1,060 families
El Salvador	Red Solidaria (RS)	2005	0.27% (2006)	35 families
Honduras	Programa de Asignación Familiar (PRAF)	1998	0.20% (2001)	629 persons
Jamaica	Program of Advancement Health/Education (PATH)	2001	0.19% (2006)	175 persons
Mexico	Progresa-Oportunidades (PROP)	1997	0.39% (2005)	5,000 families
				24,060 persons
Nicaragua	Red de protección Social (RPS)	2000	0.22% (2005)	24 families
Panama	Red de Oportunidades (RO)	2006		34 families
Paraguay	Red de Promoción y Protección Social (RPPS)	2005		9 families
Peru	Peru Juntos (PJ)	2005	0.11% (2006)	71 families
Uruguay	Plan de Atención N. la Emerg Social (PANES)	2005	0.60% (2006)	83 persons

Source. Arim and Vigorito (2006); Braun and Chudnovsky (2005); Cohen and Franco (2006b); Cohen and Villatoro (2006); CEPAL (2007); Britto (2007); Draibe (2006); Francke and Mendoza (2006); Golbert (2006b); Ivo (2006); Largaespada-Fredersdorff (2006); Levy (2006b); Lindert, Skoufias, and Shapiro (2006); Núñez and Cuesta (2006); Ponce (2006); Presidencia República Dominicana (2006); and the following websites: www .mides.gob.pa, www.redsolidaria.gob.sv, www.worldbank.org, and www.npep.jm.

Related to this, a CCT network or coalition of "transnational policy actors" (Béland and Orenstein 2009) has also emerged and gathered strength.[2] This network is made up of policymakers from different countries (including the original architects of pioneering and national-level programs), scholars, national and international evaluators, and international development organizations. This powerful coalition financially supports CCT programs, politically promotes them, and symbolically legitimates them in Latin America and elsewhere as an instrument to combat poverty in the context of budget restraints. Sharing the discourse of the aforementioned epistemic community (investment in human capital), it maintains "dense exchanges of information and services" (Keck and Sikkink 1999) in order to design, implement, and evaluate CCT programs. Moreover, the circulation of a common code that is congruent with the Washington Consensus facilitates the participation of officials and technical personnel from international financial institutions like the World Bank (WB) and the Inter-American Development Bank (IDB).

This transnational coalition has given impetus to the diffusion of CCT programs in several ways (Béland and Orenstein 2009, 12–19): the creation of an agenda regarding "the need to reform" social policies in order to combat poverty through targeting; dissemination of ideas through conferences, seminars, and other forums to facilitate "the sharing of experiences"; the portrayal of initial experiences as "models," particularly Mexico's *Progresa-Oportunidades*, Brazil's *Bolsa Familia*, and Chile's *Chile Solidario*; and by financing the programs themselves and the related evaluation process through loans made available by the IDB and World Bank.

Local and national actors of this transnational coalition have also contributed to the design of CCT programs. This was the case in Brazil, where several programs were created on the local (municipal) level in the 1990s (Aguiar 2006; Borges Sugiyama 2011); in Mexico, where the first national-level program was created, with a tripartite focus on education, health, and food (Levy and Rodríguez 2005; Rubalcava 2008); and in Chile, whose antipoverty program linked transfers to the broader supply of public services, not only in education, health, and food (Martínez Franzoni and Voorend 2011). Thus, the spread of CCT programs has not been due simply to the translation and incorporation of foreign ideas into national public policies but rather gained impetus from strategic contributions at the local and national levels.

National actors, themselves members of the epistemic communities and transnational coalitions focused on CCT policies, have generated their own "advocacy coalitions" (Sabatier and Weible 2007).[3] In this way, they have been influential, especially where these programs were first implemented, in drawing attention to extreme poverty, in "framing" the problem in terms of human capital (Joly and Marris 2001), and in pointing toward the need to stimulate investment in education, health, and food among the poorest households (Aguiar 2006; Borges Sugiyama 2011; Martínez Franzoni and Voorend 2011; Rubalcava 2008; Teichman 2007). These national-level actors have also played an important role in the implementation of CCT programs by adjusting original designs to fit with specific welfare regimes (Martínez Franzoni and Voorend 2011) and by securing international financing.

In general, these national-level advocacy coalitions comprise a select group of high-ranking public officials, specialists, and technocrats who have very little direct contact with the social demands of organized civil society (Martínez Franzoni and Voorend 2011). While the top-down policymaking schemes that they promote have become dominant in the region, there are also cases in which municipal authorities with diverse political origins have taken the initiative, giving rise to bottom-up schemes like *Bolsa Familia* in Brazil (Borges Sugiyama 2011), as well as cases like Argentina where social demands were taken into consideration in the context of an acute crisis (Golbert 2006b).

One feature of CCT programs that has undoubtedly contributed to their popularity is their low cost in terms of gross domestic product (GDP) and in comparison with social expenditure in general. In Latin America, where CCT programs are particularly popular, they represent an investment of scarcely 0.32 percent of the GDP (Valencia Lomelí 2008), this in countries where the average social expenditure is 12.5 percent of the GDP. Although the budgets of the CCT programs amount to only around 2.5 percent of social expenditure in these countries, they now serve a large number of Latin American households.

According to Morley and Coady (2003), CCT contributions in the region represent around 5 percent of total government expenditures on education, 15 percent of them focused on primary education. Moreover, the support and direct participation by international financial institutions has been rising (Aguiar 2006; Golbert 2006a; Gómez-Hermosillo Marín 2006). Indeed, support from the Inter-American Development Bank alone accounted for $4.5 billion during 2000–2005, a period in which the largest number of CCT programs were being created in Latin America (IDB 2006).

In spite of this rapid expansion, there is much controversy surrounding CCT programs. This chapter reviews the principal theoretical arguments that have been advanced to justify CCT programs in Latin America, as well as the empirical evidence regarding how well they have worked to improve outcomes in the areas of education, health, and nutrition and the degree to which they have functioned to reduce poverty. The main argument, summarized in the conclusion, is that the transnational coalition that promotes CCT programs has generated a number of illusions regarding their effectiveness; that a more balanced, nuanced, and objective analysis suggests that they are far from constituting a "magic bullet"; and that sustained progress toward the elimination of poverty requires reinvigorating the public institutions that offer basic universal welfare services.

Transfers for Relief Versus Development

The theory behind CCT programs in Latin America is quite new. If we consider the earliest designs, the earliest actions of pioneer governments, the earliest evaluations, the first publications, and the first wave of new programs promoted by international financial institutions, the bulk of CCT history occurs in the second half of the 1990s. This short period covers the operational design of the first programs in Brazil and Mexico and their subsequent implementation, evaluation, and synthesis into a theoretically coherent framework for application elsewhere. Of particular importance were evaluations done by officials in international financial organizations and prominent academics, who together had political and technical goals in promoting their wider adoption internationally (Rawlings 2005). These early studies also had the practical consequence of setting the stage for further evaluations, which were generally required by the international organizations providing funds (Morley and Coady 2003), that is, the transnational coalition in action.

The first CCT program to be evaluated was Mexico's *Progresa*, which began in 1997 under President Ernesto Zedillo and was continued by his successor, Vicente Fox, and the next president, Felipe Calderón (although in 2001 it was renamed *Oportunidades*, hence the acronym PROP used in table 8.1 and the remainder of this article).[4] A research protocol was included as part of the project's original design, and early in 1998 those running the program asked the International Food Policy Research Institute (IFPRI) to coordinate a first round of evaluations. The IFPRI assembled a team of some twenty researchers who presented their conclusions in 2000 (Skoufias 2000). In their detailed analysis of the effect of PROP's educational transfers, Morley and Coady (2003) concluded that rising interest in CCT programs after 2000 stemmed from the positive conclusions reached in these early evaluations, in regard to the relative efficiency and effectiveness of CCTs in reducing poverty in the short term and in promoting gender equality and improving educational outcomes. These outcomes were deemed to be particularly important in regard to redressing human capital deficits of poor individuals and households.

A number of studies have underscored the connection between early research and later adoptions of the CCT as a strategy of poverty reduction—poverty understood in basic needs rather than income terms (Britto 2004). Over the years, there seems to have been a process of cross-fertilization and mutual influence between policymakers in different countries. For example, the RPS program in Nicaragua was influenced by the *Bolsa Familia* (BF) program in Brazil and the FA program in Colombia, as well as PROP in Mexico and PRAF in Honduras. Then Nicaragua itself, according to Largaespada-Fredersdorff (2006), went on to influence later programs such as RS in El Salvador, RPPS in Paraguay, and PS in the Dominican Republic. The general impact of BF in Brazil and PROP in Mexico, and more recently CHS in Chile, can be seen in the new round of CCT programs inaugurated in Latin America after 2000 representing thirteen of the countries listed in table 8.1.

The enthusiasm and speed with which CCT programs were received in parts of the academy is astonishing, and their enthusiastic embrace by international financial institutions is even more surprising. For Rawlings and Rubio (2003, 26), whose bibliography focuses on evaluations made by the IFPRI in Honduras, Nicaragua, and Mexico, the rapid expansion of CCT programs reflects "solid evidence of their positive impact on the accumulation of human capital." In her analysis of the first generation of evaluations (in Brazil, Mexico, Nicaragua, and Colombia), Rawlings (2005) found that CCT programs were "administratively efficient" and offered an "effective means" of promoting the accumulation of human capital by poor households. In a more recent study for the Inter-American Development Bank, Bouillon and Tejerina (2006) concluded that in evaluations done between 1997 and 2003 (in Costa Rica, Ecuador, and Honduras, as well as in Brazil, Mexico, Nicaragua, and Colombia), cash transfer programs were found to be "very effective tools" for reducing poverty and inequality "in the long term" and the relief of poverty "in the short term."

In its annual report for 2005, the IDB (2006) concluded that CCT programs "have been particularly successful" in reducing levels of poverty in the region, as well as in promoting human capital accumulation and access to social services. And in a recent study of public transfers for the World Bank, Lindert, Skoufias, and Shapiro (2006, 46) found that CCT programs were promising not just because of their redistributive effects on income but also because of "their demonstrated impacts on human capital" and "their ability to break the intergenerational transmission of poverty." They went on to underscore the "emerging popularity" of the CCT programs in Latin America, labeling them "islands of success" in the region's large sea of social protection.

Another study by the World Bank concluded, "Evidence from several countries demonstrates that these programs are directed to the right population, reduce the poverty of the poorest households, and improve the education and the health of the children" (World Bank 2007b, 1).

In a very short time, therefore, evaluators, consultants, and academics close to international financial institutions have achieved a remarkable consensus about the principal strengths of CCT programs: they reach the poorest inhabitants directly, they promote the accumulation of human capital, they reduce poverty in the short term and long term, they lower income inequality, they break the intergenerational transmission of poverty, and, finally, they are cost-effective. These are strong conclusions to reach so soon after the start of a major social experiment. In considering the theoretical conventions that have built up around CCT programs in Latin America, we may distinguish ten salient features, which though not necessarily shared by all promoters of CCT programs are nonetheless present in most theoretical and technical discussions about them.

First, although CCT programs entail public interventions on the demand side, they are generally more respectful of market principles than the usual supply-side interventions (Levy 1991; Levy and Rodríguez 2005; Braun and Chudnovsky 2005; Rawlings 2005; Bouillon and Tejerina 2006; Cohen and Franco 2006a; World Bank 2007b). In a very real sense, CCT programs represent a continuation of broader economic reforms in Latin America during the 1980s and 1990s, which have sought to develop instruments of social policy that would be "compatible with the logic of the market" and to undertake interventions that would avoid "distortions in relative prices" (Levy and Rodríguez 2005).

Second, a key premise of CCT programs is that "a fundamental reason for the reproduction of poverty over various generations is the lack of investment in human capital in the areas of education, health and nutrition" (Villatoro 2004, 10). In other words, deficiencies in health, education, and nutrition interact to yield a vicious cycle of poverty within which individuals and families become enmeshed (Levy 1991). In essence, children from poor households are assumed to experience additional disadvantages above and beyond their immediate material deprivation because the low quality and limited amount of schooling leads to low worker productivity and depressed incomes in the future (Morley and Coady 2003).

Third, CCT programs combine the traditional role of social assistance in public programs with the newer role of social investment (Morley and Coady 2003; Lindert, Skoufias, and Shapiro 2006). Over the short term they raise the income of poor households through transfers of cash, goods, and services, and in the long term they encourage investments in human capital formation by offering economic incentives and conditional rewards for continued schooling among children. In doing so, they combine the three classic components of human capital—education, health, and nutrition—into a single package, although some programs emphasize education whereas others focus on the interaction between all three components (Rawlings and Rubio 2003) and assume strong complementarities between them (Levy 1991).

Fourth, CCT theorists argue that households and families are central to the reproduction of poverty from one generation to the next and that strategic interventions can break the vicious circle of deprivation (Cohen and Franco 2006b). They focus on mothers as key actors determining the nutrition, health, and education of children (Morley and Coady 2003). It was not immediately obvious in early discussions of conditional transfers, however, that this focus would emerge. At least in Mexico, it was taken up only after considerable debate and tied to concrete proposals put forward by government demographers such as José Gómez de León (López and Salles 2006; Rubalcava 2008).

Fifth, CCT programs concentrate their interventions at carefully chosen points in the life cycle, focusing particularly on nutrition and health during pregnancy and the first years of life and on the continuation of education during transitions from primary to secondary school and, at least in Mexico, from secondary to preparatory school (Levy and Rodríguez 2005; Cohen and Franco 2006a). To encourage education, programs generally offer extra cash transfers or educational grants when children continue in school. To promote better nutrition and health, they also transfer cash to promote the education of mothers and enable the purchase of certain nutritious food items. In some countries, programs offer participating households a standard package of medical care and nutrition, which includes food supplements for small, undernourished children, pregnant women, and nursing mothers (Rawlings and Rubio 2003).

Sixth, programs seek to change the behavior of poor households by conditioning the receipt of transfers, goods, and services on specific behavioral outcomes, such as continued school enrollment, regular rates of school attendance (generally at least 80 percent), participation in courses on health and nutrition, and the receipt of periodic health checkups. The conditional nature of the transfers is hypothesized to be "likely to lead households to make more efficient educational decisions" (Morley and Coady 2003, 6) by transforming them into rational cost-benefit calculations (Braun and Chudnovsky 2005). Conditioning enables the programs to "address market failures" and to "internalize the positive externalities accrued through increased investments in health and education among the young" (Rawlings 2005, 6).

Seventh, CCT programs seek to promote education not only by covering the direct costs of schooling but also by offsetting the opportunity costs generated by having children go to school instead of work (Rawlings 2005), while at the same time seeking "to avoid eroding the incentive for self-help or enhancing the incentives for higher fertility" (Morley and Coady 2003, 30). CCT theorists assume that the benefits of education "are permanent" because they give children the tools they need "to earn their way out of poverty" later in life. They argue that more education means greater future productivity and higher adult incomes. Children with better health and nutrition perform better at school and achieve higher future earnings from their labor (Cohen and Franco 2006a).

Eighth, because social programs are always subject to budget constraints, CCT programs generally channel their benefits to the neediest cases in order to "achieve the greatest effect with the budget on a determined relief of poverty, or to use alternative terms, to produce a determined effect at the lowest budget cost" (Coady, Grosh, and Hoddinott 2004, 1). They use a combination of approaches to identify needy households (Coady, Grosh, and Hoddinott 2004), including a proxy means test to collect information about household characteristics (Chile was first to use this approach), geographic clustering of poverty, and in some cases community-based targeting and self-selection (Morley and Coady 2003; Rawlings and Rubio 2003; Britto 2004; Braun and Chudnovsky 2005; Rawlings 2005; Villatoro 2005b; Bouillon and Tejerina 2006; Lindert, Skoufias, and Shapiro 2006; Cohen and Franco 2006a). The most commonly used mechanism is the proxy means testing of living standards, often codified as a point system (World Bank 2007b).

Ninth, by transferring resources directly to specific households, national governments attempt to establish direct relationships with individuals rather than rely on bureaucratic intermediaries (Rawlings 2005), a relationship that is in theory structured to be "apolitical" (Britto 2006) and "nonparty" (Levy and Rodríguez, 2005). In most cases, transfers are paid directly to female householders to avoid "intermediate local leaders or corporative groups that might require commitments other than those established in the program or wish to seize them for other purposes" (Levy and Rodríguez 2005, 177).

Finally, CCT programs usually have an evaluation design built into their operation from the very start, in some cases embracing experimental or quasi-experimental features (Rawlings and Rubio 2003; Bouillon and Tejerina 2006; Cohen and Franco 2006a). According to one study by the World Bank, Mexico was a pioneer in this regard, and the evaluation of the *Progresa-*

Oportunidades program went well beyond the simple construction of summary indices and concentrated instead on real "measures of impact" (World Bank 2004c). According to Behrman and Skoufias (2006), the evaluation of PROP in Mexico underscored the gains of making a serious evaluation over a reliance on "myths," a priori beliefs, and "vested interests," biases that all too often predominate in determining the effectiveness of social programs.

Assessment of Performance and Achievements

It appears, based on the large research literature that has now developed, that important sectors of academia and key representatives of international financial organizations are convinced of the social relevance, administrative efficiency, theoretical relevance, and financial viability of CCT programs. Nonetheless, it is important to evaluate their performance a decade after their initiation, particularly since the orthodoxy built up around CCT programs may be riding on a number of illusions. In this case, the positive effects of these social development programs may turn out to be ephemeral or, in the best of cases, flimsy, their positive achievements diluted. More generally, does a balanced assessment of the pros and cons of the CCT accord with the enthusiasm of CCT coalitions and networks and support their theoretical justifications?

Performance in Education

Studies evaluating the effect of CCT programs on educational outcomes generally conclude that CCTs seem to be relatively successful in achieving their explicit goal of increasing rates of school enrollment and attendance and that these outcomes translate into higher average levels of schooling among children in families receiving aid (Behrman, Sengupta, and Todd 2000; Bouillon and Tejerina 2006; Braun and Chudnovsky 2005; Britto 2004; Cohen and Franco 2006a; Cruz, de la Torre, and Velázquez 2006; De Janvry and Sadoulet 2006; Draibe 2006; Duryea and Morrison 2004; Levy and Rodríguez 2005; Morley and Coady 2003; Núñez and Cuesta 2006; Ponce 2006; Rawlings 2005; Rawlings and Rubio 2003; Reimers, De Shano da Silva, and Trevino 2006). Moreover, in at least some cases, CCT programs have contributed to reducing gender differentials in educational attainment. They also show some positive effects in reducing dropout rates, although this is not an explicit objective in many programs. Some authors, such as De Janvry and Sadoulet (2006), go so far as to conclude that conditions imposed with the transfers have yielded effects that would not have been achieved by the transfers alone, especially in Mexico but also in Brazil.

However, the positive results in regard to school enrollment and participation are not as promising with respect to the impact on actual learning. According to Villatoro (2005a), learning is one of the "least clear aspects" of CCT programs, and most studies are unable to document positive results (Behrman, Sengupta, and Todd 2000; Draibe 2006; Levy and Rodríguez 2005; Ponce 2006; Reimers, De Shano da Silva, and Trevino 2006).

As Morley and Coady (2003) point out repeatedly, it is not enough simply to raise enrollment and attendance rates; the quality of education must also be improved because without good classroom instruction, CCT programs cannot be considered to be efficient. However, to be fair, improving the quality of education is not an explicit objective of most CCT programs, which focus on enrollment and attendance rates (Morley and Coady 2003). As a result, issues such as learning and the quality of education are often ignored in evaluations.

To date, the quality of education has generally been taken for granted and has not been incorporated into the design of CCT programs, which, according to some, constitutes a serious deficiency. Reimers, De Shano da Silva, and Trevino (2006), for example, severely criticize this omission and conclude that at the end of the day, the implicit theory of these programs is that the accumulation of human capital is the same as the accumulation of years of schooling. They question this assumption and point out that educational quality for the poor is often substandard and that years of schooling do not yield the same benefits for poor children as for privileged children. They criticize CCT enthusiasts for treating instruction as a black box. In sum, an essential aspect for evaluating the effectiveness of CCT programs is left in doubt: whether or not they really succeed in improving the scholarly abilities of the poor students who participate.

Health, Consumption, and Nutrition

Studies evaluating the influence of CCT programs on a variety of health outcomes generally suggest a positive influence on the receipt of preventive infant care (checkups during pregnancy, after birth, and in early childhood), vaccinations, visits to health care centers, and illness rates (Villatoro 2005a). In some cases, they also find a reduction in maternal and infant mortality and improved knowledge of health among participants. In addition, studies of CCT programs in Latin America also point toward improvements in nutrition and consumption (Levy and Rodríguez 2005; Bouillon and Tejerina 2006; Britto 2006; Cohen and Franco 2006b), although nutrition results are somewhat mixed. Most studies show improvements in the variety of food consumed, greater height and weight among participating children, and reduced malnutrition in CCT families, but many analyses found no improvement with respect to anemia. Moreover, evaluations in Honduras found no positive influence on any nutritional outcome; neither the amount of food consumed, the variety of comestibles, the pace of physical development, nor exposure to anemia showed a positive influence. In fairness, however, these negative results probably reflect the small size of the transfers (Cohen and Franco 2006a).

One case that stands out is Nicaragua's RPS, during which a drop in the price of coffee and a serious drought brought about a severe reduction in consumption among households in the control group but not those in the treatment group (Rawlings and Rubio 2003). Despite this salient example, results are as mixed for Nicaragua as they are for Mexico. Indeed, in regard to Mexico, Neufeld, Sotres Álvarez, Gertler, et al. (2005, 41) conclude that for the period 1998–2003, "it was not possible to detect an impact from *Oportunidades* on the prevalence of anemia or on weight to height ratios" among rural children aged two to six years. They found that anemia continues to be a serious problem, with 20 percent to 30 percent of children showing iron deficiency and low stature. The evaluators also pointed out serious problems in the distribution of food supplements, in that "the type of iron [used] is not properly absorbed" (Neufeld, Sotres Álvarez, Gertler, et al. 2005, 42), indicating problems in their formulas.

Neufeld, Sotres Álvarez, García Feregrino, et al. (2005) also documented serious problems with respect to nutritional education and showed that in urban areas anemia continued to be a severe problem, present in nearly a quarter of the program participants aged two to three years in 2004. They also found the program did not have a significant effect in reducing anemia among urban children (Neufeld, Sotres Álvarez, García Feregrino, et al. 2005). The persistence of anemia despite the cash transfers is a serious concern because it is well established that iron deficiencies can impede cognitive development and thereby undermine the learning and long-term human capital formation of anemic children.

Poverty Reduction

The balance of results in poverty reduction from CCT program evaluations offers only tempered conclusions. In general, the size of poverty-reducing effects is quite small. A short-term reduction in poverty is to be expected, of course, given the size of most transfers in comparison to family income. The key issue is how to measure the longer-term effects on the incidence and intensity of poverty. The debate has generally concluded that the effects of CCT programs are greater in reducing the intensity than the incidence of poverty. That is, transfers succeed in lowering the gap between a household's income and the poverty threshold, as indicated in table 8.2, but generally do not lift households above this line (Draibe 2006; Cortés, Banegas, and Solís 2007).

Morley and Coady (2003) argue that it is wrong to assess the effect of CCT programs simply by comparing measures of poverty before and after their implementation. They argue that the comparison should contrast treatment and control groups and that in the absence of such a comparison, researchers

Table 8.2
Size of Cash Transfers by CCT Programs in Latin America

Program and Country	Amount Transferred (US$)	Year	Relative Weight of Cash Transfer
BF, Brazil	$91 (PPP) per family in extreme poverty	2003	20%–21% of family consumption
CHS, Chile	$33 (PPP) per family in extreme poverty first six months	2004	18%–50% of poverty line
FA, Colombia			9%–29% of poverty line
PJ, Peru			88% of income per family in extreme poverty
PROP, Mexico	$239 (PPP) maximum per family with high school students; $24 (PPP) in food assistance	2005	20%–21% family consumption; 15%–98% nutritional poverty line
RPS, Nicaragua			20%–21% of family consumption; 70% of poverty line
RS, El Salvador	$15 average per family, $20 maximum	2007	37%–50% of poverty line

Source. Cohen and Franco (2006b); Cohen and Villatoro (2006); Britto (2007); Draibe (2006); Francke and Mendoza (2006); Largaespada-Fredersdorff (2006); Morley and Coady (2003); Núñez and Cuesta (2006); Presidencia República Dominicana (2006); Skoufias, Davis, and de la Vega (2001); and Soares et al. (2007).
Note. PPP = purchasing power parity.

should compare the cost of the program with the size of the posttransfer poverty gap. Putting this proposal into effect, they find a reduction in the overall level of poverty of 3.0 percent to 3.9 percent in Mexico and Brazil, with a reduction of around 14 percent of the poverty gap in rural areas. However, the decline in poverty was only 0.4 percent and 0.8 percent in Honduras and Nicaragua, respectively. In their comparison of treatment and control groups in Mexico, Morley and Coady (2003) found a 17.4 percent reduction in the rate of poverty in rural Mexican communities between 1997 and 1999 and a 36.1 percent reduction in the size of the rural poverty gap, confirming other appraisals by Skoufias, Davis, and de la Vega (2001), Levy and Rodríguez (2005), and Cohen and Franco (2006b). In more recent calculations, Alvarez (2006), using the latest data from the Inter-American Development Bank, found that between 1997 and 2003, changes in the incidence of poverty were limited, with only 9 percent of the rural poor managing to rise above the poverty line.

At the national level, evaluations in Mexico suggest that PROP transfers made a significant contribution to poverty reduction during 2000–2002 (World Bank 2004c; Villatoro 2005a), but according to Cortés, Banegas, and Solís (2007), the transfers produced only modest improvements in national poverty rates (*pobreza de capacidades*) thereafter, with reductions of 3.6 percent in 2002, 3.6 percent in 2004, and 5.1 percent in 2005, although effects were greater in rural areas than in urban areas. They based their analysis on estimates calculated from the National Survey of Household Income. With respect to general poverty rates, the reduction was around only 1 percent per year. In terms of change over time (the difference between instantaneous poverty rates in the years 2002 and 2005), the contribution of transfers was calculated to be even less—just 0.22 percent in the poverty rates (*pobreza de capacidades*). Nonetheless, these authors agree with other studies that the effect of PROP was greater in reducing the intensity than the incidence of poverty, lowering the size of the gap by 11.5 percent, 9.7 percent, and 12.1 percent during 2002, 2004, and 2005, respectively.

This conclusion is consistent with the results of qualitative studies, which after five years of fieldwork confirmed that although PROP did reduce the economic vulnerability of households in Mexico, the reduction was not enough to do away with deprivation or to "eradicate poverty" (González de la Rocha 2006, 166). Other factors tended to dominate in generating poverty, and, compared with these, transfers appeared "to acquire a secondary role." More important factors included "the domestic cycle, the structure of the households and the options for generating resources by means of man-power" (González de la Rocha 2006, 166).

Other studies agree that CCT programs do not go very far in reducing poverty rates. Bourguignon, Ferreira, and Leite (2003) estimate a reduction of only 4 percent in Brazil in 1999, but like other investigators they report a larger effect in reducing the gap between household income and the poverty threshold (9.8 percent). According to Morley and Coady (2003), the modest results of Bourguignon, Ferreira, and Leite reflect the fact that the goal of the program in Brazil was to improve education rather than reduce poverty per se, so that amounts transferred were very small. Likewise, Argentina's program had a minor effect on the overall poverty rate but a major effect in reducing the rate of indigence (Braun and Chudnovsky 2005), and in Uruguay the Citizen Income transfer program achieved a 1.4 percent reduction of poverty in 2006 and reduced the poverty gap by 7.8 percent (Arim and Vigorito 2006).

In sum, recent studies yield conclusions close to what Skoufias, Davis, and de la Vega (2001, 37) originally observed: "Targeted programs, such as PROGRESA, may be quite successful at reducing the poverty gap or the severity of poverty but have a negligible impact on the headcount ratio."

In terms of long-term poverty reduction, of course, the effects of CCT programs obviously cannot be measured. Children from the first households to receive transfers in the 1990s are only now beginning to leave school and enter the workforce, and the really massive CCT interventions occurred only within the past five years. Even those who accept the conventional thinking about CCT programs agree that there are no answers to questions about "long-term impacts on welfare" and poverty reduction (Rawlings and Rubio 2003).

The only evidence to base conclusions on at this point are simulations of possible future incomes. In the initial evaluation of PROP in Mexico, for example, simulations suggested that an increase of 0.66 years in schooling as a result of transfers would ultimately yield 8 percent higher future wages and that as a result of food supplements, future earnings would be 2.9 percent higher (Skoufias, Davis, and de la Vega 2001). In their analysis, Morley and Coady (2003) estimated the future incomes of workers who received grants in Nicaragua's transfer program would be 9 percent greater owing to increased time spent in school. Of course, these estimates do not address whether future earners will actually be able to emerge from poverty, only whether future earnings are likely to be higher as a result of the additional time spent in school, leaving the critical question of poverty alleviation unaddressed. In Mexico in 2002, a third of all households earning only wage income were poor, and 22 percent experienced poor nutrition (Cortés 2006a).

The assumptions made by Morley and Coady (2003) in their simulations are largely untested. Growth in the number of workers with more years of schooling does not necessarily translate into greater future income-producing capacities, as Morley and Coady themselves admit. In this regard, Villatoro (2005a) speaks of growing uncertainty surrounding the effect of education on wages, given rising levels of schooling throughout Latin America. The implicit assumption of most CCT evaluations is that in the future, better educated workers will find sufficient demand in the labor market for their services, an assumption that Duhau (2000) calls heroic. Even Levy (2007, 1), a strong promoter of PROP in Mexico when it started in 1997, who defined the original program as "transfers of income linked to investment in human capital today, and higher personal income tomorrow," concluded, nearly ten years later, that PROP workers will not achieve higher personal incomes if they have access to small parcels of poor quality land in rural areas or are self-employed in the streets of urban areas, even if they are employed in microbusinesses. "Without businesses that have more capital and are larger," he says, "the higher personal incomes tomorrow will not happen. Where are the companies that are going to hire, and register with the social security institute, the millions of workers from *Oportunidades*?" (Levy 2007, 58).

According to Cohen and Franco (2006a, 52), the connection between receiving transfers and "the insertion of the worker in a decent job is full of questions." Certainly the critical nexus—investment in human capital today for productive work in the future—is far from ensured, for it requires a socioeconomic context in which abilities can be realized and skills can be translated into higher earnings (Gendreau 2000). Without generating new productive employment, CCT programs in Latin America can be expected to have limited effects on the future earnings and poverty of poor families. From the point of view of public policy, in the long term it is not possible to separate actions in favor of the capacities of poor households from employment policy. In the absence of meaningful job creation, the future social effectiveness of CCT programs will be limited.

In terms of inequality, Soares et al. (2007) suggest that the methods of selection used in Latin America generally produce small effects on income redistribution. They calculate just a 5 percent reduction of inequality in Mexico during 1996–2004 and a 5 percent reduction in Brazil during 1995–2004, with no effect in Chile during 1996–2003. The actual contribution of CCT programs to reductions in Mexico and Brazil was estimated to be 21 percent, yielding an overall impact on equality of just 1 percent during the periods covered. The clear implication is that the CCT programs do not constitute a solution to the enormous problems of inequality in these countries.

Influence on Gender Relations

The balance of findings with respect to gender relations yields contradictory conclusions. Although studies reveal that CCT programs usually strengthen the position of women in participating households—increasing the influence of mothers within the family, raising their self-esteem, and reducing educational gaps between men and women—they also document a frequent overloading of women with new responsibilities emanating from the program itself, and many studies find that cash transfers to mothers simply reinforce a traditional division of labor that confines women strictly to domestic roles (Cohen and Franco 2006a; García-Falconi 2004).

Most CCT programs in Latin America grant women a central role by design, transferring funds directly to mothers on the assumption that they are better administrators of family resources than fathers (Serrano 2005; Fonseca 2006). This design feature generated considerable debate when the programs were first implemented (see Rubalcava 2008) and when the first evaluations were done (Riquer-Fernández 2000). Nonetheless, the conventional theory that emerged from this early work confirmed that women were instrumental in program success (Skoufias, Davis, and de la Vega 2001). Given an unequal balance of power within the household, conditional transfers gave mothers an "effective commitment device" with which to defend the welfare of children (De Janvry and Sadoulet 2006).

Women are thus central to the accumulation of human capital. The longer a mother stays in school, the longer other members of her family stay in school. Moreover, if girls from poor families stay in school longer, in the future they will keep their own children in school longer, yielding significant downstream effects on the health and nutrition of children (Morley and Coady 2003). Indeed, the first program evaluations in Mexico emphasized the positive effect of CCT programs in empowering women—improving male recognition of their importance in family welfare and reducing gender differentials in education while not increasing mothers' time burden (Skoufias, Davis, and de la Vega 2001; Adato 2004). These themes were repeated in later assessments (Villatoro 2005a), even though many programs did not incorporate an explicit gender focus in their design or implementation (for example, Colombia; see Núñez and Cuesta 2006).

To sum up, CCT programs do appear to encourage women to become active agents in improving the welfare of their families, but only within the restrictions of traditional gender relations, thus raising questions about the extent to which these relations limit the potential of women to break the intergenerational cycle of poverty. Without a program design that confronts and overcomes maternalism and familism, women will continue to have serious difficulties integrating themselves into productive employment in less precarious ways that are less conducive to continuing the reproduction of poverty.

Conditional Cash Transfers as Social Policy

The foregoing review supports several generalizations about the influence of CCTs in Latin America. CCT programs have generally acted to increase school enrollment and attendance (though not in every case), raised years of schooling completed, and in some cases lowered the rate of leaving school. CCTs have increased access to preventative medical care and vaccinations, raised the number of visits to health centers, and reduced the rate of illness while raising overall consumption and food consumption, with positive results on the growth and weight of children, especially among the smallest. With respect to poverty, the consensus is that, in the short term, CCT programs have a greater effect in reducing the intensity of poverty than in lowering its incidence. By narrowing the gap between a family's resources and the poverty threshold, they reduce vulnerability and slightly lower overall levels of income inequality.

CCT programs appear to be relatively efficient in reaching targeted populations, typically defined as those in extreme poverty, though not without certain problems of design and implementation. Although limited, interactions between CCT program participants reinforce community social relations, and social networks are empowered by income transfers that raise the security of households and the possibility of participating in networks. Evidence suggests that CCT programs improve the standing of women, which enhances female self-esteem, promotes relationships with other women, and reduces gender gaps in education. Transfers made directly to mothers also help them negotiate a stronger bargaining position within patriarchal households.

However, the foregoing review also highlights several limitations of CCT programs. In general, they appear to have little or no effect on performance in school, on the amount learned in school, or on cognitive development generally, and their effects on rates of anemia have been limited. The persistence of anemia among children in most CCT programs suggests the possibility of long-term cognitive impairment. In the end, the long-term effects of CCT programs are still unknown. Despite simulations suggesting that accumulations of human capital will improve the future earnings, it is not clear that more years of schooling will necessarily yield improved human capabilities and higher incomes. The current link between education and earnings may not prevail in the future as levels of education rise, especially in the absence of significant job creation.

With regard to social relations, people in targeted populations often do not understand the methods by which CCT participants are selected, which gives rise to tensions in the community between those selected for participation and those not. Although conventional program designs emphasize the role of women in fomenting change, the way that transfers are made also reinforces the traditional household division of labor and at times increases the work burden of mothers receiving them.

Thus, a careful and balanced evaluation of the accumulated research yields conclusions that are notably more muted than the triumphal proclamations of ideological boosters, who generally rest their case on six pillars: (1) CCT programs attend to the poorest of the poor, (2) they are administratively efficient, (3) they reduce inequality, (4) they reduce poverty in the short term and long term, (5) they are effective at encouraging the accumulation of human capital, and (6) they are capable of breaking the intergenerational transmission of poverty. Although empirical support for points 1–3 is fairly clear, the evidence is weak or uncertain for points 4–6. Although conventional CCT theorists have tended to highlight the great progress made to date, in reality they have been around for only a decade, and it is too early to know their ultimate effects.

The desire of CCT theorists to show positive results and the urgency with which they promoted these social experiments seem to have played a key role in constructing a very optimistic vision and in promoting CCT programs as a model of successful social policy. Nonetheless, the pyramid of suppositions on which CCT programs are constructed leaves many uncertainties (Villatoro 2005b). Although it is clearly a good thing that children consume more food and experience less illness and that inequality and poverty are reduced, if only by a little, these outcomes do not mean that CCT programs are the best strategy for dealing with poverty or that they constitute "the cornerstone of the national strategy for welfare in each country" (Rawlings 2005, 7). It is still too early to determine their effects on long-term development at either the individual level or the national level (Soares et al. 2007), and the doubts that have accumulated in ten years of research must be addressed by further research and independent, multiple evaluations. Even Rawlings (2005) recognizes that CCT programs are limited in scope as instruments of national policy and must be set in a broader framework of social welfare and economic development.

The current debate must therefore widen its horizons to embrace a more general vision, with public interventions that focus not only on the demand side but on the supply side as well (Gendreau 2000; Barba Solano et al. 2005; Bouillon and Tejerina 2006). Particularly with respect to education and health, the search for interventions that do not distort markets has obscured the need for reforms on the supply side and paradoxically has limited the scope of possible actions on the demand side. A false dichotomy between targeted coverage and universal coverage makes it impossible to understand that CCT programs are embedded within institutions that are universal in character (Gendreau 2000). How can the capacities of the poor be improved without substantial improvement in the quality of health and education services more generally?

The answer to this question leads inevitably to larger discussions about the reform of social institutions and the character of welfare regimes more generally in Latin America (Filgueira 2005; Huber 2006; Barba Solano 2007). Given the minimalist view of social policy (De Ferranti et al. 2004) that has become possible in the region, it may make sense to focus public action on the limited reach of CCT programs, but to do so still leaves enormous gaps in coverage because it excludes broader social institutions and concerns itself only with protecting the poor (Huber 2005; Serrano 2005). A more comprehensive approach is required, seeking equity to connect actions on behalf of the poor with reform of the basic institutions of social security.

International financial organizations and governments now recognize that the CCT programs will last longer than originally expected and that the problems of chronic or structural poverty will require both long-term and short-term actions (Alvarez 2006). Unfortunately, social security coverage in Latin America dropped from 61.2 percent in 1980 to 52.4 percent in 2000 (Mesa Lago 2005), and this fracturing of public welfare systems in the region yields bleak economic prospects down the road: high poverty at the regional level, weak reductions in chronic poverty, high and rising inequality, weakened social institutions, and growing sociopolitical resistance to dealing with these problems. If these trends continue, then the current segmentation of social institutions could become more marked, with some categories of people being well insured, others only temporarily protected, and most occupying a no-man's-land of complete exclusion from public insurance and social protection (Lautier 2004).

In societies with emerging two-track systems of social welfare, such as Brazil and Mexico, this dualism could become permanent, enabling us to speak of institutionalized segmentation (Valencia Lomelí 2007). The key issue, then, is how to integrate CCT programs within existing social security institutions so as to overcome traditional pressures for segmentation of Latin America. An integrated view of social policy would incorporate the objective of strengthening social citizenship more generally (Barba Solano et al. 2005; Palma and Urzúa 2005; Serrano 2005; Barba Solano 2007; ECLAC 2006). Under present conditions, CCT programs cannot be expected to contribute to the construction of integrated citizenship if they are not thought of as vehicles for guaranteeing rights and if they do not increase the civil and political participation of those included (Irarrázaval 2005).

Whereas CCT programs partially fortify the access of the poor to basic services, they see themselves not as vehicles for exercising a right but simply as an instrumental administrative action (Sottoli 2008). As an administrative action, "the entitlement to rights is temporary" (Fonseca 2006, 16), and their enjoyment is left to the mercy of the vagaries of politics and subject to the arbitrary nature of selection criteria (World Bank 2007b). Civic participation by citizens within CCT programs is generally limited to requirements for coresponsibility, with a few notable exceptions that demand greater civic action (in particular in PJJ in Argentina; see Golbert 2006a, 2006b) or some changes in accountability. The idea of coresponsibility is assumed to strengthen social citizenship, with rights and duties shared between authorities and citizens (Palma and Urzúa 2005), but it can also be seen as the coercive tutelage of individuals by authorities demanding the strict fulfillment of responsibilities within a context of frank inequality between officials and presumed beneficiaries, yielding a kind of Social Taylorism.

The debate should not be limited to a comparison of extremes—either a neoliberal welfare regime of targeted programs or a universal system with a guaranteed minimum income (see Lindert, Skoufias, and Shapiro 2006)—but rather include a consideration of the variety of Latin American regimes in between (Filgueira 2005; Barba Solano 2007). There is no reason that nations cannot advance toward a recognition and validation of social rights (Sottoli 2008; ECLAC 2006) in ways that are sustainable socially, politically, and financially (Filgueira et al. 2006; Townsend 2007). According to Simões (2006, 310), CCT programs represent instruments that in practice can confront the denial of basic social rights while endeavoring to promote an "equality of conditions for exercising one's social rights." Although attention to segments of the population traditionally excluded from public attention is itself a positive initiative, broader reforms are needed to promote equity and coverage, strengthen program financial capacities, and consolidate a broader network for social security. Paradoxically, further enhancing the effect of targeted CCT programs in Latin America now requires reinvigorating the state institutions that offer basic services, especially those pertaining to education and health.

Conclusion: The CCT Is More of an Illusion Than an Achievement

An economic illusion has been created in that the discourse of investment in the human capital of individuals who, once healthy, better fed, and educated, will be able to deal with the market, though isolated from economic relations and without economic restrictions. One of the original promoters of these programs, Santiago Levy (2007), casts doubt on the initial dream of CCT programs: first, transfers to invest in student's human capital; later, higher incomes in the labor market. The assumption that the poor, armed with more human capital, will find better jobs thanks to the CCTs comes up against several questions along the trajectory of the scholarship holder until his or her labor market insertion (Cohen and Franco 2006a, 2006b).

An educational illusion has been created: the idea that increasing the number of years spent at school means by itself a greater accumulation of human capital that will empower the poor so they can get out of their situation of backwardness on their own. The quality of the education provided is taken virtually for granted (Morley and Coady 2003), and no strong action is taken to address the problem of deficiencies in the quality of the schools for the poor or to improve the learning by the students. At the very least, the strengthening of people's capacities for associating with a changing and insecure world and the overcoming of vulnerabilities in their own portfolios of assets in the context of restricted opportunities (González de la Rocha and Escobar Latapí 2008) are left in uncertainty.

A social illusion also has been created in the discourse of CCT programs being efficient in reducing poverty in the short term and in the long term. Recent evaluations and research papers show the frailty of reductions in the incidence of poverty in the short term; the most widely known achievements are in the reduction of the severity of poverty (Cortés, Banegas, and Solís 2007; Skoufias, Davis, and de la Vega 2001). Basically, CCT programs are not designed to reduce poverty in the short term. To think that these programs can provide a strategy for reaching the goal of a reduction in extreme poverty, as agreed in the Millennium objectives, is an illusion.

A political illusion has been created in the concept of a direct relation between individuals and the state in order to build a kind of free coalition of corporatist and party interests or to prevent the discretional use of CCT programs by politicians. Targeted transfers, supported by sophisticated technical means, were to be the instrument of this new relation. However, the lack of a focus on social rights may favor the room to find new mechanisms of clientelistic relations. This has certainly been the case in Mexico, where *Oportunidades*'s rules were modified regarding the selection (at first election) of local "promoters"—that is, beneficiaries that serve as a link between their community and the administrators of the CCT program—in such a way as to give rise to a bureaucratic structure dominated by members of the governing political party on the federal level (Valencia Lomelí 2011).

In addition, a sociocultural illusion has been created in the discourse on how central women are in CCT programs, as the transfers are given directly to them in the hope that they will administer the resources better and show more care for family necessities. The so-called "gender focus" of these programs, which encourages the women's agency and does give a certain empowerment, has a biased, traditionalist view of women as mothers or housewives (familialization), which makes it hard for women running families to engage in productive employment outside the home in a less precarious way and burdens women at home with heavier tasks without explicitly promoting a different vision of family labor division (Martínez Franzoni and Voorend 2008; Molyneux 2007).

Finally, a systemic illusion has been created in that the discourse of respect for market principles with interventions on the demand side has left to one side or ignored the weaknesses on the supply side of basic services of protection or social security. Efforts to create a synergy between encouraging demand for basic services through the programs and a possible improvement in the institutions providing the services, along the line of a "basic universalism" (*universalismo básico*) (Molina 2006), have been relatively few. The urge for low administrative costs has left institutional supply to its fate, but the focus on a minimal state is challenged by the very results of the programs, which generate an increased demand for services that are generally in short supply. Paradoxically, further enhancing the effect of targeted CCT programs (especially in the case of programs with a large coverage) requires reinvigorating the public institutions that offer basic services, that is, social security and social protection institutions.

Author's Note

This chapter includes modified versions of parts of two articles that were previously published, one by the *Annual Review of Sociology* (Valencia Lomelí 2008) and the other by *Global Social Policy* (Valencia Lomelí 2009). Contact the author at Centro de Investigación Observatorio Social, Universidad de Guadalajara, Guadalajara, Jalisco, Mexico; e-mail: enrivalo@gmail.com.

Notes

1. An "epistemic community" is a group of professionals specializing in a particular field that seeks, or claims, to have knowledge that is relevant to public policies in the field or in the area of a particular issue and that shares a common political project for problems associated with its field of knowledge (Haas 1992, 3).

2. Following Béland and Orenstein (2009, 9), these transnational actors can be seen as "individual or collective actors that seek to influence policy in multiple countries through the advocacy of specific, well-elaborated policy proposals." They can be "international organizations, transnational activist networks, epistemic communities, individual policy entrepreneurs, and the like."

3. "Advocacy coalitions" are made up of those participating in the design of public policy, in this case social policy, who form alliances with others sharing the same policy core beliefs and keep up a degree of coordination in work aimed at common objectives (Sabatier and Weible 2007, 194).

4. The *Oportunidades* program consists of a cash transfer to households in extreme poverty under well-defined education and health conditions to be met by the beneficiaries, especially *titulares* (female head of households), 98 percent of whom are women. About five million households receive this benefit that amounts to a minimum of $16 a month per household for food plus additional amounts for health and other items. Households are eligible for higher payments depending on the educational attainment of their young members: for instance, if the child is assisting to third grade (primary school), the household receives $11, but it receives $69 when the child reaches twelfth grade (senior high school).

Part III

Pathways out of Rural Poverty

9

Pathways out of Rural Poverty in Mexico

Darcy Tetreault

For the first time in over twenty-five years, the World Bank's *World Development Report 2008: Agriculture for Development* (WDR-08) focuses on the agricultural sector. It distinguishes between three types of developing countries (agricultural based, transforming, and urbanized), and it outlines policies designed to help facilitate three pathways out of poverty: farming, labor, and migration. Policy recommendations vary somewhat according to each country type, but the guiding principles remain the same: trade liberalization and privatization.

Mexico is the darling of this report. During the second half of the twentieth century, Mexico underwent a rapid process of urbanization, spurred on by import-substituting-industrialization policies that favored the urban sector and large-scale commercial farming. Then, in the late 1980s and early 1990s, neoliberal reforms where applied to the rural sector, accompanied by a series of compensatory programs designed to help farmers adjust to the new structural conditions. Accordingly, nearly everywhere Mexico's agricultural and social policies are mentioned in the WDR-08, they are mentioned in a positive light, as a model for other developing countries to imitate. So what exactly are these policies? And how have they affected different sectors of the rural population?

This chapter begins with a brief analysis of the WDR-08. From there it goes on to summarize the structural adjustments applied to rural Mexico over the past twenty years, pointing out how these have been accompanied by agricultural subsidy programs that channel public resources to large farms and agrofood corporations. The next section analyzes poverty trends, observing that the incidence of income poverty in rural Mexico has stagnated during the neoliberal period at an alarmingly high level of over 60 percent. With this in mind, the chapter goes on to critically analyze the three pathways out of rural poverty proposed by the World Bank. Empirical evidence is presented, suggesting that existing structural conditions have made small-scale commercial farming largely unviable, with the minor but important exception of organic coffee. At the same time, rural labor markets have contracted, spurring on urban and international migration. The last section of this chapter presents alternatives that have come from below. It is argued that the proposals and demands of independent peasant organizations, currently rallying under the banners of "food sovereignty" and "*sin maíz no hay país*," constitute national-level policy alternatives that are more conducive to successful small-scale farming, creating jobs in rural areas, strengthening national-level food sovereignty, and protecting the environment.

Critical Analysis of the 2008 WDR

As mentioned, twenty-five years have passed since the first time the World Bank put agriculture at the center of its annual flagship report. During this interval, the Bank systematically underfunded agricultural development and promoted neoliberal structural adjustments in the rural sector. In this context, several authors have welcomed the World Bank's renewed interest in agriculture, while remaining critical of the analysis and agenda contained in the WDR-08.[1] This section examines the report and summarizes some of the most important criticisms that have been leveled against it.

The WDR-08 classifies countries into three worlds of agriculture, based on agriculture's share of national economic growth and on the share of aggregate poverty in rural areas. In this way, most of the countries in sub-Saharan Africa are categorized as "agricultural based"; most of South and East Asia, North Africa, and the Middle East and some of Europe and Central Asia are considered to be "transforming"; and most countries in Latin American and Central Asia are seen as "urbanized." At the same time, the Bank recognizes the existence of regional heterogeneity within countries, reflecting the three worlds of agriculture on a subnational level.[2]

Across these three worlds of agriculture, the Bank conceives of three major pathways out of poverty: farming, wage labor in the rural nonfarm economy, and migration to urban centers. In this view, a few entrepreneurial farmers are able to increase their landholdings, adopt modern technologies (including genetically modified seeds), and plug into transnational supermarket chains. Subsistence farmers are essentially doomed to extinction. However, the Bank suggests that subsistence farming can and should be enhanced in order to help the rural poor meet their basic needs while they acquire new skills for the labor market. In this way, for the vast majority of rural dwellers, nonfarm employment and migration from the countryside represent the greatest opportunities for overcoming poverty.

This vision does not bode well for small-scale farmers and indigenous groups that have a strong attachment to their land, vocation, and community. As Akram-Lodhi (2008, 1153) observes, the WDR-08 "offers a dose of agropessimism that reflects a quite unilinear path-dependent vision of the future of food and agriculture." Indeed, the WDR-08 seems to adhere to an antiquated modernization paradigm, one in which the peasantry gradually disappears and indigenous groups are assimilated into the modern world. This paradigm is also reflected in the Bank's three-tiered typology of agricultural worlds in which countries "follow evolutionary paths that can move them from one country type to another" (World Bank 2008, 4). Clearly, this implies a unilinear evolution from "agricultural based" and "transforming" to "urbanized," characterized by a relative decline in rural populations and in agriculture's share of the national economy. According to Veltmeyer (2009, 398), while there may be "considerable historical evidence of a long-term trend that can be theorised in these terms," this does not imply that these trends represent "an immutable historic process" and that "the only possible response . . . is to adjust to them." From this perspective, capitalist development is associated with a process of (semi-)proletarianization, whereby peasants are dispossessed of their land (often violently) in order to allow large-scale enterprises to exploit natural resources for private gain. From this view, the continuation of this type of development is not inevitable; it can be resisted through collective action.

As we will see in the case of Mexico, there has indeed been widespread resistance to the type of development promoted by the World Bank. However, from the Bank's perspective, resistance is not a viable pathway out of poverty; it is treated as unreasonable political pressure for market-distorting subsidies and protectionist policies that do more harm than good in the long run. Accordingly, the WDR-08 promotes a reformist agenda that adheres to the basic tenets of neoliberalism: trade liberalization, deregulation, and privatization. Along these lines, it encourages all countries to reduce subsidies in the agricultural sector, and it appeals to transnational corporations (TNCs) to adhere to the norms of Corporate Social Responsibility. In addition, it promotes the strengthening of property rights, market-based land reform, improved access to financial services, public-private partnerships, and better management of natural resources. While the reformist elements of this agenda are meant to create greater opportunities for the rural poor, the essence of the report is remarkably consistent with prior World Bank policy, as several critics have noted (for example, Akram-Lodhi 2008; Devereux, Scoones, and Thompson 2009; Kay 2009; Veltmeyer 2009).

Another criticism that has been leveled against the WDR-08 has to do with its benign view of agribusiness. Along these lines, Amanor (2009, 261) observes, "The World Bank depicts agribusiness as creating favourable conditions for smallholder famers, in spite of considerable evidence to the contrary." Although the Bank recognizes a "growing concentration" in agricultural input markets, it offers little advice for countering oligopoly power, aside from encouraging more public investment in agricultural research and creating an investment climate that is more conducive to the entry of small- and medium-sized firms. Presumably, from the Bank's perspective, private monopolies are a lesser evil than public ones. In any case, the WDR-08 justifies its favorable view of agribusiness by giving credence to Malthusian fears. It states, "With growing resource scarcity, future food production depends more than ever on increasing crop yields and livestock productivity" (World Bank 2008, 66). With this in mind, it stresses the need to increase global food production via technological innovation, assigning a central role to agribusiness. In McMichael's opinion, this amounts to "market intensification, via agribusiness, aided by the state" (2009a, 236). Moreover, as we have seen in the context of the current food crisis, the problem is not one of low agricultural production but rather one of poor asset distribution. As Holt-Giménez (2009) points out, in 2008 the world witnessed record levels of per capita food production, paradoxically combined with record numbers of hungry people and record corporate-food profits. He and many other researchers have suggested that, to the extent that agricultural production needs to be increased in order to keep up with population growth, smallholder farmers can take a lead role by adopting agroecological technology, which tends to be more accessible, socially appropriate, and ecologically sustainable (see chapter 10).

Nevertheless, the WDR-08 pays scant attention to agroecology and totally ignores the proposals put forth by peasant organizations grouped together on the international level under the banner *Vía Campesina*, particularly with regard to achieving food sovereignty on the national level through small-scale farming. Instead the Bank sees agribusiness as the driver of technological innovation and the supplier of modern inputs for all farmers, including small-scale farmers. Similarly, transnational supermarkets are supposed to provide small farms with higher prices for their produce. Although the report recognizes that there are difficulties associated with incorporating small-scale farmers into commodity chains controlled by agrofood TNCs, it suggests that these difficulties can be overcome by helping them create producer cooperatives, thereby leveraging up their bargaining power. Critics are skeptical, however, arguing that these proposals do not realistically take into account the asymmetrical power relations that exist between TNCs and small-scale farmers, even when these are organized into producer cooperatives (see, for example, Akram-Lodhi 2008; Amanor 2009; McMichael 2009a).

In sum, from a critical point of view, the WDR-08 represents a continuation of past World Bank policy; it is geared toward market intensification, and it favors the consolidation of the corporate food regime. Correspondingly, its three proposed pathways out of poverty only consider ways in which poor peasants can adapt to current structural conditions; resistance and structural change do not enter into the picture. Given these limitations, Kay (2009, 125) concludes, "The policy proposals presented by the report are unlikely to benefit the majority of the rural poor, especially the poorest of the poor." As we will see, in the case of Mexico, there is ample empirical evidence to support this sort of skepticism.

Mexico's Agricultural Policy During the Neoliberal Era

The Mexican government began applying structural adjustments to the rural sector in the mid-1980s, in the context of the debt crisis. However, it was not until Carlos Salinas's presidential term (1988–94) that the bulk of the reforms were carried out. Subsequent administrations have consolidated these reforms and introduced antipoverty programs aimed at rural households living in extreme poverty. In this section, we briefly review these rural policies and their consequences.

When the debt crisis hit in 1982, the Mexican government immediately adopted austerity measures that spelled the demise of rural development programs that had been operating since the 1970s, including PIDER, CO-PLAMAR, and SAM.[3] Then, beginning in the mid-1980s, quotas and tariffs on agricultural imports were gradually reduced, culminating in the North American Free Trade Agreement (NAFTA), which set a fifteen-year timetable for phasing out remaining protectionist policies. During the same period, dozens of state-owned enterprises linked to the rural sector were dismantled and privatized, including the National Company for Popular Subsistence (CONASUPO), which was in charge of buying, storing, and marketing basic grains. CONASUPO was gradually replaced by a federal agency called Support and Services for Agricultural Trading (ASERCA), which was meant to be less market distorting.

Until 1988, Mexican farmers were provided with guaranteed producer prices for twelve crops (maize, beans, wheat, rice, sorghum, safflower, soybean, cotton, sesame, coconuts, sunflower, and barley). During Salinas's presidential term, all of these were eliminated, with the exception of maize and beans. As a result, producer prices dropped throughout the 1990s, as cheap grains flooded in from the United States at levels well above the quotas set by NAFTA. At the same time, farmers were faced with rising input costs.

Until the 1990s, agricultural inputs were highly subsidized in Mexico. Publicly owned companies such as Mexican Fertilizers (FERTIMEX) and the National Seeds Producer (PRONASE) provided inputs for the national market, making the country virtually self-sufficient in seed and fertilizer production. Since then, however, these state-owned companies have been dismantled or privatized, and a handful of large and powerful TNCs have gained control of the national market (for example, Cargill, Archer Daniels Midland, Bunge, and Dreyfus). Under these conditions, input costs have risen dramatically, first in the early 1990s, then again since 2006.[4]

Between 2005 and mid-2008, international prices for basic grains hiked up steeply, leading some analysts to suggest that this would create more favorable market conditions for Mexican farmers. However, what we have seen is that these higher prices have been only weakly transmitted to small-scale producers. As with agricultural inputs, Mexico's domestic grain market has become dominated by a handful of multinational and national corporations, including Cargill, Archer Daniels Midland, Minsa, and Maseca. Under oligopolistic conditions, these corporations have been able to squeeze small-scale farmers on both ends (with higher input costs and lower producer prices) and capture the lion's share of higher food prices. In this way, in 2008, Cargill's profits increased by 81 percent, Archer Daniels Midland's increased by 86 percent, and Bunge's increased by a stunning 1,452 percent (Guzmán-Flores 2008). Lack of credit is another problem. Under Salinas, subsidized agricultural credit was almost completely eliminated, as well as government-backed crop insurance. The National Bank for Rural Credit (BANRURAL) was downsized and reoriented toward medium-sized commercial farmers. Large-scale farmers were expected to obtain credit from private banks, while small amounts of subsidized credit were made available to poor farmers through antipoverty programs such as Credit on Word (*Crédito a la Palabra*) and Regional Solidarity Funds (*Fondos Regionales de Solidaridad*). The net result of all of this was a dramatic increase in the real cost of credit, accompanied by a severe contraction in its availability. This situation was exacerbated by the 1995 economic crisis, and it has not improved significantly since then. In 2001, BANRURAL was privatized. Today, only 15 percent of Mexico's farmers have access to seasonal credit; 5 percent have access to credit for long-term productive investments, and these tend to be the medium- and large-scale producers.

The last element of the neoliberal strategy was to make changes to Article 27 of the constitution and to the Agrarian Law in order to put an official end to land redistribution and to pave the way toward the privatization of the *ejido*. As part of this reform, the Program for Certification of Ejidal Rights and Titling of Urban Parcels (PROCEDE) was created in 1993 as a mechanism for strengthening land-tenure security and facilitating the renting and selling of *ejidal* land. At first there was widespread resistance, not to the program per se but rather as an expression of a broader resistance to the neoliberal reforms in their entirety. Entry into PROCEDE was supposed to be voluntary. However, during Ernesto Zedillo's presidential term (1994–2000), government officials began exerting pressure on noncomplying *ejidos* and indigenous communities, inter alia, by threatening to exclude them from exiguous subsidy programs, most important the Program for Direct Support for Agriculture (PROCAMPO). These heavy-handed tactics provoked internal conflicts in many agrarian communities, and to a large extent they worked: by late 2003, almost 80 percent of Mexico's 31,000 *ejidos* and indigenous communities had accepted PROCEDE. Resistance has continued, though, especially in the south, where Mexico's indigenous population is concentrated. In Chiapas and Oaxaca, for example, only 28 percent and 21 percent of agrarian communities, respectively, have accepted the program (De Ita 2003).

Although some critics warned that the changes made to Article 27 of the constitution would lead to significantly higher land concentration, so far this has not been the case, at least not in terms of land sales. On the other hand, a dramatic increase in land rentals has led to a de facto concentration of some of the best irrigated land, especially in the northwestern states of Sinaloa and Sonora, where up to 80 percent of *ejidal* land is rented by large-scale farmers and agribusiness that use state-of-the-art technology to produce mainly maize and beans (De Ita 2003). In Jalisco, too, there is widespread renting of *ejidal* land, in this case, by agave-producing companies that offer leases of up to eight years, often applying large quantities of agrochemicals to the land in order to get the most out of it during their contract (Tetreault 2009). Farmers who rent their land benefit by securing a low-risk income without having to invest their own time or money. This allows them to search for jobs outside of farming, often implying migration to the United States.

To cushion some of the adverse effects of these structural reforms and to help farmers adjust by "modernizing" their production and by switching to high-value export crops, the Mexican government created a number of agricultural subsidy programs; the three most important in terms of budget are, in descending order, the Program for Direct Support for Agriculture (PROCAMPO), Acquisition of Productive Assets (previously known as *Alianza para el Campo*), and Income Objective (*Ingreso Objetivo*).

PROCAMPO was created in 1993 to help farmers adjust to neoliberal reforms. It was originally supposed to be terminated in the year 2008, but in the context of the global food crisis and the current government's legitimacy crisis, Felipe Calderón extended it until the end of his presidential term. The program provides cash payments of approximately $100 for every hectare of land cultivated, made directly to landowners. In 2005, PROCAMPO benefited approximately 2.5 million Mexican farmers, including about 1.6 million small-scale farmers with less than five hectares (Fox and Haight 2010).[5] In this way, it is by far the most progressive agricultural subsidy program in Mexico. On the other hand, because payments increase according to the number of hectares seeded, large-scale producers are able to capture a far greater share of the program's resources. Indeed, farmers with less than five hectares—which represent 75 percent of the beneficiaries—receive only 37 percent of the program's transfers, whereas those with more than 20 hectares—which represent only 3 percent of the beneficiaries—obtain 23 percent (Scott 2010). Furthermore, the program does not even reach hundreds of thousands of the country's poorest farmers. According to Fox and Haight (2010), it excludes 93 percent of farmers with less than one hectare, 81 percent with between one and two hectares, and 61 percent with between two and five hectares. The program has also been criticized for various forms of corruption and clientelism, including the illegal transferring of benefits to public servants, payments that exceed the 100,000 peso per person limit, and payments made to dozens of well-known drug traffickers and their immediate family members (Fox and Haight 2010; Espinosa 2009).

Acquisition of Productive Assets (APA) is Mexico's second most important agricultural subsidy program. It was created in 1996 under the name Alliance for the Countryside, with the following goals in mind: to improve the standard of living in rural areas, to increase agricultural production, to create jobs, to reduce poverty, and to stimulate exports. As its original name suggests, APA seeks to forge partnerships between different actors, namely, the federal government, state governments, farmers, and the private sector. The main thrust of the program is to help farmers acquire capital goods such as tractors, irrigation systems, high-yield seeds, and so on. Unfortunately, it is even more regressive than PROCAMPO: farmers with more than twenty hectares of land receive 57 percent of the funds, while those with less than ten hectares receive only 21 percent (FAO 2000). Even its subprogram, *Programa de Desarrollo Rural*, which is explicitly directed toward low-income farmers, is highly regressive, channeling 55 percent of its resources to the richest 10 percent of agricultural producers (Scott 2010). Highly bureaucratic application procedures are part of the problem, making the APA inaccessible to poor farmers with low levels of formal education, especially indigenous farmers whose first language is not Spanish.

The third subsidy program mentioned previously, Income Objective, provides additional direct payments to approximately 150,000 large-scale producers. It has served as de facto price control mechanism to compensate elite farmers for the difference between national and international prices. Eighty-five percent of the transfers go to the top 10 percent of farmers (Scott 2010). In fact, Income Objective is part of a complex package of programs called Commercialization Support, administered by ASERCA in a discretional and nontransparent fashion. The budget for Commercialization Support has swollen over the past ten years, helping to channel payments to national and transnational companies that buy, sell, and process basic grains. In this way, in 2008, the Mexican government was able to transfer over $60 million to Maseca, Cargill, Minsa, and Archer Daniels Midland (Fox and Haight 2010).

Taking a step back and looking at the neoliberal reforms in their entirety, we can see what their net implications have been for the agricultural sector. Our first observation is that public investment in Mexico's rural sector dropped in global terms by over 60 percent between 1982 and 2008 (Chávez 2008). Second, between 1980 and 2006, agricultural production fell by 6.9 percent in per capita terms (González-Chávez and Macías Macías 2007). Third, although Mexico's food exports more than doubled since NAFTA came into effect (from $3,995 million to $9,431 million between 1994 and 2003), food imports increased at an even greater rate (from $4,766 million to $12,866 million in the same time period), resulting in an expanding agricultural trade deficit equal to $3,435 million in the year 2004 alone (Quintana 2007) and reaching over $5 billion in 2007. In this way, Mexico's food dependency and vulnerability has increased substantially, not just because of this growing deficit but also because Mexico tends to export nonstrategic items (such as beer, tequila, fruits, vegetables, and live beef), while importing strategic items such as basic grains (most important, maize, soya, rice, and wheat). Finally, the subsidy programs put in place over the past twenty years, ostensibly to help farmers adjust to free trade, have mostly served as an interventionist mechanism for massively transferring public funds to large farms and agribusiness.

The Evolution of Income Poverty in Rural Mexico in the Neoliberal Era

After GDP growth rate, poverty-level estimates have become the second most important performance indicator for the Mexican government during the neoliberal era. As mentioned in chapter 6, President Fox was particularly eager to show a reduction in poverty. To establish an officially accepted measuring method, he created the semiautonomous Technical Committee for Measuring Poverty, which was replaced in 2004 by the National Council for the Evaluation of Social Development Policy (CONEVAL). While recognizing the need to eventually adopt a more multidimensional approach, the Technical Committee chose to start with the poverty line method, arguing that it was the most common and transparent (Comité Técnico 2002, 14).[6] Originally, it came up with the following three poverty lines: PL1, equal to 21.73 pesos per day per person in rural areas; PL2, equal to 28.12 pesos; and PL3, equal to 34.91 pesos. Boltvinik and Damián (2003) argue that if the PL3 had been calculated correctly, it would have been equal to 41.82 pesos per day in rural areas. In any case, the government rejected PL3 (presumably because it would have indicated too dire a situation of widespread poverty) and inserted a line between PL1 and PL2, resulting in the three official lines used today: "food poverty" (equal to PL1), "capacities poverty" (invented by the government), and "patrimonial poverty" (equal to PL2). Between 2006 and 2008, in the context of the global food crisis, the cost of the basket of essential goods in Mexico rose by 18 percent (CONEVAL 2008), resulting in an increase in the three official poverty lines. Thus, in 2008, the food-poverty line was equal to 23.57 pesos in rural areas, and the patrimonial poverty line was equal to 42.73 pesos (CONEVAL 2009).

Between 2006 and 2008, there was a sharp rise in the incidence of all three types of poverty: the percentage of the rural population (defined as settlements with fewer than 15,000 inhabitants) with income below the food poverty line rose from 24.5 percent to 31.8 percent, the incidence of capacities poverty increased from 32.7 percent to 39.1 percent, and patrimonial poverty rose from 54.7 percent to 60.8 percent (CONEVAL 2009).

According to CONEVAL, the 2008 levels are not as high as they were in 2000. During Vicente Fox's presidential term (2000–2006), the official statistics show a decrease of 17.9 percent, 17.2 percent, and 14.5 percent of the rural population living under the food, capacities, and patrimonial poverty lines, respectively. While the Fox administration and the World Bank were quick to attribute this success to the expansion of opportunities, increased remittances from the United States, and an increase in real wages, independent researchers expressed strong skepticism, not just to the official explanation of causal factors but also to the very possibility that there has been such a spectacular reduction in poverty. In this vein, Julio Boltvinik—perhaps Mexico's most renowned expert on poverty—argued that it is extremely unlikely that the incidence of poverty declined so abruptly between 2000 and 2006, considering that the GDP per capita grew at about only 1 percent annually in the same period. He attributes the apparent drop to an illusion created by major changes made to the ENIGH questionnaire and sampling method, resulting in the registration of more income (Boltvinik 2006b).[7]

Not everyone agrees. For example, Fernando Cortés—a distinguished member of the Technical Committee for Measuring Poverty—rejects the possibility that changes to ENIGH have had a significant impact on the raw data (Cortés 2006b). Through statistical analysis, he comes to the conclusion that there has in fact been a decrease in the incidence of all three types of income poverty in rural Mexico. However, when we take statistical margins of error into consideration, the decrease is minimal. Moreover, he demonstrates that the reductions are due more to increased remittances from the United States than to the expansion of PROP (Cortés, Banegas, and Solís 2007).

Be this as it may, there is one aspect of the debate that has received relatively little attention, that is, what constitutes rural Mexico. The most common definition is—or at least it used to be—communities with fewer than 2,500 inhabitants.[8] This is the definition that the Ministry of Social Development (SEDESOL) uses to design and operate its antipoverty programs, most important, PROP. However, for some unexplained reason, CONEVAL has chosen to define rural Mexico as the sum of localities with fewer than 15,000 inhabitants. This not only bumps up the rural population from 24 million to 38 million people but also makes the incidence of poverty seem less on the national level, since the official basket of basic goods is calculated to be cheaper in rural areas.

Using the same ENIGH data and defining rural Mexico as the sum of communities with fewer than 2,500 inhabitants, Enrique Hernández-Laos (2006) calculated poverty levels in rural Mexico between 1992 and 2004. He uses a poverty line of $3.35 per person per day, which is almost exactly the same as the government's patrimonial poverty line but based on a different basket of basic goods. With this more focused definition of rural Mexico, the incidence of income poverty appears to have hovered at over 60 percent since 1992, affecting as much as 75 percent of the rural people in 1996, at the height of the so-called "peso crisis." In 2008, 69 percent of Mexicans living in communities with fewer than 2,500 inhabitants had incomes below the patri-monial poverty line.[9]

Farming, Labor, and Migration: Three Pathways out of Rural Poverty?

The Farming Pathway out of Poverty

Under NAFTA, Mexican farmers have been forced to compete toe-to-toe with highly subsidized and better-endowed producers in the United States. Whereas US farmers receive on average $21,000 of subsidies annually, Mexican farmers receive only $700 (Quintana 2007). Farmers and agricultural workers in the United States and Canada have on average 1.6 and 1.8 tractors, respectively; in Mexico, there are only 2 tractors for every 100 people employed in the agricul-tural sector. In the United States, there are on average 59.1 hectares of arable land per person in the agricultural sector; in Canada, the figure is 117.2; in Mexico, it is only 3.1 (Calva 2002).

The architects of NAFTA were aware of these asymmetries; they knew that the vast majority of Mexican farmers would be at a disadvantage. How-ever, from a neoliberal perspective, this was not necessarily a bad thing. The more competitive farmers would find ways to adapt, and the rest of the rural population would either find nonagricultural jobs in the rural sector or emi-grate from the countryside.

Next, we analyze labor and migration as pathways out of rural poverty; here we ask how competitive small-scale commercial farmers were expected to adapt. The most common vision put forth by neoliberal economists was that they were expected to switch from traditional crops such as maize and beans to export-oriented crops with a comparative advantage, especially fruits and vegetables. What the past fifteen years have shown, however, is that small-scale farmers have simply been unable to overcome the obstacles to make this transi-tion. Fruit and vegetable production requires high initial capital investment, technical know-how, and timely commercialization. But without government support, small-scale producers have had little to no access to credit, techni-cal training, and marketing networks. Consequently, growth in this sector has been highly concentrated in the hands of large- and medium-scale producers, linked to TNCs and largely oriented toward export markets (Rello and Saave-dra 2007).

There is one export-oriented crop, though, that is dominated by small-scale producers: organic coffee. Mexico is the world's number one producer of organic coffee, and the vast majority of its 12,000 producers are indigenous peasants, organized into producer cooperatives. These farmers harvest approximately 6,000 tons of coffee per year (Bray, Sánchez, and Murphy 2002), most of which is channeled through fair trade, where producers receive higher prices for ecological and socially responsible production.[10] With minimum fair-trade prices at about $2.80/kilogram, this translates into about $16.8 million per year in foreign revenue. This revenue has had a significant impact on raising the incomes of poor indigenous farmers in coffee-producing communities, concentrated in the south of Mexico (Roozen and VanderHoff 2002). In addition, organic coffee production has helped protect the natural environment, and it has helped to finance small-scale community development projects (Moguel and Toledo 1999). However, the economic success of this movement needs to be kept in perspective: $16.8 million represent less than 0.2 percent of Mexico's agricultural export earnings in 2004.

The organic fair-trade coffee movement forms part of the larger agroecology movement analyzed in chapter 10, with the peculiarity of being oriented toward international markets. It has come from below, with virtually no support from the Mexican government. NGOs have been key players in conducting agroecological research, providing technical assistance, and constructing fair-trade networks. Financial support has come primarily from international institutions (Gómez-Cruz, Tovar, and Rindermann 2004). And, of course, most of the credit must be given to the indigenous farmers themselves for their productive and organizational capacity.

In sum, with the small but important exception of organic coffee, commercial farming has provided very few pathways out of rural poverty in Mexico. The structural reforms applied to the country's agricultural sector in the late 1980s and early 1990s have translated into adverse economic conditions for small-scale commercial farmers. During the 1990s and first years of the twenty-first century, these farmers were faced with a drop in producer prices, dramatically higher input costs, little or no access to credit, and the removal of marketing support. Although international grain prices have increased significantly over the past five years, small-scale farmers have been unable to benefit from this, given the oligopolistic market conditions, the concomitant rise in input costs (fertilizers, seeds, and fuel), and the unavailability of credit.

Rural Labor Markets and Wages

To what extent have rural labor markets provided more opportunities for Mexico's peasantry during the neoliberal era? The short answer is not at all. Between 1993 and 2006, the number of people employed in the agricultural sector dropped by over 30 percent, from 8.84 million to 6.03 million

(INEGI 2007). Furthermore, in approximately the same time period (1993 to 2004), real wages in the agricultural sector fell by 10 percent, and they were 40 percent lower than the national average (CEPAL 2005). Between 2000 and 2006, about 546,600 nonagricultural jobs were added to the rural sector. However, in the same period, over 1 million agricultural jobs were lost, resulting in a deficit of 640,000 jobs (González-Chávez and Macías Macías 2007). In short, the neoliberal reforms have resulted in fewer jobs that pay less. Moreover, labor conditions in the agricultural sector are deplorable. Agricultural workers are often exposed to dangerous agrochemicals, they live in cramped housing conditions, and they lack social security, among many other hardships.

Migration

To begin with, it is important to mention that migration is not a new phenomenon in Mexico. There has been migration from Mexico to the United States for well over a hundred years, and rural-urban migration has also been around long before neoliberal policies were put in place, reaching its apogee in the post–World War II period. However, it was not until the early 1990s that the Mexican government adopted rural policies that were explicitly designed to reduce the rural population.

So what has been the result? Has there been a mass exodus? In relative terms, the rural population has been decreasing rapidly since import-substituting industrialization policies were put in place that favored the urban industrial sector. In 1940, Mexico had a population of 20 million people, 65 percent of whom lived in rural areas. Today the population is 106 million, and only 23.5 percent live in rural areas (that is, in communities with fewer than 2,500 inhabitants). However, it was not until the beginning of the twenty-first century that the rural population began to diminish in absolute terms. Between 2000 and 2005, it decreased by half a million people, in spite of the fact that fertility rates are over 50 percent higher in the countryside (INEGI 2008).

The declining rural population is due, on one hand, to rural-urban migration and, on the other, to international migration. Although internal migration patterns in Mexico have become more complex during the past two decades, rural-urban migration is still an important phenomenon. Between 1995 and 2000, approximately 864,000 peasants migrated to urban centers (Anzaldo-Gómez 2003). Most of them end up working in the informal sector, where remuneration is very low.

As David Barkin (2001) observes, rural-urban migration does not always imply an abandonment of the countryside; it is often part of a temporary or multifaceted family strategy for generating the much-needed monetary income required to maintain roots in rural communities of origin. From this perspective, peasant and indigenous groups are not an anachronism destined to disappear but rather a manifestation of living cultures that have adapted and survived for centuries in spite of public policies that militate against them. From a different angle, precarious and low-paying labor markets in urban areas have forced rural migrants to stay connected with their communities of origin in order to reduce the risk of temporary unemployment and minimize the cost of raising a family (Grammont 2009).

International migration, for its part, is not usually associated with extreme poverty, because of the high cost of crossing the border illegally and of getting set up to work in the United States. On the other hand, since the 1990s, there has been an increase in the number of US-bound migrants from marginalized rural areas in Mexico, including the predominantly indigenous regions in the south. Like others, these migrants take advantage of social networks in order to overcome the costs and obstacles associated with international migration (Escobar 2005).

In this way, migration to the United States has burgeoned during the neoliberal era, in spite of the US government's attempts to control the border. In 1990, there were 4,447,000 Mexicans in the United States; over the course of the next decade, this number almost doubled, to 8,072,000. By 2007, the number had risen to 11,812,000 (CONAPO 2008). Approximately 40 percent of these people come from rural areas. So, in net terms, this translates to more than 200,000 people who leave rural Mexico and make it to the United States each year, though this appears to have tapered off significantly in the context of the current financial crisis.

Remittances have grown even faster. Between 1991 and 2001, money sent back from the United States increased by a factor of 3.5, from $2.66 billion to $8.90 billion. By the year 2004, this figure had increased to $16.6 billion, representing more than the total amount of foreign direct investment in Mexico during the same year, more than Mexico's foreign-currency earnings in tourism, and about 80 percent of its petroleum-export earnings (Durand 2007).[11] During the next four years, remittances grew at a somewhat slower rate to over $25 billion in 2008. However, in the context of the financial crisis, in 2009, remittances shrank by about 12 percent, according to Mexico's Central Bank.

It has been calculated that approximately 40 percent of remittances go to rural areas (CONAPO 2008). As we have seen, this influx of money is the main factor in preventing the countryside from falling deeper into poverty. From a different angle, although migration may be a pathway out of *income* poverty, it is not necessarily a pathway out of poverty conceptualized in more complex terms. Rural-urban migration usually implies having to live in urban slums, where violent crime and drugs run rampant. And international migration is wrought with sacrifices and dangers: hundreds of people die each year trying to cross the border, families are separated, women are left behind with heavier workloads, and illegal immigrants in the United States generally form part of the most marginalized segments of the US population. Taking all of this into consideration, one cannot help wonder if there are not alternative policies to overcoming poverty in rural Mexico.

Protests and Demands From Below

In the WDR-08, the World Bank stresses the need to foster the participation of independent peasant organizations in the formulation of agricultural policies. Ironically, this endorsement is accompanied with a caveat: "the challenge in building pro-agricultural coalitions . . . is to avoid creating political pressure for 'misinvestment' or to resist reforms" (World Bank 2008, 249). In other words, independent peasant organizations are welcome to participate in policy processes, as long as they go along with the neoliberal agenda.

Ruling politicians in Mexico seem to have the same view. For the past two decades, independent peasant and indigenous organizations have been proposing and demanding, inter alia, land redistribution, significantly higher levels of public investment in the rural sector, subsidies and marketing support for small-scale farmers, protectionist policies against dumping and volatile international markets, and constitutional changes designed to protect the special collective rights of indigenous groups. These demands, however, have fallen on deaf ears.

When Carlos Salinas assumed the presidency in 1988, he created the Permanent Agrarian Congress (CAP) and invited both independent and government-affiliated peasant organizations to participate. Then, by controlling negotiations with CAP, sidestepping resistance, and ignoring demands from below, he went on to carry out the structural reforms recently outlined, culminating in NAFTA.

The Zapatistas staged their uprising the same day that NAFTA came into effect. By their own account, Salinas's neoliberal reforms were the straw that broke the camel's back. After centuries of exclusion and oppression, Mexico's indigenous peoples said, "Enough!" The government entered into negotiations with them, and in 1996, representatives of the Zedillo administration signed the San Andrés Accords, designed to meet the demands of indigenous groups with respect to autonomy and self-determination. These accords were supposed to be the first of a series; however, the Mexican government has yet to honor them, forcing the Zapatistas to break off negotiations and turn toward autochthonous development in their base communities, without government support.

Negotiations with organizations representing small- and medium-scale commercial farmers have also resulted in broken agreements. In the mid-1990s, independent peasant organizations—linked to the international movement *La Vía Campesina*—began staging protests in the western and northern parts of the country, sometimes blocking roads with their tractors. Their demands included the renegotiation of the agricultural chapter of NAFTA, higher subsidies for the production of basic grains, guaranteed minimum prices, and the provision of credit at affordable rates. President Ernesto Zedillo responded by suspending some farmers' interest payments and providing other partial concessions, which helped to calm protests until the end of his term.

The protests, however, resumed in the first years of Vicente Fox's term, as small- and medium-sized farmers began to rally under the banner "*el campo no aguanta más*" (the countryside cannot take anymore). As part of this movement, in 2002, over a dozen national-level independent peasant organizations articulated a series of proposals for the salvation of the Mexican countryside, including the renegotiation of NAFTA's agricultural chapter, the participation of independent peasant organizations in policymaking processes, support for organic agriculture, and the assignment of 3 percent of Mexico's GDP to productive, social, and sustainable development in the countryside.[12] A year later, these proposals were partially incorporated into the National Accord for the Countryside (ANP), signed by the Fox administration but only superficially honored thereafter.

Since Felipe Calderón took office in 2006, smallholder farmer organizations have regrouped around the slogan "*Sin maíz no hay país y sin frijol tampoco*" (without maize or beans there is no country).[13] On January 1, 2008, the day that the last of NAFTA's import quotas was lifted, these organizations blocked a border entry from the United States and began staging protests throughout the country. Their demands are not new, and they are congruent with the *La Vía Campesina*'s demands on the international level (see chapter 10). They include the renegotiation of NAFTA's agricultural chapter, genuine participation of independent peasant organizations in policymaking processes, higher public investment in the rural sector (to increase agricultural production, improve rural diets, create nonagricultural jobs, and provide farmers with subsidized credit, technical training, and extension services), the application of the precautionary principle with regard to genetically modified organisms, government support for organic farming, reversals of the changes made in 1992 to Article 27 of the constitution and to the Agrarian Law, and the honoring of the San Andrés Accords (CNDSARC 2008). So far, the Calderón administration has shown no intention of meeting these demands. Instead, the Mexican government's reaction to the worldwide food crisis has been to increase the food-subsidy component of PROP and to further liberalize agricultural trade by lifting all tariffs and quotas on agricultural imports, regardless of their country of origin.

Conclusion

Under neoliberal reforms, economic conditions have greatly deteriorated in Mexico's agricultural sector. Small-scale commercial farmers have been especially hard hit with increased production costs, virtually no access to credit, and a lack of marketing support. In this way, the incidence of income poverty has stagnated at distressingly high levels, with remittances and *Oportunidades* being the two main factors preventing the countryside from falling deeper into income poverty.

Without jobs or commercial-farming opportunities in rural areas, peasants have migrated en masse toward urban centers and to the United States. While this often represents a pathway out of *income* poverty, it hardly represents an ideal solution for the 25 million Mexicans who still live in rural areas, many of them indigenous, linked to their communities of origin through tradition, family, and detailed knowledge of local ecosystems. Migration implies many risks and sacrifices. Mexico's cities are oversaturated with families living in slums and working in the informal sector, and the US government is trying desperately to prevent more illegal immigrants from entering the United States, making it progressively more dangerous to cross the border. Furthermore, once across the border, illegal immigrants face job insecurity and generally form part of the most marginalized segments of the US population.

On the international level, the neoliberal agenda has created a situation in which a handful of TNCs have come to dominate the agricultural-inputs markets, food processing, and supermarket chains. Under these conditions, over the past five years there has been a sensational rise in the cost of fertilizers and seeds. Food prices have also skyrocketed, driven by a host of factors, including increased interest in biofuels, rising demand for beef and cereals in developing countries, oligopolistic market conditions, and market speculation. The result is a global food crisis.

The *World Development Report 2008* promotes a continuation of the neo-liberal policy agenda, with some modest proposals for reform. This agenda is geared toward strengthening the corporate food regime. In contrast, independent peasant and indigenous organizations have articulated demands and proposals designed to make small-scale agroecological farming the cornerstone of an integrated rural development strategy. These demands include protectionist policies against the dumping of cheap grains and against the need to import expensive basic staples, the reorientation of existing subsidized programs in order to channel them primarily toward small-scale farmers, an increase in public investment in the rural sector, the reconstitution of inalienable *ejidal* rights, government support for organic agriculture, and the recognition of indigenous groups' right to autonomy and self-determination. The protagonists of *La Vía Campesina* and *sin maíz no hay país* argue that these alternatives represent a more a viable path for overcoming poverty in rural Mexico, one that would allow indigenous groups and peasants to remain in their communities of origin and increase their monetary income through farming, one that is more conducive to reducing food dependency and vulnerability on the national level, and one that lends itself to creating jobs in rural areas, conserving the natural environment, and preserving the positive elements of indigenous cultures.

Author's Note

An earlier version of this chapter was published in the *European Review of Latin American and Caribbean Studies* 88 (April 2010): 77–94.

Notes

1. The WDR-08 has been critically analyzed by several scholars of agrarian issues, for example, Akram-Lodhi (2008); Devereux, Scoones, and Thompson (2009); Kay (2009); and Veltmeyer (2009). Also see the five articles included in a special section of the WDR-08 in the *Journal of Agrarian Change* 9, no. 2 (2009).

2. In this typology, Mexico is considered to be an urbanized country, with agricultural-based regions, especially in the south, where the indigenous population is concentrated.

3. PIDER is the Spanish acronym for the Investment Program for Rural Development, SAM is the Mexican Food System, and COPLAMAR refers to the National Plan for Depressed Areas and Marginalized Groups.

4. Fertilizer prices have been particularly dynamic. Since 2006, the price of urea has increased by 150 percent, and the price of ammonium phosphate has increased sixfold (González Amador 2008). Under these conditions, Cargill's subsidiary, Mosaic Fertilizer, saw profits rise by 1,200 percent in the first quarter of 2007 (Holt-Giménez 2009).

5. Estimates regarding the number of PROCAMPO's beneficiaries vary. Because the government has organized information according to registered payment instead of individual farmers, it is impossible to know the exact number of beneficiaries. In any case, the figures frequently cited by top government officials tend to inflate the number (Fox and Haight 2010, 27).

6. The poverty line method is an indirect and unidimensional measurement of poverty based on income. Basically, it works as follows: a basket of essential goods is defined normatively, the cost of this basket is calculated, and then it is compared to household income. If a household's income is less than the cost of the basket, then the household is considered to be "poor." If the basket of goods includes only food, as is often the case, then to calculate less severe levels of poverty that take into consideration more than just nutritional needs, the cost of the basket is multiplied by an "expansion factor," generally defined as the inverse of Engel's coefficient. In this way, the poverty line method provides a head count of those whose incomes are below a certain level. This method is limited, however, in that it says nothing about how far one's income is below the poverty line or about the distribution of income among the poor. Moreover, it reflects an extremely limited conceptualization of poverty that does not take into consideration the satisfaction of quantifiable and nonquantifiable basic needs (Max-Neef 1986), the provision of basic public services, and the empowerment of marginalized groups.

7. ENIGH is the Spanish acronym for the National Survey of Income and Expenditure of Households, applied every two years to almost 30,000 households. Leaving aside the changes made to the questionnaire and sampling method in 2002, Boltvinik and others have argued that the income data collected through ENIGH is not reliable enough in itself to determine the evolution of poverty. From this point of view, it is necessary to make adjustments to national accounts. This is just one of the many points of controversy in the methodological debates regarding the poverty line method. For a review of these debates in the Mexican context, see Tetreault (2006).

8. For decades, the official definition of rural Mexico has been communities with fewer than 2,500 inhabitants. With an eye on population growth and nonpermanent migration patterns, Barkin (2006) and others argued that this underestimates the size of the rural population. The National Population Council (CONAPO) defines localities with fewer than 2,500 inhabitants as "rural" and those with between 2,500 and 14,999 inhabitants as "rural semi-urbanized." Of course, any dividing line is somewhat arbitrary, and choices must be based on research-specific regionalization criteria, taking into consideration data availability and comparability. For the purposes of this study, rural Mexico is defined as the population living in conglomerates of fewer than 2,500 people. In these areas, over half of the economically active population (EAP) is employed in the agricultural sector (including ranching, fishing, and hunting). By contrast, in towns of between 2,500 and 14,999 inhabitants, only 20 percent of the EAP is employed in this sector (INEGI 2007). Furthermore, Boltvinik and Damián (2003) observe that the poverty profile of these medium-sized towns is similar to that of larger urban centers.

9. Author's calculation, following CONEVAL's method and using data collected through the ENIGH 2008.

10. Although there is a strong overlap between organic production and fair trade in the coffee sector, the two do not necessarily go hand in hand; much of the coffee produced by Mexico's peasants is not organic and is not marketed as such.

11. As Durand (2007) observes, part of this dramatic increase in remittances is due to better accounting methods used by the Bank of Mexico. Other factors include (1) an increase in

the number of illegal migrants (who tend to send back more money than legal migrants) and (2) a moderate decrease in the transaction costs of sending money back from the United States, due to increased competition and denouncements against Money Gram and Western Union, which used to control the market and charge exorbitant fees.

12. Gómez-Cruz, Tovar, and Rindermann (2004) put forth a more detailed proposal with regard to how the Mexican government could support organic agriculture. The following elements are included in this proposal: (1) support for the formation of an independent National Organization of Organic Producers, (2) better defined laws and standards for organic farming, (3) creation of a National Certification System for Organic Production, (4) provision of direct and indirect subsidies for organic producers (for example, cash transfers, subsidized credit, reduced bureaucracy and costs for certification, and exemption from taxes), (5) actions geared toward fostering an internal market for organic products, and (6) creation of a National Centre for the Development of Organic Agriculture in Mexico, whose main responsibilities would be to carry out research and development in support of organic agriculture, to collect and disseminate pertinent information, to provide organic farmers with technical assistance, and to promote farmer-to-farmer knowledge transfer by training "peasant promoters."

13. The organizations affiliated with this movement include *Asociación Mexicana de Uniones de Crédito del Sector Social* (AMUCSS), *Asociación Nacional de Empresas Comercializadoras de Productores del Campo* (ANEC), *Central Campesina Cardenista* (CCC), *Central Independiente de Obreros Agrícolas y Campesinos, A.C.* (CIOAC), *Coalición de Organizaciones Democráticas Urbanas y Campesinas, A.C.* (CODUC), *Coordinadora Nacional de Organizaciones Cafetaleras* (CNOC), *Coordinadora Nacional Plan de Ayala* (CNPA), *Frente Democrático Campesino de Chihuahua* (FDCChih), *Red Mexicana de Organizaciones Campesinas Forestales* (RED MOCAF), *Unión Campesina Democrática* (UCD), *Unión Nacional de Organizaciones Regionales Campesinas Autónomas* (UNORCA), and *Unión Nacional de Trabajadores Agrícolas* (UNTA). It is interesting to note that seven of these organizations (UNORCA, ANEC, CCC, CIOAC, CODUC, CNPA, and FDCChih) are also officially affiliated with *La Vía Campesina*.

10

Agroecology and Food Sovereignty
The Peasant Pathway out of Poverty

Darcy Tetreault

Small-scale traditional farming is still widespread in Latin America. In fact, the peasant sector contributes significantly to national agricultural production, ranging from 27 percent in Chile to 67 percent in Nicaragua (ECLAC 2009). Despite decades of development policies hostile toward small farms, the number of peasants in the region has remained at about 75 million since the 1980s (Altieri 2010). So, why haven't they disappeared, as modernization theory would have it? From the perspective of the World Bank (2008), agricultural production under the model advanced by traditional and indigenous communities in the region is seen as not viable, unable to resist the forces of change that require of producers access to modern technology, markets, and capital. The farming path envisioned by the World Bank ultimately requires conversion into capitalist entrepreneurs who are also able to take advantage of economies of scale and organize production on the basis of the corporate capital model. Small-scale producers who are unable to compete are expected to abandon farming and find employment in other sectors of the economy or as agricultural wage laborers. In this view, the peasantry is destined to disappear, making room for more technologically advanced models of industrial agriculture.

We argue on the contrary that the proposals put forth by *La Vía Campesina* and the social movements in the region are both viable and more sustainable, allowing for smallholder farmers and ranchers to stay in their communities of origin and enjoy a high standard of living. In this chapter we describe and analyze agroecology and food sovereignty in Latin America, two overlapping and complementary movements that represent an alternative to the dominant mode of industrial agriculture and the existing corporate food agenda. Agroecology has proven to be an effective approach to increasing agricultural yields in a socially and ecologically sustainable manner, while the food sovereignty movement strives to radically reorient food and agricultural policy on the international and national levels. The confluence of these two movements seeks to put multifunctional small-scale farming at the center of a rural development strategy geared toward eradicating poverty; producing abundant, high-quality, and culturally appropriate food; and protecting the natural environment.

Agroecology

Agroecology is both a science and a movement. As a science it uses ecological theory to study, design, manage, and evaluate agricultural systems in an effort to make them more productive in an ecologically sustainable way. It goes beyond the technical considerations of organic farming by taking into consideration the cultural, socioeconomic, and environmental specificities of local settings. In Latin America, this has translated into an approach that uses traditional peasant and indigenous technologies as a starting point; applies modern science and participatory experimental procedures to increase yields, recycle nutrients, and conserve soil and water; and then disseminates successful ideas and techniques through farmer-to-farmer meetings and workshops. Instead of providing technical recipes for how to grow food, like in the industrial model, agroecology promotes a set of principles, including diversity, recycling of nutrients, and increased biological interactions and synergies (Rosset et al. 2011). As Altieri, Rosset, and Thrupp (1998) observed over ten years ago, "there are thousands of examples where rural producers in partnership with NGOs and other organizations, have promoted and implemented alternative, agroecological development projects which incorporate elements of both traditional knowledge and modern agricultural science, featuring resource-conserving yet highly productive systems such as polycultures, agroforestry, the integration of crops and livestock, etc."

As a movement, agroecology can be traced back to the 1970s, when social activists and NGOs—inspired by Paulo Freiri's approach to popular education, liberation theology, and participatory action research—began working with marginalized rural communities in different parts of Latin America. By this time, agrochemicals and other Green Revolution technologies had made their way into many traditional peasant and indigenous communities, often with the help of government extension services, leading to a host of environmental problems (for example, loss of soil fertility, pest infestations, and declining yields). NGOs sought to address these problems, to improve local diets, and to contribute to the development of locally appropriate technologies. Through the praxis of reflection-action-reflection, they also sought to facilitate a process of empowerment among the rural poor (Altieri 1990; Holt-Giménez 2006).

Along these lines, Holt-Giménez (2006) describes how the work of World Neighbors, a US-based NGO, helped to develop and spread simple composting and terrace-building techniques among Kaqchikel Mayan farmers, in Chimaltenango, Guatemala. These techniques allowed subsistence farmers to double or even triple their yields in just one or two years, leading to further experimentation and the establishment of a 900-member cooperative named Kato-Ki. As Holt-Giménez explains, this cooperative helped to train visiting farmers from Mexico, Panama, Costa Rica, and Honduras, before it was dismantled by the Guatemalan army during the 1980s anti-insurgency campaigns. Thereafter, with the help of NGOs, some of the cooperative's promoters managed to find jobs in sustainable agriculture projects in Mexico, Honduras, and Nicaragua (Holt-Giménez 2006). In this way, agroecology began to spread throughout the region, with exceptional rapidity in Nicaragua where peasants were well organized and receptive because of the Sandinista Revolution.

In Mexico, several NGOs were founded during the 1970s and 1980s to promote agroecology (for example, the Center for Ecodevelopment, the Environmental Studies Group, and Rural Studies and Peasant Assistance), generally staffed by urban middle-class professionals. Linkages were formed with indigenous peasant organizations to preserve and defend traditional ecological knowledge (Carruthers 1996). In this way, indigenous farmers emerged early on as the main protagonists of the agroecological movement in Mexico (Nigh 1992; Toledo 1992). Most of their produce was destined for autoconsumption or stayed in local markets. At the same time, in Oaxaca, the Union of Indigenous Communities of the Isthmus Region (UCIRI) was formed with the help of a Dutch priest by the name of Frans VanderHoff, who used liberation theology to help organize indigenous peasants to produce organic coffee for emerging niche markets in the global North (Roozen and VanderHoff 2002). This marked the beginning of organic fair-trade production in Mexico, which is now the largest exporter of certified organic coffee in the world. Although this movement has since revealed its limits and pitfalls, not the least of which is high levels of dependence on volatile international markets, it has contributed significantly to raising the incomes and consciousness of approximately 12,000 indigenous farmers in Mexico, organized into producer cooperatives.

According to Carruthers (1996), smallholder farmers in Mexico turned to agroecology in the context of the debt crisis, when the state began to withdraw subsidies for agricultural inputs and support for marketing. In this regard, many agriculturalists were simply too poor to buy agrochemicals. Likewise, in other parts of Latin America, "NGOs emerged as an attempt to fill the vacuum left by the withdrawal of the State (either by policy definition as in Chile or by lack of economic resources due to the debt as in Bolivia, Peru and most Central American countries) from peasant assistance programs" (Altieri 1990, 117). Working directly either with grassroots groups or with the cooperatives and unions that are in direct contact with the grassroots, these NGOs helped to develop alternative farming techniques aimed at improving the production of basic foods for autoconsumption, minimizing risk through increased crop and animal diversity, and enhancing the natural resource base through water, soil, and local germplasm conservation (Altieri 1990). This implied reevaluating peasant and indigenous technologies, then building on them with experimental techniques that rely on locally available inputs.

In the late 1980s and early 1990s, research began to emerge that shed new light on traditional and indigenous farming systems. For example, by examining six case studies of activities pursued by indigenous peoples in rain forest areas of Central America and South America, Clay (1988) observed efficient use of nutrients, intimate knowledge of local ecosystems, crop diversity, and other ecologically rational behavior. While warning not to romanticize about these systems, he recommended further research in order to draw lessons regarding their sustainability, before it is too late. From a different angle, Toledo (1990) stressed the ecological rationality of peasant production, characterized by energy efficiency, minimal external inputs, small plots of land, polycultures, and so on. Following Chayanov (1985), he also noted that these systems are geared primarily toward the reproduction of the basic peasant economic unit (that is, the family), and they are designed for long-term stability, as opposed to maximum production in one growing season.

By definition, subsistence farming produces very little surplus for the market. Hence, comparisons between traditional and modern farm-system prototypes have generally concluded that the former are less productive per unit of land. However, as Wilken (1987) and many others since him have pointed out, these comparisons are usually based on single-crop output, failing to take into account the multiple uses of land and labor in traditional agricultural systems. In any case, agroecology is not just about resuscitating traditional farming technology but also about making it more productive with modern science. Along these lines, recent research has found that small farms adhering to agroecological principles tend to be more productive than large monoculture farms, when total produce is taken into account (Altieri 2010). Furthermore, there is much evidence that small farmers make better stewards of natural resources, conserving biodiversity and better safeguarding the sustainability of production (see, for example, Bray, Sánchez, and Murphy 2002; Moguel and Toledo 1999; Rosset 2000).

As case studies of successful agroecological projects began accumulating throughout Latin America during the 1980s, it became apparent that broader institutional capacity was required to strengthen the movement and further disseminate knowledge and methodologies. With this in mind, eleven NGOs from eight Latin American countries joined together in 1989 to create the Latin American Consortium on Agroecology and Development (CLADES), with the mission to prevent the collapse of peasant agriculture by transforming it into a more sustainable and productive enterprise. More recently, the Latin American Scientific Society of Agroecology (SOCLA), headed by Miguel Altieri, was founded to promote the discussion and exchange of scientific information regarding agroecology. Among other projects, SOCLA set up the Latin American Agroecology Doctoral Program at the National University of Colombia. It also bears mentioning that there are numerous graduate and undergraduate university programs on agroecology throughout the region.

More important for our analysis, over the past few years the peasant and small-farm organizations that make up *La Vía Campesina* have incorporated agroecology into their agenda on food sovereignty. An important example is the Brazil's Landless Workers' Movement (MST), the largest rural movement in Latin America, with roots that date back to the late 1970s. Through land invasions and legal channels, the MST has redistributed over 14 million hectares to more than 1 million landless peasants, including former slum dwellers who go through a process of "repeasantization." Although the MST initially promoted a conventional agricultural production model in its settlements, when this proved to be economically and ecologically unsustainable in the 1990s, it turned to agroecology (Holt-Giménez 2009). Since 2000, the MST has made agroecology a national policy for orienting production in its settlements and for educational purposes.

Perhaps even more impressive is the Cuban experience with agroecology. After the collapse of the Soviet Union in 1989, and faced with a tightening US trade embargo, the country experienced acute food shortages. In the context of the Cold War, the agricultural sector had been heavily oriented toward export crops, especially sugarcane, and it had become highly dependent on Green Revolution technologies. With the sudden disappearance of 85 percent of their trade, Cuban farmers had to scramble to reorient production toward domestic needs, with far less access to external inputs. Between 1986 and 1995, per capita agricultural production dropped by over 5 percent, only to rebound in the late 1990s, as diesel-consuming tractors were replaced by animal traction, and petrochemicals were replaced by biological fertilizers and pest controls (Rosset et al. 2011). However, the most dramatic gains have been made since 2000, when agroecology began to spread rapidly through the countryside via the farmer-to-farmer methodology, with the organizational support of the National Association of Small Farmers (ANAP), linked to *La Vía Campesina*. Urban dwellers also adopted agroecology in the 1990s, planting gardens on rooftops and in backyards. The National Urban Agriculture Group (GNAU), a governmental agency working in concert with decentralized units on the provincial and local levels, helped to facilitate and coordinate this process (Koont 2008). The net result was a dramatic increase in the production of vegetables, beans, roots, tubers, and other crops, greatly surpassing precrisis levels, with only a fraction of the agrochemicals used in the 1980s (Rosset et al. 2011). In this way, the Cuban experience points toward the potential of agroecology as a strategy to increase global food production, without having to rely on petrochemicals and fossil fuels.

La Vía Campesina and Food Sovereignty

La Vía Campesina was formed in 1993, during an international meeting of peasant leaders from around the world, in Mons, Belgium. As Desmarais (2007) recounts, it had a "difficult birth" due to a conflict of interests between representatives of farm organizations and those of NGOs, the Paulo Freire Stichting Foundation in particular. The latter sought to speak on behalf of smallholder farmers and to use *La Vía Campesina* as a platform for participatory research. The peasant leaders gathered at Mons had a grander vision of forming "a farmer-led, autonomous peasant and farm movement of progressive organizations that would strive to build the capacity to articulate joint positions and policies in opposition to the neo-liberal model advocated by many national governments and international institutions" (Desmarais 2007, 94). To make this happen, farmers felt that they needed to make their own voices heard, implying the need for NGOs to step aside and limit their participation to a facilitative role. Those who were unwilling to do so, like the Paulo Freire Stichting Foundation, were pushed aside for the sake of autonomy. Within *La Vía Campesina* democratic decision making is sought through a participatory process that revolves around international conferences, held once every three or four years, to discuss and determine overarching strategies. These are preceded by regional conferences that are meant to ensure that peasant voices are being heard from the bottom up. Outside of the international conference, the International Coordinating Commission is the main decision-making and coordinating body, with equal gender and regional representation (Desmarais 2007).

Once consolidated into an autonomous coordinating network for peasant organizations worldwide, *La Vía Campesina* began challenging the neoliberal agenda in the agricultural arena. Its first appearance on the international stage was in 1995, at the Global Assembly on Food Security, held in Quebec City. The next year, it introduced the concept of food sovereignty at the World Food Summit in Rome, defining it as "the right of each nation to maintain and develop its own capacity to produce its basic foods respecting cultural and productive diversity" (*Vía Campesina*, cited in Wittman, Desmarais, and Wiebe 2010, 197). Subsequently, the concept was elaborated to include "the right of peoples to define their agricultural and food policies" (p. 200). Food sovereignty, defined in this way, is meant to challenge the once hegemonic notion of "food security" that had been woven into the neoliberal discourse since the 1980s.[1] In an oft-cited definition, the FAO defines "food security" as "a situation that exists when all people, at all times, have physical, social and economic access to sufficient, safe and nutritious food that meets their dietary needs and food preferences for an active and healthy life" (cited in Patel 2009, 664). Here, there is no mention of how, where, and by whom food shall be produced. From a neoliberal perspective, all of this is determined by market forces, which supposedly allocate the factors of production in the most efficient way possible. In contrast, by alluding to "the right of each nation," food sovereignty puts the onus on the state to support peasant production and to ensure a certain level of food self-sufficiency on the national level. This includes incentives for supporting sustainable agriculture and upholding health and safety standards. To give countries in the global South the ability and the right to protect and nurture their small-farm sector, *La Vía Campesina* seeks to radically revamp international trade agreements. At the same time, by making reference to "the right of peoples," the architects of food sovereignty recognize the importance of indigenous groups and local spaces for building radical alternatives to the corporate food regime.

The existing international order is often referred to as "the corporate food regime" in order to contrast it with earlier regimes[2] and to make reference to the dominance of large transnational corporations (TNCs) in agricultural-input markets, processing, and food distribution. To illustrate the point, just two companies, Archer Daniels Midland and Cargill, control three-quarters of the world grain trade (Vorley 2003), and the top four seed companies (Monsanto, DuPont, Syngenta, and Groupe Limagrain) control 44 percent of the global market (ETC Group n.d.). Likewise, food processing is increasingly concentrated in the hands of food giants like Nestlé, Tyson Foods, and Kraft, and food distribution is concentrated in national and international supermarket chains (Walmart, Loblaws, Carrefour, etc). According to the World Bank (2008), in some Latin American countries, as much as 60 percent of food is sold through supermarkets. Under these conditions, access to food—which should be a right, according to *La Vía Campesina*—is controlled by TNCs whose modus operandi is to maximize profits. Not surprisingly, these same TNCs have enjoyed record profits over the past five years, in the context of the current food crisis. Since 2006, grain and food prices have soared, due to a number of factors, including increased production of biofuels, rising demand for beef and cereals in developing countries, oligopolistic market conditions, and financial speculation. At the same time, the number of chronically hungry people in the world has swelled to over one billion.

How can food sovereignty supplant the corporate food regime and address this crisis? Part of the answer lies in the mobilization of the peasantry and alliance building with progressive segments of civil society. *La Vía Campesina* has taken a lead role in the antiglobalization movement (more accurately the "alternative globalization movement"), with a visible presence among participants in protest marches around the world, especially during WTO meetings. Recently, *La Vía Campesina* participated in, and helped to coordinate, protests and an alternative forum around the United Nations Climate Change Conference (COP-16) in Cancún, at the end of 2010. At this event, internationally organized peasants sent out a clear message: small-scale farming, based on the principles of agroecology, not only helps to cool the planet and mitigate the pernicious effects of climate change but also is the best way to overcome poverty. It does not depend on fossil fuels, and it is more resilient to extreme weather events such as hurricanes and droughts, as evidenced by the research conducted in Honduras and Cuba by Holt-Giménez (2000) and Rosset et al. (2011), respectively.

During the 1990s, trade liberalization and the withdrawal of government subsidies and marketing support for Latin American farmers led to an influx of underpriced grains from the United States and Europe, combined with high prices for conventional farming inputs (for example, agrochemicals, seeds, machinery, irrigation, and credit). As a result, small-scale commercial farming became economically unviable for millions of Latin American peasants, forcing them to leave the countryside (temporarily or permanently) in search of more lucrative opportunities in urban centers or abroad. Agricultural policies were reoriented to support agroindustrial export-oriented production, with an increased emphasis on high-value luxury food items consumed by the upper and middle classes. Basic grains were imported cheaply from the United States and elsewhere at prices well below their cost of production, thanks to heavy government subsidies, captured mainly by transnational agribusiness. This seemed to make sense from a Ricardian point of view, which stresses the virtues of specialization and free trade, based on the principle of comparative advantage. However, since 2006, the price of basic grains has shot up, peaking first in 2008 and reaching unprecedented heights during the first months of 2011. Under these conditions, countries that are net importers of food—including most Latin American countries—have had to pay dearly for their dependence on foreign markets.

Food sovereignty implies greater food self-sufficiency on the local and national levels, without going to the extremes of autarky. This requires a reversal of many of the neoliberal reforms implemented during the 1980s and the 1990s, including protectionist policies to guard against dumping and volatile markets. From this perspective, the availability of food should not depend on the whims of speculative investment and the profit-maximizing strategies of TNCs. Thus, *La Vía Campesina* calls on governments to foster a turn toward sustainable family-farm-based production, instead of subsidizing corporate-led and export-oriented production. Public policy should encourage organic farming based on indigenous knowledge and sustainable agricultural practices (that is, agroecology). The idea is to develop local food economies, grounded in diversified small-scale farming and local processing.

What measures need to be taken in order to facilitate this transition? In a statement titled *Priority to Peoples Food Sovereignty*, prepared in 2001 by *La Vía Campesina* and a number of other organizations belonging to the Our World Is Not For Sale Coalition, the following proposals were made: (1) ban dumping and put in place market policies that ensure adequate prices for all farmers (that is, tariffs and price controls); (2) abolish all direct and indirect export supports and phase out domestic production subsidies that promote unsustainable agriculture and inequitable land-tenure patterns; (3) implement genuine agrarian reform to ensure that peasants have access to land, seed, water, and other resources; (4) target support at integrated family farms with low external input; and (5) regulate large companies, inter alia, by prohibiting biopiracy and patenting life, banning the production of and trade in genetically modified organisms, and putting in place labeling and other quality control mechanisms. Of course, because of the existing global economic structures, this agenda is politically difficult to implement, even where progressive governments are willing to do so. Accordingly, the aforementioned coalition (led by *La Vía Campesina*) also seeks radical reforms on the international level, starting with one clear demand: get the WTO out of food and agriculture! From this perspective, the WTO cannot be radically reformed. In its place, the coalition proposes an alternative international framework for sustainable production and trade of food and agricultural goods with the following characteristics: (1) a reformed and strengthened United Nations, (2) an independent dispute-settlement mechanism to prevent dumping (administered by an international Court of Justice), (3) a legally binding international treaty linked to the UN Charter of Human Rights to define the rights of peasants, and (4) an international convention constructed around the concept of food sovereignty.

Conclusion

According to the World Bank (2008), another Green Revolution is needed to increase food production at a sufficient rate to feed the world's population, which continues to grow at a rate of just over 1 percent per year. The Malthusian threat, in this view, must be kept in check with profit-motivated technological innovation and ever-increasing levels of economic efficiency, best achieved through free trade, international competition, and economies of scale. The problem, however, is not that there is not enough food; today there is more food per capita available than ever before.[3] This has resulted in a situation that Raj Patel (2008) calls "stuffed and starved" whereby "half the world is malnourished, the other half obese—both symptoms of the corporate food monopoly."

While the Green Revolution of the post–World War II period was enormously successful in increasing aggregate food production on the global level, the costs and benefits have been poorly distributed. Today, approximately one-sixth of humanity suffers from chronic hunger. Extreme poverty is largely concentrated in rural areas, where peasants eke out a living on marginal farmlands. Moreover, the first generation of Green Revolution technologies (hybrid seeds, monocultures, mechanization, and technically exact combinations of irrigation, chemical fertilizers, herbicides, and pesticides) has caused diverse forms of environmental deterioration, denounced in the early 1960s by Rachel Carson. In addition to the health risks posed by toxic contamination, the industrialized agriculture model has had to confront problems of declining soil fertility, plagues, depletion of aquifers, salinization, and so on, especially in the global South.

The latest stage of the Green Revolution has been centered on genetically modified (GM) seeds, with dubious benefits and considerable health and environmental risks. There is much scientific debate surrounding GM seeds, inextricably intertwined with ideological positions and political agendas. What is certain is that GM seeds have genetically contaminated landrace varieties in unexpected places such the Sierra Norte, Oaxaca. In this and other ways, the spread of GM seeds threatens to displace landrace varieties, which have been developed over the course of thousands of years, adapted to local ecosystems and palates, and conserved in situ by traditional peasants and indigenous groups. These landrace varieties constitute an invaluable pool of genetic resources, ironically needed to replenish the properties of commercial seeds, so as to make them more resistant to new plant diseases and pest infestations.

With all of this in mind, it is extremely unlikely that a corporate-led continuation of the Green Revolution will address third world hunger. We argue that an alternative approach based on the principles of agroecology and food sovereignty is needed. This alternative assigns agriculture a multifunctional role that goes far beyond mere commodity production; it includes overcoming poverty, reducing social and gender inequality, reversing environmental degradation, stabilizing rural communities, and stopping the hemorrhage of emigration. As McMichael and Schneider (2011) suggest, it comes down to a question of whether agriculture should be a servant to economic growth or recognized as an activity that performs these multiple functions, all of which revolve around the production of safe, abundant, and culturally appropriate foods. Insofar as there has been a confluence between agroecology and food sovereignty (Holt-Giménez 2009; Holt-Giménez and Shattuck 2011), the 149 organizations grouped together in *La Vía Campesina* (including 57 from Latin America) are struggling toward making this alternative vision a reality. This is happening in peasant communities all over the region, where farmer-to-farmer technology transfers are reshaping agricultural practices, and it is happening on the world stage, through peaceful actions of protest and demand. Success will ultimately depend on global political forces and the ability of radical social movements to tip the balance of power in favor of progressive change.

Notes

1. For a conceptual and etymological analysis of food sovereignty and food security, see Patel (2009).

2. The concept of "food regimes" was developed by Friedmann and McMichael (1989) and further analyzed by McMichael (2009b) to identify three periods in the structure of global trade, food production, and distribution. The first encompasses the period between 1870 and the 1930s, during the first liberal era of free trade, with Great Britain at the center of the world economy, when Europe imported tropical commodities from its colonies in the global South, combined with basic grains and livestock from ex-colonial and settler states in temperate zones (that is, the United States, Canada, Australia, Argentina, Uruguay, South Africa). After the Great Depression and World War II, a second regimen emerged under US hegemony, with grain surpluses redirected to postcolonial states in the form of food aid, in an effort to secure loyalty in the context of the Cold War. During this period, which lasted until the 1970s, most Latin American countries adopted an import-substituting-industrialization strategy, assigning the main role of food production to large-scale commercial farming units, nurtured with subsidies, protective trade barriers, and Green Revolution technologies. The corporate food regime emerged in the late 1980s in the context of the debt crisis and the ascendance of free trade, privatization, and deregulation. In Latin America and elsewhere, this translated into the dismantling of state agencies that had provided farmers with subsidized agricultural inputs and marketing support, the rise of transnational agribusiness and supermarket chains, and an increased focus on industrial, export-oriented agricultural production.

3. While 2010 may have been a bad year for basic grain production on the global level (FAO 2010), it is too early to tell whether this marks the beginning of a new trend toward falling production, something that has been predicted for years with an eye on climate change and soil exhaustion.

Bibliography

Abrahamson, Rita. 2004. "The Power of Partnerships in Global Governance." *Third World Quarterly* 25, no. 8: 1453–67.

Adams, Dale, Doug Graham, and J. D. Von Pischke, eds. 1984. *Undermining Rural Development with Cheap Credit*. Boulder, CO: Westview.

Adato, Michelle. 2004. "Programas de Transferencias Monetarias Condicionadas: Beneficios y Costos Sociales." In *La Pobreza en México y el Mundo: Realidades y Desafíos*, edited by J. Boltvinik and A. Damián, 348–63. Mexico DF: Siglo XXI.

Adelman, Irma. 1986. "A Poverty Focused Approach to Development Policy." In *Development Strategies Reconsidered*, edited by J. P. Lewis. Reprinted in Wilber, C. K., *The Political Economy of Underdevelopment*, 4th ed., 493–507. New York: Random House.

Aguiar, Marcelo. 2006. *Educacao e Oportunidades: O Exemplo Mexicano*. Brasília: Missao Crianca.

Akram-Lodhi, Haroon. 2008. "(Re)imagining Agrarian Relations? The World Development 2008: Agriculture for Development." *Development and Change* 39, no. 6: 1145–61.

———. 2011. "Critical Rural Development Studies." In *The Critical Development Studies Handbook: Tools for Change*, edited by H. Veltmeyer, 172–74. Halifax: Fernwood.

Akram-Lodhi, Haroon, Saturnino Borras Jr., and Cristóbal Kay, eds. 2007. *Land, Poverty and Livelihoods in an Era of Neoliberal Globalization: Perspectives from Developing and Transition Countries*. London: Routledge.

Alarcon, Diana. 2004. *Priorities and Strategies in Rural Poverty Reduction: Experiences from Latin America and Asia*. Washington, DC: Inter-American Development Bank.

Alcaldias Municipales. 2000. *Estrategia de Reducción de la Pobreza: Leon Norte*. Leon Norte: Ibis.

Alkire, Sabina, and Maria Emma Santos. 2010. "Acute Multidimensional Poverty: A New Index for Developing Countries." Oxford Poverty and Human Development Initiative Working Paper No. 38. http://www.ophi.org.uk/wp-content/uploads/ophi-wp38.pdf.

Allen, Katie. 2010. "Food Prices to Rise by Up to 40% Over Next Decade, UN Report Warns." *The Guardian*, June 15. http://www.guardian.co.uk/business/2010/jun/15/food-prices-rise-un-report.

Alonso, Jorge. 1998. "FOBAPROA: Another State Party Crime." *Envio Digital*, no. 207. Accessed August 20, 2010. http://www.envio.org.ni/articulo/1357.

Alove, Robert F. 1995. "Education as Contested Terrain in Nicaragua." *Comparative Education Review* 39, no. 1: 28–53.

Altieri, Miguel. 1990. "Agroecology and Rural Development in Latin America." In *Agroecology and Small Farm Development*, edited by M. Altieri and S. Hecht, 113–18. Boca Raton, FL: CRC Press.

———. 2010. "Scaling Up Agroecological Approaches for Food Sovereignty in Latin America." In *Food Sovereignty: Reconnecting Food, Nature and Community*, edited by H. Wittman, A. Desmarais, and N. Wiebe, 120–33. Halifax: Fernwood.

Altieri, Miguel, Peter Rosset, and Lori Ann Thrupp. 1998. "The Potential of Agroecology to Combat Hunger in the Developing World." In *Food First Policy Brief*, no. 2. Oakland: Institute for Food and Development Policy.

Alvarez, Carola. 2006. "Oportunidades: Presente y Futuro. Temporalidad y Graduación." Presented at the seminar Oportunidades: Presente Futuro, Instituto Nacional de Salud Público, Juitepec, Mexico, Universidad Iberoamerica, CIDE, CIESAS.

Amanor, Kojo Sebastian. 2009. "Global Food Chains, African Smallholders and World Bank Governance." *Journal of Agrarian Change* 9, no. 2: 247–62.

Amin, Sajeda, Ashok S. Rai, and Giorgio Ropa. 2003. "Does Microcredit Reach the Poor and Vulnerable? Evidence from Northern Bangladesh." *Journal of Development Economics* 70, no. 1: 59–82.

Anaya-Zamora, Juan Manuel. 2007. "El Programa Oportunidades y la Generacioón de Capital Social en Tatahuicapan de Juárez, Veracruz. La Experiencia de Tres Actores: Beneficiarias, Vocales y Enlaces Municipales." Master's thesis, CIESAS, Guadalajara.

Angelucci, Manuela, and Attanasio Orazio. 2009. "Oportunidades: Program Effect on Consumption, Low Participation, and Methodological Issues." *Economic Development and Cultural Change* 57, no. 3: 479–506.

Anzaldo-Gómez, Carlos. 2003. *Tendencias Recientes de la Urbanización*. Mexico DF: CONAPO.

Arana, Mario. 1997. "General Economic Policy." In *Nicaragua without Illusions: Regime Transition and Structural Adjustment in the 1990s*, edited by T. W. Walker. Delaware: Scholarly Resources.

Arim, Rodrigo, and Andrea Vigorito. 2006. *Las Políticas de Transferencias de Ingresos y Su Rol en Uruguay, 2001–2006*. Washington, DC: World Bank. Accessed March 1, 2012. http://siteresources.worldbank.org/INTURUGUAYINSPANISH/Resources/TRANSFERENCIAINGRESOSDic06.pdf.

Armas Dávila, Amparo. 2004. "La Equidad de Género y el Programa del Bono de Desarrollo Humano en Ecuador." In *Aprender de la Experiencia: El Capital Social en la Superación de la Pobreza*, edited by I. Arriagada. Santiago, Chile: CEPAL.

Arriagada, Irma, and Carlos Barba Solano. 2007. *¿Reducir la Pobreza o Construir Ciudadanía Social para Todos? América Latina: Regímenes de Bienestar en Transición al Iniciar el Siglo XXI*. Guadalajara: Universidad de Guadalajara.

Arriagada, Irma, and Charlotte Mathivet. 2007. "Los Programas de Alivio a la Pobreza Puente y Oportunidades: Una Mirada desde los Actors." In *Serie Políticas Sociales*, no. 134. Santiago, Chile: CEPAL.

Arriagada, Irma, and Francisca Miranda. 2005. "Propuestas para el Diseño de Programas de Superación de la Pobreza desde el Enfoque de Capital Social." In *Aprender de la Experiencia: El Capital Social en la Superación de la Pobreza*, edited by I. Arriagada, 197–228. Santiago, Chile: CEPAL.

Arroyo-Picard, Alberto. 2003. "Crítica de dos Décadas de Política Salarial y Fundamento para una Alternativa Viable." In *Hacia la Transformación de la Política Social en México*, edited by M. Gendreau and E. Valencia. Puebla y Guadalajara: Universidad Iberoamericana Puebla, ITESO, Universidad de Guadalajara, UNICEF, INDESOL/SEDESOL.

Assmann, Hugo. 1980. "El 'Progresismo Conservador' del Banco Mundial." In *Banco Mundial: Un Caso de "Progresismo Conservador,"* edited by H. Assmann. San José: Departamento Ecuménico de Investigaciones.

Atal, Yogesh, and Else Yen, eds. 1995. "Poverty and Participation in Civil Society." Proceedings of a UNESCO/CROP Round Table, World Summit for Social Development, Copenhagen, Denmark, March.

Atria, Raúl, ed. 2004. *Social Capital and Poverty Reduction in Latin America and the Caribbean: Towards a New Paradigm.* Santiago, Chile: ECLAC.

Ayres, Robert. 1983. *Banking on the Poor: The World Bank and World Poverty.* London: MIT Press.

Babb, Florence E. 1996. "After the Revolution: Neoliberal Policy and Gender in Nicaragua." *Latin American Perspectives* 23, no. 1: 27–48.

Babb, Sarah. 2009. *Behind the Development Banks: Washington Politics, World Poverty, and the Wealthy of Nations.* Chicago and London: University of Chicago Press.

Bailey, John. 1994. "Centralism and Political Change in Mexico: The Case of National Solidarity." In *Transforming State-Society Relations in Mexico: The National Solidarity Strategy,* edited by W. Cornelius, A. Craig, and J. Fox, 97–119. La Jolla, CA: Center for US-Mexican Studies.

Banegas, O., S. Jarrin, S. Escobar de Pabon, B. Rojas, H. Nusselder, and A. Sanders. 2002. *HIVOS Outreach and Impact of Microcredit: Case Studies of Banco Solidario (Ecuador) and Caja los Andes (Bolivia).* Centro de Estudios para el Desarrollo Rural. Free University of Amsterdam, mimeo San Jose.

Banerjee, Abhijit V., and Esther Duflo. 2003. "Inequality and Growth: What Do the Data Say?" *Journal of Economic Growth* 8, no. 3: 267–99.

———. 2011. *Poor Economics: A Radical Rethinking of the Way to Fight Global Poverty.* New York: Public Affairs.

Barba Solano, Carlos. 2006. "Las Reformas Económica y Social en América Latina: Regímenes de Bienestar en Transición." In *Alternancia, Políticas Sociales y Desarrollo Regional en México,* edited by G. Ordónez, R. Enriques, I. Román, and E. Valencia, 51–83. Tijuana and Guadalajara: El Colegio de la Frontera Norte, ITESO, Universidad de Guadalajara.

———. 2007. *¿Reducir la Pobreza o Construir Ciudadanía Social para Todos? América Latina: Regímenes de Bienestar en Transición al Iniciar el Siglo XXI.* Guadalajara: Universidad de Guadalajara.

———. 2010a. "La Reforma de la Ley General de Salud en México y la Creación del Seguro Popular: ¿Hacia la Cobertura Universal?" In *Perspectivas del Universalismo en México,* edited by E. Valencia, 87–102. Guadalajara: ITESO y Universidad de Guadalajara.

———. 2010b. "Los Estudios sobre la Pobreza en América Latina." Special issue, *Revista Mexicana de Sociología* 71: 9–49.

Barba Solano, Carlos, Anete B. L. Ivo, Enrique Valencia Lomelí, and Alicia Ziccardi. 2005. "Research Horizon: Poverty in Latin America." In *The Polyscopic Landscape of Poverty Research: "State of the Art" in International Poverty Research,* edited by E. Oyen, 29–60. Bergen, Norway: CROP.

Barkin, David. 2001. "La Nueva Ruralidad y la Globalización." In *La Nueva Ruralidad en América Latina,* edited by E. Pérez Correa and M. A. Farah Quijano, 21–40. Bogotá: Pontificia Universidad Javeriana.

———. 2006. "Building a Future for Rural Mexico." *Latin American Perspectives* 33, no. 2: 132–40.

Barros, Flávia. 2005. "Banco Mundial e ONGs Ambientalistas Internacionais: Ambiente, Desenvolvimento, Governança Global e Participação da Sociedade Civil." Diss., Universidade Nacional da Brasília, Brazil.

Batista Jr., Paulo Nogueira. 1996. "O Plano Real à Luz da Experiência Mexicana e Argentina." *Estudos Avançados* 10, no. 28: 129–97.

Bebbington, Anthony. 2005. "Estrategias de Vida y Estrategias de Intervención: El Capital Social y los Programas de Superación de la Pobreza." In *Aprender de la Experiencia: El Capital Social en la Superación de la Pobreza*, edited by I. Arriagada, 21–46. Santiago, Chile: ECLAC.

Bebbington, Anthony, Samuel Hickey, and Diana C. Mitlin, eds. 2008. *Can NGOs Make a Difference? The Challenge of Development Alternatives*. London: Zed Books.

Bebczuk, Ricardo. 2008. "Financial Inclusion in Latin America and the Caribbean: Review and Lessons." *Documento de Trabajo*, no. 68. Mayo, CEDLAS, Universidad Nacional de La Plata.

Behrman, Jere, Lia Fernald, Paul Gertler, Lynnette Neufeld, and Susan Parker. 2008. "Evaluación de los Efectos a Diez Años de Oportunidades en el Desarrollo, Educación y Nutrición en Niños entre 7 y 10 Años de Familias Incorporadas desde el Inicio del Programa." In *Evaluación Externa del Programa Oportunidades 2008, a Diez Años de Intervención en Zonas Rurales (1997–2007)*, edited by SEDESOL, 15–18. Mexico DF: SEDESOL.

Behrman, Jere, Alejandro Gaviria, and Miguel Székely, eds. 2003. *Who's In and Who's Out: Social Exclusion in Latin America*. Washington, DC: Inter-American Development Bank.

Behrman, Jere, Susan Parker, and Petra Todd. 2009. "Schooling Impacts of Conditional Cash Transfers on Young Children: Evidence from Mexico." Accessed March 2, 2012. http://athena.sas.upenn.edu/~petra/papers/schoolingimpactsedcc.pdf.

Behrman, Jere, Piyali Sengupta, and Petra Todd. 2000. "El Impacto de Progresa sobre el Rendimiento Escolardurante el Primer Año de Operación." In *Progresa. Educación. Evaluación de resultados del Programade Educación, Salud y Alimentación*, 125–83. Mexico DF: SEDESOL.

Behrman, Jere, and Emmanuel Skoufias. 2006. "Mitigating Myths about Policy Effectiveness: Evaluation of Mexico's Antipoverty and Human Resource Investment Program." *American Academy of Political Science* 606: 244–75.

Béland, Daniel, and Mitchell Orenstein. 2009. "How Do Transnational Policy Actors Matter?" Paper presented in annual meeting of the Research Committee 19 of the International Sociological Association, Montreal, August.

Bello, Walden. 2008. "*Globalization, Development, and Democracy: A Reflection on the Global Food Crisis.*" CASID keynote lecture, University of British Colombia, Vancouver, June 6.

———. 2009. "The Global Collapse: A Non-Orthodox View." Accessed February 22, 2009. http://www.zmag.org/znet/viewArticle/20638.

Beneria, Lourdes, and Breny Mendoza. 1995. "Structural Adjustment and Social Emergency Funds: The Case of Honduras, Mexico, and Nicaragua." *European Journal of Development Research* 7, no. 1: 53–76.

Berberoglu, Berch. 2002. *Labor and Capital in the Age of Globalization*. Lanham, MD: Rowman and Littlefield.

Berger, Marguerite, Lara Goldmark, and Tomas Miller. 2006. *An Inside View of Latin American Microfinance*. Washington, DC: Inter-American Development Bank.

Bertelsen, Mette Frost, and Soren Kirk Jensen. 2002. "Poverty Reduction Strategies: A Possibility for Participatory Economic Policy Making? The Central American Experience." Accessed March 2, 2012. www.eurodad.org/uploadstore/cms/docs/honduras_and_nicaragua_PRSp .pdf.

Bessis, Sophia. 1985. "De la Exclusión Social a la Cohesión Social." *Síntesis del Coloquio de Roskilde*. World Summit for Social Development, Copenhagen, Denmark, March.

Bienefeld, Manferd. 2000. "Structural Adjustment: Debt Collection Device or Development Policy?" *Review Fernand Braudel Center* 23, no. 4: 533–87.

Birdsall, Nancy. 1997. "On Growth and Poverty Reduction: Distribution Matters." Remarks at the Conference on Poverty Reduction, Harvard Institute for International Development, February 8.

Boisier, Sergio, Francisco Sabatini, Verónica Silva, Ana Soja, and Patricio Vergara. 1992. *La Descentralización: El Eslabón Perdido de la Cadena Transformación Productiva con Equidad y Sustentabilidad*. Santiago, Chile: Cuadernos de CEPAL.

Boltvinik, Julio. 2004. "Políticas Focalizadas de Combate a la Pobreza en México: El PROGRESA/ Oportunidades." In *La Pobreza en México y el Mundo: Realidades y Desafíos*, edited by J. Boltvinik and A. Damián, 315–47. Mexico DF: Siglo XXI.

———. 2006a. "La Ley General de Desarrollo Social: Génesis, Logros, Limitaciones y Riesgos." In *Alternancia, Políticas Sociales y Desarrollo Regional en México*, edited by G. Ordónez, R. Enriques, I. Román, and E. Valencia, 123–46. Tijuana and Guadalajara: El Colegio de la Frontera Norte, ITESO, Universidad de Guadalajara.

———. 2006b. "Los Fracasos de Fox/ II." *La Jornada*, June 2.

———. 2010. "Ingreso Ciudadano Universal y Economía Moral." In *Perspectivas del Universalismo en México*, edited by E. Valencia, 179–94. Guadalajara: Universidad de Guadalajara e ITESO.

Boltvinik, Julio, and Araceli Damián. 2003. "Evolución y Características de la Pobreza en México." *Comercio Exterior* 53, no. 6: 519–31.

———, eds. 2004. *La Pobreza en México y el Mundo: Realidades y Desafíos*. Mexico DF: Siglo XXI.

Booth, David. 2003. "PRSPs: Introduction and Overview." *Development Policy Review* 21, no. 2: 131–59.

———. 2005. "Missing Links in the Politics of Development: Learning from the PRSP Experiment." Working Paper, ODI. Accessed April 1, 2008. www.odi.org_uk/publications/ working_ papers/ wp256.pdf.

Borges Sugiyama, Natasha. 2011. "Bottom-up Policy Diffusion: National Emulation of a Conditional Cash Transfer Program in Brazil." *Publius: The Journal of Federalism* 42, no. 1: 25–51.

Bouillon, Céasar, and Luis Tejerina. 2006. "Do We Know What Works? A Systematic Review of Impact Evaluations of Social Programs in Latin America and the Caribbean." Working Paper, Unit Poverty Inequality, Sustainable Development, IDB, Washington, DC.

Bourguignon, François, Francisco Ferreira, and Phillippe Leite. 2003. "Conditional Cash Transfers, Schooling and Child Labor: Micro-simulating Bolsa Escola." Working Paper 2003–07, Department of Labor, CNRS, EHESS, ENS, Paris.

Bourguignon, François, Francisco Ferreira, and Nora Lustig. 2005. *The Microeconomics of Income Distribution Dynamics in East Asia and Latin America*. Washington, DC: World Bank and Oxford University Press.

Braathen, Einar. 2006. *A Participatory Pathbreaker? Experiences with Poverty Reduction Strategy Paper from Four African Countries.* Oslo: Norwegian Institute for Urban and Regional Research.

Bradshaw, Sarah, and Brian Linneker. 2002. "Civil Society Responses to Poverty Reduction Strategies in Nicaragua." *Progress in Development Studies* 3, no. 2: 147–58.

Bradshaw, Sarah, Brian Linneker, and Ana Quiros Viquez. 2004. *Evaluation of the Development of the Poverty Reduction Strategy in Nicaragua.* Managua: La Coordinadora Civil.

Brand, Ulrich. 2005. "Order and Regulation: Global Governance as a Hegemonic Discourse of International Politics." *Review of International Political Economy* 12, no. 1: 155–76.

Braun, Miguel, and Mariana Chudnovsky. 2005. *Transferencias Condicionadas en Efectivo Como Estrategia de Reducción de la Pobreza: Un Estudio Comparativo en América Latina.* Washington, DC: BID.

Bray, David, José Luis Plaza Sánchez, and Ellen Contreras Murphy. 2002. "Social Dimensions of Organic Coffee Production in Mexico: Lessons for Eco-Labeling Initiatives." *Society and Natural Resources* 15: 429–46.

Brenner, Robert. 2003. *O Boom e a Bolha: Os Estados Unidos na Economia Mundial.* Rio de Janeiro: Record.

Bresser-Pereira, Luiz Carlos. 2006. "El Nuevo Desarrollismo y la Ortodoxia Convencional." *Economia UNAM* 4, no. 10: 7–29.

Britto, Tatiana. 2004. "Conditional Cash Transfers: Why Have They Become So Prominent in Recent Poverty Reduction Strategies in Latin America?" Working Paper 390, ISS, The Hague, Netherlands.

———. 2006. "Conditional Transfers in Latin America." *Poverty in Focus*, 3–5.

———. 2007. "Challenges of El Salvador's Conditional Cash Transfer: Red Solidaria." *Country Study*, no. 9.

Brown, David. 2004. "Participation in Poverty Reduction Strategies: Democracy Strengthened or Democracy Undermined?" In *Participation: From Tyranny to Transformation?*, edited by S. Hickey and M. Mohan. London: Zed Books.

Brown, Michael Barrat. 1995. *Africa's Choices after Thirty Years of the World Bank.* Boulder, CO: Westview.

Bruhn, Kathleen. 1996. "Social Spending and Political Support: The 'Lessons' of the National Solidarity Program in Mexico." *Comparative Politics* 28, no. 2: 151–77.

Bryceson, Deborah Fahy, and Leslie Bank. 2001. "End of an Era: Africa's Development Policy Parallax." *Journal of Contemporary Africa* 19, no. 1: 5–23.

Bulmer-Thomas, Victor. 1996. *The New Economic Model in Latin America and Its Impact on Income Distribution and Power.* New York: St. Martin's Press.

Burbach, Roger, and Barbara Flynn. 1982. *Agroindústria nas Américas.* Rio de Janeiro: Zahar.

Burkett, Paul. 1990. "Poverty Crisis in the Third World: The Contradictions of World Bank Policy." *Monthly Review* 42, no. 7: 20–32.

Bustelo, Pablo. 1999. *Teorías Contemporáneas del Desarrollo Económico.* Madrid: Editorial Sintesis.

Calva, José Luis. 2002. "Disyuntiva Agrícola." *El Universal*, November 8.

Cammack, Paul. 2002a. "Ataque a los Pobres." *New Left Review* 13: 104–12.

———. 2002b. "The Mother of All Governments: The World Bank's Matrix for Global Governance." In *Global Governance: Global Perspectives*, edited by R. Wilkenson and S. Hughes, 36–53. Oxford: Routledge.

————. 2004. "What the World Bank Means by Poverty Reduction, and Why It Matters." *New Political Economy* 9, no. 2: 189–211.

Carroll, Toby. 2005. "Efficiency of What and for Whom? The Theoretical Underpinnings of the Post-Washington Consensus Socio-institutional Neoliberalism." Working Paper No. 122, Asia Research Centre. Accessed December 10, 2006. http://www.arc.murdoch.edu.au/wp/wp122.pdf.

Carruthers, David. 1996. "Indigenous Ecology and the Politics of Linkage in Mexican Social Movements." *Third World Quarterly* 17, no. 5: 1007–28.

Castellanos, Antonio, and Roberto González Amador. 2002. "Subieron Pasivos del Fobaproa 46.8 por Ciento en Cuatro Años." *La Jornada*, May 22.

Castro-Monge, Ligia María. 2001. "Nicaragua and the HIPC Initiative: The Tortuous Journey to Debt Relief." *Canadian Journal of Development Studies* 22, no. 2: 417–53.

Catalan-Aravena, Oscar. 2000. "A Decade of Structural Adjustment in Nicaragua: An Assessment." *International Journal of Political Economy* 30, no. 1: 55–71.

Caufield, Catherine. 1996. *Masters of Illusion: The World Bank and the Poverty of Nations.* New York: Henry Holt.

Cavero, Ramiro, Juan Carlos Requena, Juan Carlos Nuñez, Rosalind Eyben, and Wayne Lewis. 2002. "Crafting Bolivia's PRSP: Five Points of View." *Finance and Development* 39, no. 2: 13–16.

CCER (Coordinadora Civil de la Emergencia y la Reconstrucción). 2001. *La Nicaragua que Queremos: Enfoque y Prioridades para una Estrategia: Resultado del Proceso Consulta, Debate y Analysis.* Managua: Editronic.

CDF (Credit and Development Forum). 1998. *Credit and Development Forum Statistics.* Vol. 6. Dhaka, Bangladesh: CDF.

Cecchini, Simone, and Aldo Madariaga. 2011. "Programas de Transferencias Condicionadas: Balance de la Experiencia en América Latina y el Caribe." In *Cuadernos de la CEPAL,* 95. Santiago, Chile: CEPAL.

CEFP (Centro de Estudios de las Finanzas Públicas). 2009. *Proyecto de Presupuesto de Egresos de la Federación 2010: Evolución del Gasto Social 2003–2010.* Mexico: LXI Legislatura Camera de Diputados.

CEPAL (Comisión Económica para América Latina y el Caribe). 1996. *Situación de la Pobreza en Chile.* Encuesta CASEN 1994. Santiago, Chile: CEPAL.

————. 1998. *Economic Survey of Latin America and the Caribbean, 1997–1998.* Santiago, Chile: CEPAL.

————. 2003. *La Inversión Extranjera en América Latina y El Caríbe.* Santiago, Chile: CEPAL.

————. 2005. *México: Crecimiento Agropecuario, Capital Humano y Gestión del Riesgo.* Santiago, Chile: CEPAL.

————. 2007. *Panorama Social 2006.* Santiago, Chile: CEPAL.

————. 2008. *Social Panorama of Latin America 2008.* Santiago, Chile: CEPAL.

————. 2009. *Social Panorama of Latin America 2009.* Santiago, Chile: CEPAL.

Chambers, Robert, and Jethro Pettit. 2004. "Shifting Power to Make a Difference." In *Inclusive Aid: Changing Power and Relationships in International Development,* edited by L. Groves and R. Hinton, 137–62. London: Earthscan.

Chávez, Marcos. 2008. "Sacrificio Presupuestal: Política Agraria Calderonista." *La Jornada del Campo,* no. 13. Mexico DF: Universidad Nacional Autónoma de México.

Chávez-Juárez, Forian Wendelspiess. 2010. "The Impact of Oportunidades on Inequality of Opportunity in Rural and Urban Areas in Mexico." Master's thesis, University of Lausanne. http://www.wendelspiess.eu/download/MScE_Thesis_FWChJ.pdf.

Chayanov, Alexander. 1985. *La Organización Económica de la Unidad Campesina*. Buenos Aires, Argentina: Nueva Visión.

Chen, Shaohua, and Martin Ravallion. 2008. "The Developing World Is Poorer Than We Thought, but No Less Successful in the Fight against Poverty." Policy Research Working Paper 4703, World Bank, Washington, DC.

Chenery, Hollis, Montek S. Ahluwalia, C. L. G. Bell, John H. Duloy, and Richard Jolly. 1974. *Redistribution with Growth*. London: Oxford University Press.

Cheru, Fantu. 2006. "Building and Supporting PRSPS in Africa: What Has Worked Well So Far?" *Third World Quarterly* 27, no. 2: 469–88.

Chossudovsky, Michel. 1997. *The Globalization of Poverty: Impacts of IMF and World Bank Reforms*. London: Zed Books.

Christen, Robert Peck. 1999. Bulletin Highlights. *MicroBanking Bulletin*, no. 3: 19–49.

Cibils, Alan, Mark Weisbrot, and Debrayani Kar. 2000. *Argentina since Default: The IMF and the Depression*. Washington, DC: Center for Economic and Policy Research.

Cimadamore, Alberto, Hartley Dean, and Jorge Siqueira, eds. 2005. *The Poverty of the State: Reconsidering the Role of the State in the Struggle against Global Poverty*. Buenos Aires, Argentina: CLACSO/Instituto de Economía, UNICAMP.

CIVICUS. 2008. "From Consultation to Participation: Civil Society Index Report Honduras." Accessed April 2, 2008. http://www.civicus.org/new/media/CSI_Honduras_Country_Report.pdf.

Clay, Jason. 1988. *Indigenous Peoples and Tropical Forests: Models of Land Use and Management from Latin America*. Cambridge: Cultural Survival Inc.

Cling, Jean Pierre, Mireille Razafindrakoto, and Francois Roubaud, eds. 2003. *New International Poverty Reduction Strategies*. New York: Routledge.

CNDSARC (Campaña Nacional en Defensa de la Soberanía Alimentaria y por la Reactivación del Campo). 2008. "Manifiesto Campesino." *Alternativas* 3, no. 35. Accessed May 25, 2008. http://www.unorca.org.mx/trinchera/Manifiesto y llamamiento.doc.

Coady, David, Margaret Grosh, and John Hoddinott. 2003. *Targeted Antipoverty Interventions: A Selected Annotated Bibliography*. Washington, DC: World Bank.

———. 2004. *Targeting of Transfers in Developing Countries: Review of Lessons and Experience*. Washington, DC: World Bank.

Cohen, Ernesto, and Rolando Franco. 2006a. "Los Programas de Transferencias con Corresponsabilidad en América Latina: Similitudes y Diferencias." In *Transferencias con Corresponsabilidad: Una Mirada Latinoamericana*, edited by E. Cohen and R. Franco, 23–84. Mexico: SEDESOL/FLACSO.

———, eds. 2006b. *Transferencias con Corresponsabilidad: Una Mirada Latinoamericana*. Mexico: FLACSO.

Cohen, Ernesto, and Pablo Villatoro. 2006. "Chile: Puente-Chile Solidario." In *Transferencias con Corresponsabilidad: Una Mirada Latinoamericana*, edited by E. Cohen and R. Franco, 179–224. Mexico: FLACSO.

Collier, Paul. 2004. "Aid, Policy and Growth in Post-conflict Situations." *European Economic Review* 48, no. 5: 1125–45.

Comité Técnico para la Medición de la Pobreza. 2002. *Medición de la Pobreza: Variantes Metodológicas y Estimación Preliminary.* Mexico DF: Secretaría de Desarrollo Social.

CONAPO (Consejo Nacional de Población). 2008. *Series sobre Migración: Población Residente en Estados Unidos.* Mexico DF: CONAPO.

CONEVAL (Consejo Nacional de Evaluación de la Política de Desarrollo Social). 2008. *Informe de Evaluación de la Política de Desarrollo Social en México 2008.* Mexico DF: CONEVAL.

———. 2009. "Reporta Coneval Cifras de Pobreza por Ingresos 2008." Comunicado de Prensa No. 006/09. Mexico DF: CONEVAL.

———. 2011. "Coneval Informa los Resultados de la Medición de la Pobreza 2010." Comunicado de Prensa No. 007. Mexico DF: CONEVAL.

Cornelius, Wayne, and Ann Craig. 1988. *Politics in Mexico: An Introduction and Overview.* La Jolla, CA: Center for US-Mexican Studies.

Cornia, Giovanni Andrea. 1994. *Macroeconomic Policy, Poverty Alleviation and Long-Term Development: Latin America in the 1990s.* UNICEF International Child Development Centre, Florence Economic Policy Series No. 40.

Cornia, Giovanni Andrea, Richard Jolly, and Frances Stewart, eds. 1987a. *Adjustment with a Human Face.* New York: Oxford University Press.

Cortés, Fernando. 2006a. "La Incidencia de la Pobreza y la Concentración del Ingreso en México." In *La Situación del Trabajo en Meéxico*, edited by E. de la Garza and C. Salas, 91–123. Mexico: UAM/Instituto Nacional de Solidaridad/Editorial Plaza y Valdés.

———. 2006b. "¿Disminuyó la Pobreza? México 2000–2002." In *Alternancia, Políticas Sociales y Desarrollo Regional en México*, edited by G. Ordóñez, R. Enríquez, I. Román, and E. Valencia, 193–229. Tijuana and Guadalajara: El Colegio de la Frontera Norte, Instituto Tecnológico y de Estudios Superiores de Occidente, Universidad de Guadalajara.

Cortés, Fernando, Israel Banegas, and Patricio Solís. 2007. "Pobres con Oportunidades: México 2002–2005." *Estudios Sociológicos* 25, no. 73: 3–40.

Covey, Jane. 1998. "Critical Cooperation? Influencing the World Bank through Policy Dialogue and Operational Cooperation." In *The Struggle for Accountability: The World Bank, NGOs and Grassroots Movements*, edited by Jonathan Fox and David Brown. Cambridge and London: MIT Press.

Craig, David, and Doug Porter. 2003. "Poverty Reduction Strategies: A New Convergence." *World Development* 31, no. 1: 53–69.

———. 2005. "The Third Way and the Third World: Poverty Reduction and Social Inclusion Strategies in the Rise of Inclusive Liberalism." *Review of International Political Economy* 12, no. 2: 226–63.

———. 2006. *Development beyond Neo-liberalism: Governance, Poverty Reduction and Political Economy.* London: Routledge.

Cruz, Carlos, Rodolfo de la Torre, and César Velázquez. 2006. *Informe Compilatorio: Evaluación Externa de Impacto del Programa Oportunidades 2001–2006.* Cuernavaca, Mexico: Instituto Nacional de Salud Puúblico.

CTMP (Comité Técnico para la Medición de la Pobreza). 2002. *Medición de la Pobreza: Variantes Metodológicas y Estimación Preliminar.* Mexico DF: Secretaría de Desarrollo Social.

Cuesta, José. 2007. "Political Space, Pro-poor Growth, and Poverty Reduction Strategy in Honduras: A Story of Missed Opportunities." *Journal of Latin American Studies* 39, no. 2: 329–54.

Cuesta, José, and Rafael del Cid. 2003. *Aprendiendo sobre la Marcha: La Experiencia de la Estrategia de Reducción de la Pobreza en Honduras.* The Hague, the Netherlands: Institute of Social Studies.

Davis, Mike. 2006. *Planet of Slums.* London: Verso.

De Ferranti, David, Guillermo Perry, Francisco Ferreira, and Michael Walton. 2004. *Inequality in Latin America: Breaking with History?* Washington, DC: World Bank.

De Ferranti, David, and Luis Serven. 2000. *Asegurando el Futuro en una Economía Globalizada.* Washington, DC: World Bank.

De Grammont, Hubert. 2004. "La Nueva Ruralidad en América Latina." Special issue, *Revista Mexicana de Sociología* 66: 279–300.

Deininger, Klaus, and Lyn Squire. 1998. "New Ways of Looking at Old Issues: Inequality and Growth." *Journal of Development Economics* 57, no. 2: 259–87.

De Ita, Ana. 2003. *México: Impactos del Procede en los Conflictos Agrarios y la Concentración de la Tierra.* Mexico DF: Centro de Estudios para el Cambio en el Campo Mexicano.

De Janvry, Alain, and Elisabeth Sadoulet. 1995. *Poverty, Equity and Social Welfare in Latin America: Determinants of Change over Growth Spells.* Geneva: ILO.

———. 2000. "Rural Poverty in Latin America: Determinants and Exit Paths." *Food Policy* 25, no. 4: 389–409.

———. 2006. "When to Use a CCT versus a CT Approach?" Paper presented at Third International Conference on Conditional Transferencias, Istanbul, World Bank/Government of Turkey.

De la Brière, Bénédicte, and Laura Rawlings. 2006. "Examining Conditional Cash Transfer Programs: A Role for Increased Social Inclusion?" Social Protection Discussion Paper 603, Washington, DC, World Bank.

Delgado Wise, R., and James Cypher. 2005. "The Strategic Role of Labor in Mexico's Subordinated Integration into the US Production System under NAFTA." Working Paper, Doctorado en Estudios del Desarrollo, Universidad Autónoma de Zacatecas, Zacatecas, Mexico.

Deneulin, Severine, and Lila Shahani, eds. 2009. *An Introduction to the Human Development and Capability Approach: Freedom and Agency.* London: Earthscan.

Desmarais, Annette. 2007. *La Vía Campesina: Globalization and the Power of Peasants.* Halifax: Fernwood.

Devereux, Stephen, Ian Scoones, and John Thompson. 2009. Critical Responses to the World Bank's World Development Report 2008: Agriculture for Development. *Journal of Peasant Studies* 36, no. 2: 468–74.

Dezalay, Yves, and Bryant Garth. 2005. *La Internacionalización de las Luchas por el Poder: La Competencia entre Abogados y Economistas por Transformar los Estados latinoamericanos.* México: Instituto de Investigaciones Jurídicas/Universidad Nacional Autónoma de México.

Dijkstra, Geske. 2000. "Structural Adjustment and Poverty in Nicaragua." Paper presented at the Meeting of the Latin American Studies Association, Miami, March 16–18.

———. 2004. "Governance for Sustainable Poverty Reduction: The Social Fund in Nicaragua." *Public Administration and Development* 24, no. 3: 197–211.

———. 2005. "The PRSP Approach and the Illusion of Improved Aid Effectiveness: Lessons from Bolivia, Honduras and Nicaragua." *Development Policy Review* 23, no. 4: 443–64.

Dollar, David, and Aart Kraay. 2002. "Growth Is Good for the Poor." *Journal of Economic Growth* 7: 195–225.

Draibe, Sonia. 2006. "Brasil: Bolsa-Escola y Bolsa Familia." In *Transferencias con Corresponsabilidad: Una Mirada Latinoamericana*, edited by E. Cohen and R. Franco, 139–76. Mexico DF: FLACSO.

Drake, Deborah, and Elizabeth Rhyne, eds. 2002. *The Commercialization of Microfinance: Balancing Business and Development*. Bloomfield, CT: Kumarian Press.

Driscoll, Ruth, and Alison Evans. 2005. "Second-Generation Poverty Reduction Strategies: Opportunities and Emerging Issues." *Development Policy Review* 23, no. 1: 5–25.

Duhau, Emilio. 2000. "Política Social, Pobreza y Focalización." In *Los Dilemas de la Política Social: ¿Cómo Combatir la Pobreza?*, edited by E. Valencia, M. Gendreau, and A. M. Tepichín, 157–74. Guadalajara: ITESO y Universidad de Guadalajara.

Durand, Jorge. 2006. "Las Dos Caras de la Remesa." In *Alternancia, Políticas Sociales y Desarrollo Regional en México*, edited by Gerardo Ordóñez, Rocío Enríquez, Ignacio Román, and Enrique Valencia, 231–47. Tijuana and Guadalajara: El Colegio de la Frontera Norte, Instituto Tecnológico y de Estudios Superiores de Occidente, Universidad de Guadalajara.

Durand, Jorge, and Douglas Massey. 2003. *Clandestinos: Migración México-Estados Unidos en los Albores del Siglo XXI*. Zacatecas: Universidad de Zacatecas.

Durston, John. 2001. *Social Capital—Part of the Problem, Part of the Solution: Its Role in the Persistence and Overcoming of Poverty in Latin America and the Caribbean*. Santiago, Chile: ECLAC.

Duryea, Suzanne, and Andrew Morrison. 2004. "The Effect of Conditional Transfers on School Performance and Child Labor: Evidence from an Ex-Post Impact Evaluation in Costa Rica." Working Paper 505, IDB, Washington, DC.

Eastwood, Robert, and Michael Lipton. 2001. "Pro-poor Growth and Pro-poor Poverty Reduction." *Asian Development Review* 18, no. 2: 1–37.

Ebentreich, Alfredo. 2005. "Microfinance Regulation and Supervision in Peru: Current State, Lessons Learned and Prospects for the Future." Essays on Regulation and Supervision, No. 4, Microfinance Regulation and Supervision Resource Center.

Echeverria, Ruben. 1998. "Strategic Elements for the Reduction of Rural Poverty in Latin America and the Caribbean." Policy Research Paper, Washington, DC, Inter-American Development Bank.

ECLAC (Economic Commission for Latin America and the Caribbean). 1990. *Productive Transformation with Equity*. Santiago, Chile: ECLAC.

———. 2006. *La Protección Social de Cara al Futuro: Acceso, Financiamiento y Solidaridad*. Santiago, Chile: ECLAC.

———. 2009. *The Outlook for Agriculture and Rural Development in the Americas: A Perspective on Latin America and the Caribbean*. Santiago, Chile: ECLAC-IICA-FAO.

———. 2010a. *Social Panorama of Latin America*. Santiago, Chile: ECLAC.

———. 2010b. *Time for Equality: Closing Gaps, Opening Trails*. Santiago, Chile: ECLAC.

———. 2011. *Social Panorama of Latin America*. Santiago, Chile: ECLAC.

Economist, The. 2005. "The Hidden Wealth of the Poor." Special supplement, November 5.

Economy, Elizabeth. 2004. *The River Runs Black: The Environmental Challenge to China's Future*. Ithaca, NY: Cornell University Press.

Escobar, Agustín. 2005. "Pobreza y Migración Internacional: Propuestas Conceptuales, Primeros Hallazgos." In *Los Rostros de la Pobreza: El Debate*, edited by Monica Gendreau, Vol. IV, 97–128. Tlaquepaque: Instituto Tecnológico y de Estudios Superiores de Occidente.

Escobar, Agustín, and Mercedes González de la Rocha. 2006. "Vulnerabilidad y Activos de los Hogares: El Programa Progresa-Oportunidades en Pequeñas Ciudades." In *Alternancia, Políticas Sociales y Desarrollo Regional en México*, edited by G. Ordónez, R. Enriques, I. Román, and E. Valencia, 249–95. Tijuana and Guadalajara: El Colegio de la Frontera Norte, ITESO, Universidad de Guadalajara.

Espina Prieto, Mayra. 2008. *Políticas de Atención a la Pobreza y la Desigualdad*. Buenos Aires, Argentina: CLACSO.

Esping-Andersen, Gøsta. 1990. *The Three Worlds of Welfare Capitalism*. Princeton, NJ: Princeton University Press.

Espinosa, Verónica. 2009. "Del Procampo al Pronarco." Special edition, *Proceso*, no. 24: 49–51.

ETC Group. n.d. "The World's Top 10 Seed Companies—2006." Accessed April 23, 2011. http://www.etcgroup.org/en/node/656.

Eyben, Rosalind. 2004. "Who Owns a Poverty Reduction Strategy? A Case Study of Power, Instruments and Relationships in Boliva." In *Inclusive Aid: Changing Power and Relationships in International Development*, edited by L. Groves and R. Hinton, 57–75. London: Earthscan.

FAO (Food and Agriculture Organization of the United Nations). 2000. "Evaluación de la Alianza para el Campo, 1998–1999." Accessed March 16, 2006. http://www.fao.org/Regional/Lamerica/.

———. 2010. "Food Outlook: Global Market Analysis." Accessed April 23, 2011. http://www.fao.org/docrep/013/al969e/al969e00.pdf.

Feder, Ernest. 1976. "The New World Bank Programme for the Self-Liquidation of the Third World Peasantry." *Journal of Peasant Studies* 3, no. 3: 343–54.

Fernando, Nimal. 2004. "From Niche Market to Mainstream: Changing Face of the Microfinance Industry in Asia." Paper presented at the Asian Development Bank Institute workshop on Modalities of Microfinance Delivery in Asia, Manila, October 4–8.

Ferreira, Francisco, and Michael Walton. 2005. "The Inequality Trap: Why Equity Must Be Central to Development Policy." *Finance and Development* 42, no. 4: 34–37.

Filgueira, Fernando. 2005. *Welfare and Democracy in Latin America: The Development, Crisis and Aftermath of Universal, Dual and Exclusionary Social States*. Geneva: Programme Social Policy Development, UNRISD.

Filgueira, Fernando, Carlos Gerardo Molina, Jorge Papadópulos, and Federico Tobar. 2006. *Universalismo Básico: Una Alternativa Posible y Necesaria para Mejorar las Condiciones de Vida*. Washington, DC: BID.

Fine, Ben, Costas Lapavitsas, and Jonathan Pincus, eds. 2001. *Development Policy in the 21st Century: Beyond the Washington Consensus*. London: Routledge.

Finnemore, Martha. 1997. "Redefining Development at the World Bank." In *International Development and the Social Sciences: Essays on the History and Politics of Knowledge*, edited by Frederick Cooper and Randall Packard. Berkeley: University of California Press.

Fiszbein, Ariel, and Norbert Schady. 2009. *Conditional Cash Transfers: Reducing Present and Future Poverty*. Washington, DC: World Bank.

Fonseca, Ana. 2006. "Los Sistemas de Proteccioón Social en América Latina: Un Análisis de las Transferencias Monetarias Condicionadas." Accessed March 2, 2011. www.rlc.fao.org/es/prioridades/seguridad/ingreso/pdf/fonseca.pdf.

Forbes, Kristen. 2000. "A Reassessment of the Relationship between Inequality and Growth." *American Economic Review* 90, no. 4: 869–87.

FOSDEH (Foro Social de Deuda Externa y Desarollo de Honduras). 2001. *Advantages and Difficulties of the Process of Preparation of a PRSP in Honduras.* Tegucigalpa: FOSDEH.

Foust Rodríguez, David. 2010. *Filiación Política de los Coordinadores Estatales y Coordinadores de CAR Oportunidades.* Guadalajara: Universidad de Guadalajara.

Fox, Jonathan, and Libby Haight. 2010. "La Política Agrícola Mexicana: Metas Múltiples e Intereses en Conflicto." In *Subsidios para la Desigualdad: Las Políticas Públicas del Maíz en México a Partir del Libre Comercio,* edited by J. Fox and L. Haight, 9–45. Santa Cruz: University of California.

Fraga, Arminio. 2005. "A Fork in the Road: Latin America Faces a Choice between Populism and Deeper Reform." *Finance and Development* 42, no. 4: 14–16.

Franke, P., and A. Mendoza. 2006. "Peru: Programa, Juantos." In *Tranferencias con Corresponsabilidad: Una Mirada Latinoamericana,* edited by E. Cohen and R. Franco. Mexico City, FLASCO Mexico.

Freije, Samuel, Rosangela Bando, Fernanda Arce, Carlos Medina, and Raquel Bernal. 2006. "Conditional Transfers, Labor Supply, and Poverty: Microsimulating Oportunidades." *Economía* 7, no. 1: 73–124.

Friedman, Milton. 2002. *Capitalism and Freedom.* Chicago: University of Chicago Press.

Friedmann, Harriet, and Philip McMichael. 1989. "Agriculture and the State System: The Rise and Fall of National Agricultures, 1870 to Present." *Sociologia Ruralis* 29, no. 2: 93–117.

Fröbel, Folker, Jürgen Heinrichs, and Otto Kreye. 1980. *The New International Division of Labor: Structural Unemployment in Industrialised Countries and Industrialisation in Developing Countries.* Cambridge: Cambridge University Press.

Fuglesang, Andreas, and Dale Chandler. 1993. *Participation as Process—Process as Growth: What We Can Learn from the Grameen Bank.* Dhaka, Bangladesh: Grameen Trust.

Ganuza, Enrique, Arturo León, and Pablo Sauma. 1999. *Gastos Públicos y Servicios Sociales Basicos en America Latina y el Caribe: Analísis desde la Perspectiva de 20/20.* Santiago, Chile: ECLAC.

García-Falconi, Sulima. 2004. "Las Representaciones Sociales en Torno al Progresa-Oportunidades en Santiago, Mexquititlán, Amealco, Querétaro." PhD diss., Universidad de Guadalajara, Mexico.

Garuda, Gopal. 2000. The Distributional Effect of IMF Programmes: A Cross-Country Analysis. *World Development* 28, no. 6: 1031–51.

Gendreau, Mónica. 2000. "El Progresa en el Debate Actual en Torno a la Política Social: Reflexiones Finales." In *Los Dilemas de la Política Social: ¿Cómo Combatir la Pobreza?,* edited by E. Valencia, M. Gendreau, and A. M. Tepichín, 411–31. Guadalajara: Universidad de Guadalajara y ITESO.

George, Susan. 1978. *O Mercado da Fome.* Rio de Janeiro: Paz e Terra.

George, Susan, and Fabrizio Sabelli. 1996. *La Religión del Crédito: El Banco Mundial y Su Imperio Secular.* 2nd ed. Barcelona: Intermón.

Germidis, Dimitri, Denis Kessler, and Rachel Meghir. 1991. *Financial Systems and Development: What Role for the Formal and Informal Financial Sectors?* Paris: OECD.

Ghimire, Krishna, ed. 2001. *Land Reform and Peasant Livelihoods: The Social Dynamics of Rural Poverty and Agrarian Reform in Developing Countries.* London: ITDG.

Giarracca, Norma, ed. 2001. *¿Una Nueva Ruralidad en América Latina?* Buenos Aires, Argentina: CLACSO.

Gibbons, David. 1992. *The Grameen Reader.* Dhaka, Bangladesh: Grameen Bank.

Giddens, Anthony. 1998. *The Third Way: The Renewal of Social Democracy.* Cambridge: Polity Press.

Girvan, Norman, ed. 1997. *Poverty, Empowerment and Social Development in the Caribbean.* Kingston: Canoe Press.

Gleich, Albrecht von. 1999. "Poverty Reduction Strategies: The Experience of Bolivia." In *Waging the Global War on Poverty: Strategies and Case Studies,* edited by R. Halvorson Quevedo and H. Schneider. Paris: OECD-Development Centre.

Glyn, Andrew, Alan Hughes, Alan Lipietz, and Ajit Singh. 1990. "The Rise and Fall of the Golden Age." In *The Golden Age of Capitalism: Re-interpreting the Post-war Experience,* edited by S. Marglin and J. Schor, 39–125. Oxford: Clarendon Press.

Golbert, Laura. 2006a. "Aprendizajes del Programa Jefes y Jefas de Argentina." Paper presented at Reunión Expertos Gestión y Financiamiento de las Políticas que Afectan a las Familias, Santiago, Chile, CEPAL, October 16–17.

———. 2006b. "Derecho a la Inclusión o Paz Social El Programa para Jefes/as de Hogares Desocupados." In *Política y Políticas Públicas en los Procesos de Reforma América Latina,* edited by R. Franco and J. Lanzaro, 319–52. Mexico: FLACSO-Mexico, CEPAL.

Goldman, Michael. 2005. *Imperial Nature: The World Bank and Struggles for Social Justice in the Age of Globalization.* New Haven and London: Yale University Press.

Gómez-Cruz, Manuel Ángel, Laura Gómez Tovar, and Rita Schwentesius Rindermann. 2004. "Propuesta de Política de Apoyo para la Agricultura Orgánica de México." *Revista Vinculando.* Accessed May 11, 2008. http://vinculando.org.

Gómez-Hermosillo Marín, Rogelio. 2006. "Prólogo." In *Transferencias con Corresponsabilidad: Una Mirada Latinoamericana,* edited by E. Cohen and R. Franco, 9–17. Mexico DF: Facultad de Ciencias Sociales (FLACSO).

González Amador, Roberto. 2008. "Por las Nubes, el Costo de Fertilizantes: Agricultores Pequeños no Podrán Sembrar Intueft." *La Jornada,* May 22.

González Amador, Roberto, and Rosa Vargas. 2005. "Baja Pobreza Rural pero Crece Desigualdad." *La Jornada,* August 25.

González-Chávez, Humberto, and Alejandro Macías Macías. 2007. "Vulnerabilidad Alimentaria y Política Agroalimentaria en México." *Desacatos,* no. 25: 47–78.

González de la Rocha, Mercedes. 2006. "Los Hogares en las Evaluaciones: Cinco Años de Investigación." In *Procesos Domésticos y Vulnerabilidad: Perspectivas Antropológicas de los Hogares con Oportunidades,* edited by M. Gónzalez de la Rocha. Mexico: La Casa Chata.

González de la Rocha, Mercedes, and Arturo Escobar Latapí. 2008. "Vulnerabilidad y Activos de los Hogares: El Programa Oportunidades en Ciudades Pequeñas." In *Método Científico y Política Social: A Propósito de las Evaluaciones Cualitativas de Programas Sociales,* edited by F. Cortés, A. Escobar, and M. González de la Rocha, 129–202. Mexico DF: El Colegio de México.

González-Gómez, Mauricio. 1999. "Crisis y Cambio Económico en México." In *México en el Umbral del Nuevo Siglo: Entre la Crisis y el Cambio,* edited by S. K. Purcell and L. Rubio, 65–101. Mexico: Centro de Investigación para el Desarrollo A.C. Porrúa.

Gonzalez-Vega, Claudio, Mark Schreiner, Richard Meyer, Jorge Rodríguez, and Sergio Navajas. 1997. "BANCOSOL El Reto del Crecimiento en Organizaciones de Microfinanzas."

Economics and Sociology, Occasional Paper No. 2345, Rural Finance Program Department of Agricultural Economics, Ohio State University.

Gore, Charles. 2000. "The Rise and Fall of the Washington Consensus as a Paradigm for Developing Countries." *World Development* 28, no. 5: 789–804.

Government of Honduras. 2000. "Honduras: Interim-Poverty Reduction Strategy Paper." Accessed March 10, 2005. www.imf.org/external/NP/prsp/2000/hnd/01/041300.pdf.

———. 2001. "Honduras: Poverty Reduction Strategy Paper." Accessed March 10, 2005. http://poverty2.forumone.com/tiles/I-Ionduras_PRSP.pdf.

———. 2006. "Estrategia para la Reduccion de al Pobreza: Version Actualizada." Accessed March 10, 2005. www_fosdeh.net/archivos/Presentacion_CCERP_27_marzo.pdf.

Government of Nicaragua. 2001. "A Strengthened Growth and Poverty Reduction Strategy." Accessed March 10, 2005. http://poverty.worldbank.org/files/Nicaragua_PRSP.pdf.

———. 2005. "National Development Plan: The Revised PRSP." Accessed March 10, 2005. http://www.imf.org/external/pubs/ft/scr/2005/cr05440.pdf.

Gowan, Peter. 2003. *A Roleta Global: Uma Aposta Faustiana de Washington para a Dominação do Mundo.* Rio de Janeiro: Record.

Grammont, Hubert. 2009. "El Perfil de la Familia Rural y de la Familia Campesina en México." Ponencia preparado para el Congreso 2009 de la Asociación de Estudios Latinoamericanos, Rio de Janeiro, Brasil, June 11–14.

Green, Duncan. 2008. *From Poverty to Power: How Active Citizens and Effective States Can Change the World.* Oxford: Oxfam International.

Griffith-Jones, Stephany. 1996. "The Mexican Peso Crisis." *CEPAL Review,* no. 60: 155–75.

Grogg, Patricia. 2004. "Latin America: Microcredit—A Tool for Development or Profit?" *Inter Press Service.* Accessed March 1, 2012. http://www.ifad.org/media/news/2004/091204.htm.

Guillén, Arturo. 2007. *Mito y Realidad de la Globalización Neoliberal.* Mexico DF: Miguel Ángel Porrúa Editores, UAMI.

Guimaráes, João, and Nestor Avendaño. 2003. *A Strategy without Ownership: Country Report Nicaragua.* The Hague, the Netherlands: Institute of Social Studies.

Guimaraes, Roberto. 1989. *Desarrollo con Equidad: ¿Un Nuevo Cuento de Hadas para los Años de Noventa?* Santiago, Chile: CEPAL.

Gulli, Hege, and Marguerite Berger. 1999. "Microfinance and Poverty Reduction: Evidence from Latin America." *Small Enterprise Development* 10, no. 3: 16–28.

Guzmán-Flores, Jesús. 2008. "Orígenes de la 'Crisis Alimentaria' Internacional." *Rumborural,* no. 9: 30–39.

Gwin, Catherine. 1997. "U.S. Relations with the World Bank, 1945–1992." In *The World Bank: Its First Half Century,* edited by D. Kapur, J. Lewis, and R. Webb, 195–274. Washington, DC: Brookings Institution Press.

Haas, Peter. 1992. "Introduction: Epistemic Communities and International Policy Coordination." *International Organization* 46: 1–35.

Hall, Gilette, and Harry Anthony Patrinos, eds. 2005. *Indigenous Peoples, Poverty and Human Development in Latin America.* London: Palgrave Macmillan UK.

Halvorson-Quevedo, Raundi, and Hartmut Schneider, eds. 1999. *Waging the Global War on Poverty: Strategies and Case Studies.* Paris: OECD, Development Centre.

Hanmer, Lucia, and David Booth. 2001. *Pro-poor Growth: Why Do We Need It?* London: ODI.

Harper, Malcolm, and Shailendra Vyakarnam. 1988. *Rural Enterprise: Case Studies from Developing Countries.* London: ITDG Publishing.

Harvey, David. 2005. *A Brief History of Neoliberalism*. Oxford: Oxford University Press.

Havnevik, Kjell, Deborah Bryceson, Lars-Erik Birgegård, Prosper Matondi, and Atakilte Beyene. 2007. "African Agriculture and the World Bank Development or Impoverishment?" Workshop Report, Nordic Africa Institute workshop, Uppsala, Sweden, Nordiska Afrikainstitutet, Uppsala 2, March 13–14.

Hermele, Kenneth. 2005. "The Poverty Reduction Strategies: A Survey of Literature." Forum Syd, Stockholm, Sweden, SARPN, June. http://www.forumsyd.se/.

Hernández-Laos, Enrique. 2006. "Bienestar Pobreza y Vulnerabilidad en México: Nuevas Estimaciones." *Economía UNAM*, no. 009: 14–32.

Hernández-Laos, Enrique, and Jorge Velázquez-Roa. 2003. *Globalización, Desigualdad y Pobreza: Lecciones de la Experiencia Mexicana*. Mexico DF: UAM, Plaza y Valdés.

Holt-Giménez, Eric. 2000. *Midiendo La Resistencia Agroecológica Campesina ante el Huracán Mitch en Centroamérica*. Tegucigalpa: Vecinos Mundiales.

———. 2006. *Campesino a Campesino: Voices from Latin America's Farmer to Farmer Movement for Sustainable Agriculture*. Oakland: Food First Books.

———. 2009. "From Food Crisis to Food Sovereignty: The Challenge of Social Movements." *Monthly Review* 61, no. 3: 142–56.

Holt-Giménez, Eric, and Annie Shattuck. 2011. "Food Crises, Food Regimes and Food Movements: Rumblings of Reform or Tides of Transformation?" *Journal of Peasant Studies* 38, no. 1: 109–44.

Huber, Evelyne. 2005. "Inequality and the State in Latin America." Paper presented at ASPA Conference of the Presidential Task Force on Difference and Inequality in the Third World, University of Virginia, April 22–23.

———. 2006. "Un Nuevo Enfoque para la Seguridad Social en la Región." In *Universalismo Básico: Una Nueva Política Social para América Latina*, edited by C. Molina, 169–87. Washington, DC, and Mexico DF: BID and Planeta.

Hulme, David. 1999. "Impact Assessment Methodologies for Microfinance: Theory, Experience and Better Practice." Finance and Development Research Program, Working Paper No. 1, IDPM, University of Manchester.

Hulme, David, and Paul Mosley. 1996. *Finance against Poverty*. London: Routledge.

Hunt, Diana. 1989. *Economic Theories of Development*. Toronto: Harvester Wheatsheaf.

Huntington, Samuel. 1975. *A Ordem Política nas Sociedades em Mudança*. São Paulo e Rio de Janeiro: Editora da USP/Forense Universitária.

IDB (Inter-American Development Bank). 1998a. *Rural Poverty Reduction Strategy*. Washington, DC: IDB, Sustainable Development Department.

———. 1998b. *The Path out of Poverty*. Washington, DC: IDB.

———. 1998c. *Economic and Social Progress in Latin America: Facing Up to Inequality*. Washington, DC: IDB.

———. 1998d. "Family Allowance Program: Phase II." Accessed January 10, 2008. www.iadb.org/exr/doc98/apr/ho1026e.pdf.

———. 2006. *Annual Report 2005*. Washington, DC: IDB.

IFPRI (International Food Policy Research Institute). 2000. "Progresa ¿Está Dando Buenos Resultados?" Accessed September 9, 2003. http://www.progresa.gob.mx.

———. 2004. *Impact Evaluation of a Conditional Cash Transfer Program: The Nicaraguan Red de Protección Social*. Accessed November 28, 2006. www.ifpri.org/divs/fcnd/dp/papers/fcndp 1 84.pdf.

IMF and World Bank. 2005a. "The Poverty Reduction Strategy Initiative: Findings from 10 Country Case Studies of World Bank and IMF Support." Washington, DC: World Bank.

———. 2005b. "Nicaragua: Poverty Reduction Strategy Paper." IMF Country Report No. 05/440, Washington, DC, IMF.

———. 2007. "Taking Action for the World's Poor and Hungry People." Accessed March 1, 2012. www.ifpri.org.

IMF and World Bank and IDA (International Development Association). 2001. "Poverty Reduction Strategy Paper, Honduras: Joint Staff Assessment." Accessed March 10, 2008. www.imf.org/external/np/jsa/2001/hnd/eng/091701.pdf.

———. 2002. "Review of the Poverty Reduction Strategy Paper (PRSP) Approach: Main Findings." Accessed March 10, 2008. www.imf.org/externalnp/PRSpgen/review/2002/031502a.pdf.

INEGI (Instituto Nacional de Estadística, Geografía e Informática). 2007. *Encuesta Nacional de Ocupación y Empleo 2006.* Mexico DF: INEGI.

———. 2008. *II Conteo de Población y Vivienda 2005.* Mexico DF: INEGI.

Interforos. 2000. *Estrategia de Combate a La Pobreza: Propuesta de Interforos.* Tegucigalpa: Interforos.

Irarrázaval, Ignacio. 2005. *Participación Ciudadana en Programas de Reducción de la Pobreza en América Latina: Experiencias en Argentina, Chile, Peru y Uruguay.* Washington, DC: IDB.

Ivo, Anete. 2006. "Inegalités, Deémocratie et Pauvreté: Les Effets Politiques des Programmes Ciblés au Brésiln." Paper presented at Colloq. Int., Egalité/Inegalité(s) Amériques, Inst. Am., Université de Paris.

Jennings, Ray. 2000. *Participatory Development as New Paradigm: The Transition of Development Professionalism.* Washington, DC: USAID.

Johnson, Susan, and Ben Rogaly. 1997. *Microfinance and Poverty Reduction.* Oxford: Oxfam.

Joly, Pierre-Benoît, and Claire Marris. 2001. "Mise sur Agenda et Controverses: Une Aproche Comparée du Cas des OGM en France et aux Etats-Unis." Paper presented at Coloquio Risques Collectifs et Situations de Crise, Bilans et Perspectives, CNRS, Paris, February 7–9.

Kadaras, James, and Elizabeth Rhyne. 2004. *Characteristics of Equity Investment in Microfinance.* Boston: Acción International.

Kakwani, Nanak, and Ernesto Pernia. 2000. "What Is Pro-Poor Growth?" *Asian Development Review* 18, no. 1: 1–16.

Kapstein, Ethan. 1996. "Workers and the World Economy." *Foreign Affairs* 75, no. 3: 16–37.

Kapur, Devesh, John Lewis, and Richard Webb, eds. 1997. *The World Bank: Its First Half Century History.* Washington, DC: Brookings Institution Press.

Karl, Terry Lynn. 2000. "Economic Inequality and Democratic Instability." *Journal of Democracy* 11, no. 1: 149–56.

Katz, Jorge, ed. 1996. *Estabilización Macroeconómica, Reforma Estructural y Comportamiento Industrial: Estructura y Funcionamiento del Sector Manufacturero Latinoamericano en los Años 90.* Buenos Aires, Argentina: Alianza Editorial.

Kaufman, Frederick. 2010. "The Food Bubble: How Wall Street Starved Millions and Got Away with It." *Harper's Magazine,* June 22.

Kay, Cristóbal. 2009. "Development Strategies and Rural Development: Exploring Synergies, Eradicating Poverty." *Journal of Peasant Studies* 36, no. 1: 103–37.

Keck, Margaret E., and Kathryn Sikkink. 1999. "Transnational Advocacy Networks in International and Regional Politics." *International Social Science Journal* 159: 89–101.

Kemmis Betty, Adam. 2010. "Microcredit in Bolivia: What Impact on the Lives of the Poor?" The Democracy Center. Accessed March 1, 2012. http://democracyctr.org/blogfrombolivia/microcredit-in-bolivia-what-impact-on-the-lives-of-the-poor/.

Kessler, Gabriel, and María Cecilia Roggi. 2005. "Programas de Superación de la Pobreza y Capital Social: La Experiencia Argentina." In *Aprender de la Experiencia: El Capital Social en la Superación de la Pobreza*, edited by I. Arriagada, 133–60. Santiago, Chile: CEPAL.

Khandker, Shahidur. 1999. *Fighting Poverty with Microcredit*. Dhaka, Bangladesh: University Press.

Klasen, Stephen. 2000. "Measuring Poverty and Deprivation in South Africa." *Review of Income and Wealth* 42, no. 1: 33–58.

———. 2003. "In Search of the Holy Grail: How to Achieve Pro-poor Growth." In *Towards Pro-poor Policies: Proceedings from the ABCDE Europe Conference*, edited by L. Kolstad, B. Tungodden, and N. Stern. Washington, DC: World Bank.

Klugman, Jeni, ed. 2002. *A Sourcebook for Poverty Reduction Strategies*. Vols. 1–2. Washington, DC: World Bank.

Knack, Stephen. 1999. "Social Capital, Growth and Poverty: A Survey of Cross-Country Evidence." Social Capital Initiative Working Paper No. 7, World Bank, Social Development Department, Washington, DC.

Koont, Sinan. 2008. "A Cuban Success Story: Urban Agriculture." *Review of Radical Political Economics* 40, no. 3: 285–91.

Kruijt, Dirk. 1992. "Monopolios de Filantropía: El Caso de las Llamadas 'Organizaciones no Gubernamentales' en América Latina." *Polémica* 16: 41–47.

Laderchi, Caterina, Ruhi Saith, and Frances Stewart. 2003. "Does It Matter That We Do Not Agree on the Definition of Poverty? A Comparison of Four Approaches." *Oxford Development Studies* 31, no. 3: 243–73.

Lancaster, Carol. 2007. *Foreign Aid: Diplomacy, Development, Domestic Politics*. Chicago and London: University of Chicago Press.

Lapenu, Cécile, and Manfred Zeller. 2001. "Distribution, Growth and Performance of Microfinance Institutions in Africa, Asia and Latin America." Food Consumption and Nutrition Division, Discussion Paper No. 114, International Food Policy Research Institute, Washington, DC.

Largaespada-Fredersdorff, Carmen. 2006. "Nicaragua: Red de Protección Social y Sistema de Atención a Crisis." In *Transferencias con Corresponsabilidad: Una Mirada Latinoamericana*, edited by E. Cohen and R. Franco, 323–61. Mexico DF: FLACSO.

Larraín, Christian. 2007. "BancoEstado Microcreditos: Lecciones de un Modelo Exitoso." In *Serie Financiamiento del Desarrollo*, 195. Santiago, Chile: CEPAL.

Lautier, Bruno. 2004. "Les Politiques Sociales au Mexique e tau Brésil: L'assurance, l'assistance, l'absence." In *Brésil, Mexique: Deux Trajectorires dans la Mondialisation*, edited by B. Lautier and J. Marques Pereira, 165–99. Paris: Ed. Karthala.

Ledgerwood, Joanna. 1998. *Microfinance Handbook*. Washington, DC: World Bank.

Leipziger, Danny. 2001. "The Unfinished Poverty Agenda: Why Latin America and the Caribbean Lag Behind." *Finance and Development* 38, no. 1: 38–41.

Levy, Santiago. 1991. "Poverty Alleviation in Mexico: Policy Research External Affairs." Working Paper No. 679, World Bank, Washington, DC.

———. 1994. "La Pobreza en México." In *La Pobreza en México: Causas y Políticas para Combatirla*, edited by F. Vélez. Mexico: Fondo de Cultura.

————. 2006a. *Pobreza y Transición Democrática en México*. Washington, DC: Brookings Institution Press.

————. 2006b. *Progress against Poverty: Sustaining Mexico's Progresa-Oportunidades Program*. Washington, DC: Brookings Institution Press.

————. 2007. *Productividad, Crecimiento y Pobreza en México: ¿Qué Sigue Después de Progresa-Oportunidades?* Washington, DC: IDB.

————. 2008. *Good Intentions, Bad Outcomes: Social Policy, Informality and Economic Growth in Mexico*. Washington, DC: Brookings Institution Press.

Levy, Santiago, and Evelyne Rodríguez. 2005. *Sin Herencia de Pobreza: El Programa Progresa-Oportunidades de México*. Mexico DF: IDB and Editorial Planeta Mexicana.

Lindert, Kathey, Emmanuel Skoufias, and Joseph Shapiro. 2006. *Redistributing Income to the Poor and the Rich: Public Transfers in Latin America and the Caribbean*. Washington, DC: World Bank.

Lomelí-Vanegas, Leonardo. 2010. "Viabilidad Fiscal del Universalismo Básico en México." In *Perspectivas del Universalismo en México*, edited by E. Valencia, 37–44. Guadalajara: Universidad de Guadalajara e ITESO.

López, Humberto. 2004. *World Bank Pro-poor Growth: A Review of What We Know (and of What We Don't)*. Washington, DC: World Bank.

López, María de la Paz, and Vania Salles, eds. 2006. *El Programa Oportunidades Examinado desde el Género*. Mexico DF: UNIFEM y el Colegio de México.

Lotze, Conny. 2005. "Economics with a Social Face." *Finance and Development* 42, no. 4: 4–7.

Lustig, Nora. 2002. "The Tequila Effect: The Mexican Peso Crisis." In *Finance Markets and Sustainable Development*. San Francisco: ICS Press. Accessed January 12, 2004. http://www.wu-wien.ac.at/inst/vw7/TequilaEffect.pdf.

Lustig, Nora, and Omar Arias. 2000. "Poverty Reduction." *Finance and Development* 42, no. 1: 30–33.

Macdonald, Laura. 1994. "Mobilizing Civil Society: Interpreting International CSOs in Central America." *Millennium: Journal of International Studies* 23, no. 2: 267–85.

Macdonald, Laura, and Arne Rückert, eds. 2009. *Post-Neoliberalism in the Americas: Beyond the Washington Consensus*. London: Palgrave Macmillan.

Mancera Corcuera, Carlos, Leslie Serna Hernández, and Alejandra Priede Schubert. 2008. "Modalidad Educativa y Organización Multigrado como Factores Asociados con las Brechas de Aprendizaje de los Becarios del Programa Oportunidades (Primaria y Secundaria en 2007)." In *Evaluación Externa del Programa Oportunidades 2008, a Diez Años de Intervención en Zonas Rurales (1997–2007)*, edited by SEDESOL, 129–36. Mexico DF: SEDESOL.

Manning, Susan. 1996. "Politics and Economic Change in Mexico: Neoliberalism, the State, and Civil Society." Working Paper, John Hopkins University, Department of Sociology. Accessed May 25, 2001. http://www.jhu.edu/~soc/pcid/papers/19.htm.

Marglin, Stephen, and Juliet Schor. 1990. *The Golden Age of Capitalism: Reinterpreting the Postwar Experience*. Oxford: Clarendon Press.

Martínez Franzoni, Juliana, and Koen Voorend. 2008. "Transferencias Condicionadas, Regímenes de Bienestar e Igualdad de Género: ¿Blancos, Negros o Grises?" Documento de Trabajo, Instituto de Investigaciones Sociales, Universidad de Costa Rica.

————. 2011. "Actors and Ideas behind CCTs in Chile, Costa Rica and El Salvador." *Global Social Policy* 11, no. 2–3: 279–98.

Marulanda, Beatriz, and María Otero. 2005. *Perfil de la Microfinanzas en Latinoamérica en 10 Años: Visión y Características.* Boston: Acción International. Accessed March 2, 2012. http://www.fidamerica.cl/admin/docdescargas/centrodoc/centrodoc_549.pdf.

Mason, Edward, and Robert Asher. 1973. *The World Bank since Bretton Woods.* Washington, DC: Brookings Institution Press.

Matin, Imran, and David Hulme. 2003. "Programs for the Poorest: Learning from the IGVGD Program in Bangladesh." *World Development* 31, no. 3: 647–65.

Max-Neef, Manfred. 1986. "Desarrollo a Escala Humana: Una Opción para el Futuro." *Development Dialogue*, 9–94. Uppsala, Sweden: Dag Hammarskjöld Foundation.

McMichael, Philip. 2003. *Development and Social Change: A Global Perspective.* Thousand Oaks, CA: Sage/Pine Forge Press.

———. 2009a. "A Food Regime Genealogy." *Journal of Peasant Studies* 36, no. 1: 139–69.

———. 2009b. "Banking on Agriculture: A Review of the World Development Report 2008." *Journal of Agrarian Change* 9, no. 2: 235–46.

———. 2010. "The Agrofuels Project at Large." In *Imperialism, Crisis and Class Struggle: The Verities of Capitalism*, edited by H. Veltmeyer. Leiden: Brill.

McMichael, Philip, and Mindi Schneider. 2011. "Food Security Politics and the Millennium Development Goals." *Third World Quarterly* 32, no. 1: 119–39.

McNamara, Robert S. 1968. *The Essence of Security: Reflections in Office.* New York: Harper and Row.

———. 1973. *One Hundred Countries, Two Billion People: The Dimensions of Development.* New York: Praeger.

———. 1981. "The McNamara Years at the World Bank." In *Major Policy Addresses of Robert S. McNamara, 1968–1981.* Baltimore, MD: World Bank/Johns Hopkins University Press.

Mehrota, Santosh, and Enrique Delamonica. 2007. *Eliminating Human Poverty: Macroeconomic and Social Policies for Equitable Growth.* London: Zed Books.

Mehta, S. Pradeep, and Bipul Chatterjee. 2011. *Growth and Poverty: The Great Debate.* Jaipur: TS International.

Mena, Jose Manuel, and Enrique Errazuriz. 2006. *BancoEstado: Inclusive Finance: Expanding Borders.* Santiago, Chile: Banco Estado.

Mendes Pereira, João Márcio. 2010a. *O Banco Mundial Como Ator Político, Intelectual e Financeiro (1944–2008).* Rio de Janeiro: Civilização Brasileira.

———. 2010b. "O Banco Mundial e a Construção Político-Intelectual do 'Combate à Pobreza.'" *Topoi* 11, no. 21: 260–82.

Mesa Lago, Carmelo. 2005. *Las Reformas de Salud en América Latina y el Caribe: Su Impacto en los Principios de la Seguridad Social.* Santiago, Chile: CEPAL.

Mexico, Federal Government. 2008. "Oportunidades: A Program of Results." Accessed March 2, 2012. www.gobiernofederal.gob.mx.

Meyer, Richard. 2002. "Track Record of Financial Institutions in Assisting the Poor in Asia." Research Paper No. 49, Asian Development Bank Institute Research. Accessed March 1, 2012. http://www.adbi.org/research%20paper/2002/12/01/41.track.record.of.financial.institutions/.

Microcredit Summit Campaign. 1998. *Directory of Institutional Profiles.* Washington, DC: Microcredit Summit Campaign.

Mirowski, Philip, and Dieter Plehwe. 2009. *The Road from Mont Pelerin: The Making of the Neoliberal Thought Collective.* Cambridge, MA: Cambridge University Press.

MkNelly, Barbara, and Christopher Dunford. 1999. "Impact of Credit with Education on Mothers and Young Children's Nutrition: CRECER Credit with Education Program in Bolivia." Freedom from Hunger Research Paper No. 5, Freedom from Hunger, December.

MkNelly, Barbara, Chatree Watetip, Cheryl A. Lassen, and Christopher Dunford. 1996. "Preliminary Evidence That Integrated Financial and Educational Services Can Be Effective against Hunger and Malnutrition." Freedom from Hunger Research Paper No. 2, Program in International Nutrition, University of California, Davis, CA.

Moguel, Patricia, and Victor Toledo. 1999. "Biodiversity Conservation in Traditional Coffee Systems of Mexico." *Conservation Biology* 13, no. 1: 11–21.

Molenaers, Nadia, and Robrecht Renard. 2003. "The World Bank, Participation and PRSP: The Bolivian Case Revisited." *The European Journal of Development Research* 15, no. 2: 133–61.

Molina, Carlos Gerardo, ed. 2006. *Universalismo Básico: Una Nueva Política Social para América Latina*. Washington, DC, and Mexico DF: BID and Planeta.

Molinar, Juan, and Jeffery Weldon. 1994. "Electoral Determinants and Consequences of National Solidarity." In *Transforming State-Society Relations in Mexico: The National Solidarity Strategy*, edited by W. Cornelius, A. Craig, and J. Fox, 123–41. La Jolla, CA: Center for US-Mexican Studies.

Molyneux, Maxine. 2006. "Mothers at the Service of the New Poverty Agenda: Progresa/Oportunidades, Mexico's Conditional Transfer Programme." *Social Policy and Administration* 40, no. 4: 425–49.

———. 2007. "Change and Continuity in Social Protection in Latin America: Mothers at the Service of the State?" Working Paper No. 1, UNRISD, Gender Development Programme, UNRISD, Geneva.

Monje, Guillermo. 1995. "Falling from Grace? The Political Economy of Non-governmental Organizations: A Study of Competition and Dysfunction." PhD diss., Columbus, Ohio State University.

Morduch, Jonathan. 1999. "The Microfinance Promise." *Journal of Economic Literature* 37: 1569–614.

Morduch, Jonathan, and Don Johnston. 2003. "Can the Poor Pay More? Microfinance and Returns to Capital in Indonesia." Paper presented at Asian Development Bank Institute, Tokyo University, and Hitotsubashi University, June.

Morley, Samuel, and David Coady. 2003. *From Social Assistance to Social Development: Targeted Education Subsidies in Developing Countries*. Washington, DC: Center for Global Development/International Food Policy Research Institute.

Morrow, Daniel. 2001. *Poverty Reduction Strategy Papers [PRSP] and Sustainable Development*. Washington, DC: World Bank.

Mosley, Paul. 2001a. "Attacking Poverty and the Post-Washington Consensus." *International Development* 13, no. 3: 307–13.

———. 2001b. "Microfinance and Poverty in Bolivia." *Journal of Development Studies* 37, no. 4: 101–32.

Mostajo, Rossana. 2000. *Gasto Social y Distribución del Ingreso: Caracterización y Impacto Redistributivo en Paises Seleccionados de América Latina y el Caríbe*. Santiago, Chile: CEPAL.

Moyo, Sam, and Paris Yeros, eds. 2005. *Reclaiming the Land: The Resurgence of Rural Movements in Africa, Asia, and Latin America*. London: Zed Books.

Narayan, Deepa, Robert Chambers, Meera K. Shah, and Patti Petesch. 2000. *Voices of the Poor: Crying Out for Change.* Washington, DC: World Bank.

Navajas, Sergio, and Mark Schreiner. 1998. "Apex Organizations and the Growth of Microfinance in Bolivia." Economics and Sociology Occasional Paper No. 2500, Rural Finance Program, Department of Agricultural, Environmental and Development Economics, Ohio State University.

Navajas, Sergio, Mark Schreiner, Richard L. Meyer, Claudio Gonzalez Vega, and Jorge Rodriguez Meza. 2000. "Microcredit and the Poorest of the Poor: Theory and Evidence from Bolivia." *World Development* 28, no. 2: 333–46.

Navajas, Sergio, and Luis Tejerina. 2006. *Microfinance in Latin America and the Caribbean: How Large Is the Market?* Sustainable Development Department Best Practices Series MSM-135. Washington, DC: IDB.

Navarro, Jorge. 1992. "Poverty and Adjustment: The Case of Honduras." *CEPAL Review* 49: 91–101.

Neufeld, Lynnette, Fabiola Mejía, Ana Cecilia Fernández, Armando García, Ignacio Méndez, and Clara Domínguez. 2008. "Diagnóstico Situacional del Estado Nutricio de Niños Menores de Dos Años de Edad y de Sus Madres, Beneficiarios de Oportunidades en Zonas Rurales." In *Evaluación Externa del Programa Oportunidades 2008, a Diez Años de Intervención en Zonas Rurales (1997–2007)*, 121–28. Mexico DF: SEDESOL.

Neufeld, Lynnette, Daniela Sotres Álvarez, Raquel García Feregrino, Armando García Guerra, Lizbeth Tolentino Mayo, Lia Fernald, and Juan Rivera Dmmarco. 2005. "Estudio Comparativo sobre el Estado Nutricional y la Adquisición de Lenguaje entre Niños de Localidades Urbanas con y sin Oportunidades." In *Evaluación Externa del Programa Oportunidades 2004: Alimentación*, edited by B. Hernàndez Prado and M. Hernàndez Avila, Vol. III, 87–116. Cuernavaca: Instituto Nacional de Salud Público.

Neufeld, Lynnette, Daniela Sotres Álvarez, Paul Gertler, Lizbeth Tolentino Mayo, Jorge Jiménez Ruiz, Lia Fernald, Salvador Villalpando, Teresa Shamah, and Juan Rivera Dommarco. 2005. In *Evaluación Externa del Programa Oportunidades 2004: Alimentación*, edited by B. Hernàndez Prado and M. Hernàndez Avila, Vol. III, 15–50. Cuernavaca: Instituto Nacional de Salud Público.

Nigh, Ronald. 1992. "La Agricultura Orgánica y el Nuevo Movimiento Campesino en México." *Antropológicas*, no. 3: 39–50.

Noël, Alain. 2006. "The New Global Politics of Poverty." *Global Social Policy* 6, no. 3: 304–33.

Núñez, Jairo, and Laura Cuesta. 2006. "Colombia: Programa Familias en Acción." In *Transferencias con Corresponsabilidad: Una Mirada Latinoamericana*, edited by E. Cohen and R. Franco, 227–78. Mexico DF: Facultad de Ciencias Sociales.

Ocampo, José Antonio. 2004. "Social Capital and the Development Agenda." In *Social Capital and Poverty Reduction in Latin America and the Caribbean: Towards a New Paradigm*, edited by R. Atria et al., 25–32. Santiago, Chile: ECLAC.

———. 2007. "Markets, Social Cohesion and Democracy." In *Policy Matters: Economic and Social Policies to Sustain Equitable Development*, edited by J. A. Ocampo, K. S. Jomo, and S. Khan, 1–31. London: Zed Books.

Ocampo, José Antonio, K. S. Jomo, and Khan Sarbuland, eds. 2007. *Policy Matters: Economic and Social Policies to Sustain Equitable Development.* London: Zed Books.

OECD (Organisation for Economic Co-operation and Development). 2010. *Perspectives on Global Development: Shifting Wealth.* Paris: OECD.

Olave, Patricia. 1994. "Reestructuración Productiva Bajo el Nuevo Patrón Exportador." In *América Latina en los Ochenta: Reestructuración y Perspectivas*, edited by J. A. Córdova, 21–66. Mexico DF: IIEC-UNAM.

O'Malley, Anthony, and Henry Veltmeyer. 2006. "Banking on Poverty." *Canadian Journal of Development Studies* 26, no. 3: 287–307.

Onis, Ziya, and Fikret Senses. 2005. "Rethinking the Emerging Post-Washington Consensus." *Development and Change* 36, no. 2: 263–90.

Ordóñez, Gerardo. 2002. *La Política Social y el Combate a la Pobreza en México*. Mexico DF: Universidad Nacional Autónoma de México.

Ordóñez, Gerardo, and Guadalupe Ortega. 2006. "La Lucha Contra la Pobreza en el Gobierno de Fox: Continuidad en la Alternancia." In *Alternancia, Políticas Sociales y Desarrollo Regional en México*, edited by G. Ordónez, R. Enriques, I. Román, and E. Valencia, 159–92. Tijuana and Guadalajara: El Colegio de la Frontera Norte, ITESO, Universidad de Guadalajara.

Otero, Gerardo. 1999. *Farewell to the Peasantry: Political Formation in Rural Mexico*. Boulder, CO: Westview.

Padmanabhan, K. P. 1988. *Rural Credit*. London: Intermediate Technology Publications.

Palma, Julieta, and Raúl Urzúa. 2005. *Anti-poverty Policies and Citizenry: The Chile Solidario Experience*. New York: UNESCO.

Park, Albert, and Changqing Ren. 2001. "Microfinance with Chinese Characteristics." *World Development* 29, no. 1: 39–62.

Parker, Susan. 2003a. "Case Study: The Oportunidades Program in Mexico." Paper presented at the Shanghai Poverty Conference, Scaling Up Poverty Reduction, April 20. Accessed March 1, 2012. http://www.politiquessociales.net/IMG/pdf/Mexico_oportunidades.pdf.

———. 2003b. "Evaluación del Impacto de *Oportunidades* sobre la Inscripción, Reprobación y Abandono Escolar." In *Evaluación Externa de Impacto del Programa Oportunidades 2003*, edited by B. Hernández and M. Hernández. Cuernavaca, Mexico: Instituto Nacional de Salud Pública.

Parker, Susan, and Jere Behrman. 2008. "Seguimiento de Adultos Jóvenes en Hogares Incorporados desde 1998 a Oportunidades: Impactos en Educación y Pruebas de Desempeño." In *Evaluación Externa del Programa Oportunidades 2008, a Diez Años de Intervención en Zonas Rurales (1997–2007)*, edited by SEDESOL, 43–46. Mexico DF: SEDESOL.

PA-SMEC/BIT, BCEAO. 1998. "Banques de Données sur les Systèmes Financiers Décentralisés de 7 Pays de l'UMOA (Bénin, Burkina Faso, Côte d'Ivoire, Mali, Niger, Sénégal et Togo)." PA-SMEC, projet BIT/BCEAO, Dakar, Sénégal/ Genève, Suisse, 8 volumes.

Patel, Raj. 2008. *Stuffed and Starved: The Hidden Battle for the World Food System*. Brooklyn, NY: Melville House.

———. 2009. "What Does Food Sovereignty Look Like?" *Journal of Peasant Studies* 36, no. 3: 663–706.

Patten, Richard, Jay Rosengard, and Don Johnson. 2001. "Microfinance Success amidst Macro Economic Failure: The Experience of Bank Rakyat Indonesia during the East Asian Crisis." *World Development* 29, no. 6: 1057–69.

Paugam, Serge, ed. 1996. *L'exclusion: L'Etat des savoirs*. Paris: Ed. La Découverte.

Payer, Cheryl. 1980. "El Banco Mundial y los Pequeños Agricultores." In *Banco Mundial: Un Caso de "Progresismo Conservador,"* edited by Hugo Assmann. San José: Departamento Ecuménico de Investigaciones.

———. 1982. *The World Bank: A Critical Analysis*. New York: Monthly Review Press.

Peet, Richard, ed. 2004. *La Maldita Trinidad: El Fondo Monetario Internacional, el Banco Mundial y la Organización Mundial de Comercio*. Pamplona: Laetoli.

Pender, John. 2001. "From Structural Adjustment to Comprehensive Development Framework: Conditionality Transformed?" *Third World Quarterly* 22, no. 3: 397–411.

Petras, James, and Sonia Arellano López. 1997. "Non-government Organisations and Poverty Alleviation in Bolivia." In *Neoliberalism and Class Conflict in Latin America*, edited by H. Veltmeyer and J. Petras, 180–94. London: Macmillan.

Petras, James, and Henry Veltmeyer. 2001. *Globalization Unmasked: Imperialism in the 21st Century*. Halifax and London: Fernwood, and ZED Press.

———. 2005. *Social Movements and the State: Argentina, Bolivia, Brazil, Ecuador*. London: Pluto Press.

———. 2011a. *Social Movements in Latin America: Neoliberalism and Popular Resistance*. New York: Palgrave Macmillan.

———. 2011b. *Critical Rural Beyond Neoliberalism: A World to Win*. London: Ashgate.

———. 2012. *Beyond Neoliberalism: A World to Win*. London: Ashgate.

Pitt, Mark, and Shahidur R. Khandker. 1998. "The Impact of Group-Based Credit Programs on Poor Households in Bangladesh: Does the Gender of Participants Matter?" *Journal of Political Economy* 106, no. 5: 958–96.

Pitt, Mark M., Shahidur R. Khankder, Omar H. Chowdhury, and Daniel L. Millimet. 2003. "Credit Programs for the Poor and the Health Status of Children in Rural Bangladesh." *International Economic Review* 44, no. 1: 87–118.

Pochmann, Marcío. n.d. *Unequal Distribution of Income and Wealth in Brazil*. Geneva: UNRISD.

Poder Ejecutivo Federal. 1994. *Sexto Informe de Gobierno*. Mexico DF: Gobierno Federal.

———. 1997. *Progresa, Programa de Educación, Salud y Alimentación*. Mexico DF: Gobierno Federal.

———. 2008. *Vivir Mejor*. Mexico DF: Gobierno Federal.

———. 2009. "Tercer Informe de Ejecución, México, DF: Gobierno Federal." Accessed September 1, 2010. http://pnd.calderon.presidencio.gob.mx.

———. 2011. *Cuarto Informe de Ejecución*. Mexico DF: Gobierno Federal.

Ponce, Juan. 2006. "The Impact of Conditional Cash Transfer Program on Students' Cognitive Achievements: The Case of the 'Bono de Desarrollo Humano' of Ecuador." Working Paper No. 06–301, FLACSO, Ecuador.

Potter, David. 2000. "Democratization, Good Governance and Development." In *Poverty and Development into the 21st Century*, edited T. Allen and A. Thomas, 365–82. New York: Oxford University Press.

Presidencia República Dominicana. 2006. *Programas de Transferencias Condicionadas de Ingreso: Experiencia de la Repuública Dominicana*. Rome: FAO.

Psacharopoulos, George, and Harry Anthony Patrinos, eds. 2004. *Indigenous People and Poverty in Latin America: An Empirical Analysis*. Washington, DC: World Bank.

Quintana, Víctor. 2007. "Año 13: El Impacto del TLCAN en la Agricultura Mexicana." Vía Campesina. Accessed April 28, 2008. http://www.viacampesina.org.

Raczynski, Dagmar. 1998. "The Crisis of Old Models of Social Protection in Latin America: New Alternatives for Dealing with Poverty." In *Poverty and Inequality in Latin America: Issues and New Challenges*, edited by V. Tokman and G. O'Donnell, 140–68. Notre Dame: University of Notre Dame Press.

Raczynski, Dagmar, and Claudia Serrano. 2005. "Programas de Superación de la Pobreza y el Capital Social: Evidencias y Aprendizajes de la Experiencia en Chile." In *Aprender de la Experiencia: El Capital Social en la Superación de la Pobreza*, edited by I. Arriagada, 99–132. Santiago, Chile: CEPAL.

Rajan, Raguerham, and Luigi Zingales. 2003. *Saving Capitalism from the Capitalists: Unleashing the Power of Financial Markets to Create Wealth and Spread Opportunity*. New York: Crown Business.

Ramirez, Álvaro. 2004. "The Microfinance Experience in Latin America and the Caribbean." Paper presented at the Asian Development Bank Institute Workshop on Modalities of Microfinance Delivery in Asia, Manila, October 4–8.

Ravallion, Martin. 2004. *Pro-poor Growth: A Primer*. Washington, DC: World Bank.

Ravallion, Martin, and Shaohua Chen. 2009. "Weakly Relative Poverty." Policy Research Working Paper Series 4844, World Bank, Washington, DC.

Rawlings, Laura B. 2005. "A New Approach to Social Assistance: Latin America's Experience with Conditional Cash Transfer Programs." *International Social Security Review* 58, no. 2–3: 133–61.

Rawlings, Laura B., and Gloria M. Rubio. 2003. "Evaluación del Impacto de los Programas de Transferencias Condicionadas en Efectivo: Lecciones desde América Latina." In *Cuadernos Desarrollo Humano, 10*. Mexico DF: SEDESOL.

Reimers, Fernando, Carol De Shano da Silva, and Ernesto Trevino. 2006. "Where Is the 'Education' in Conditional Cash Transfers in Education?" Working Paper No. 4, UNESCO Institute for Statistics, Montreal.

Rello, Fernando, and Fernando Saavedra. 2007. *Implicaciones Estructurales de la Liberalización en la Agricultura y el Desarrollo Rural: El Caso de México*. Washington, DC: World Bank.

Republic of Bolivia. 2001. *Poverty Reduction Strategy Paper*. La Paz, Bolivia.

Rhyne, Elizabeth. 2001. *Mainstreaming Microfinance: How Lending to the Poor Began, Grew and Came of Age in Bolivia*. Bloomfield, CT: Kumarian Press.

Rich, Bruce. 1994. *Mortgaging the Earth: The World Bank, Environmental Impoverishment, and the Crisis of Development*. Boston: Beacon Press.

Riquer-Fernández, Florinda. 2000. "Las Pobres de Pobreza: Reflexiones." In *Los Dilemas de la Política Social: ¿Cómo Combatir la Pobreza?*, edited by E. Valencia, M. Gendreau, and A. M. Tepichín, 283–310. Guadalajara: Universidad de Guadalajara y ITESO.

Rivera, Leonor, Bernardo Hernández, and Roberto Castro. 2006. "Asociación Entre la Violencia de Pareja Contra las Mujeres de las Zonas Urbanas en Pobreza Extrema y la Incorporación al Programa Oportunidades." In *El Programa Oportunidades Examinado desde el Género*, edited by M. P. López and V. Salles, 69–93. Mexico DF: UNIFEM and Colegio de México.

Robinson, Marguerite S. 2001. *The Microfinance Revolution: Sustainable Finance for the Poor*. Washington, DC: World Bank.

Robinson, William I. 1997. "Nicaragua and the World: A Globalization Perspective." In *Nicaragua without Illusions: Regime Transition and Structural Adjustment in the 1990s*, edited by T. W. Walker, 23–42. Wilmington, DE: SR Books.

Rodríguez, Eduardo, and Samuel Freije. 2008. "Una Evaluación de Impacto sobre el Empleo, los Salarios y la Movilidad Ocupacional Intergeneracional del Programa Oportunidades." In *Evaluación Externa del Programa Oportunidades 2008, a Diez Años de Intervención en Zonas Rurales (1997–2007)*, edited by SEDESOL, 19–22. Mexico DF: SEDESOL.

Rodrik, Dani. 1997. *Has Globalization Gone Too Far?* Washington, DC: Institute of International Economics.

Rondinelli, Dennis, Jhon R. Nellis, and Shabbir Cheema. 1983. "Decentralization in Developing Countries: A Review of Recent Experience." World Bank Staff Paper No. 581, World Bank, Washington, DC.

Roozen, Nico, and Frans VanderHoff. 2002. *La Aventura del Comercio Justo: Una Alternativa de Globalización por los Fundadores de Max Havelaar.* Mexico DF: El Atajo.

Rosenau, James, and Ernst Otto Czempiel, eds. 1992. *Governance without Government: Order and Change in World Politics.* Cambridge: Cambridge University Press.

Rosset, Peter. 2000. "The Multiple Functions and Benefits of Small Farm Agriculture in the Context of Global Trade Negotiations." *Development* 43, no. 2: 77–82.

Rosset, Peter, Braulio Machín Sosa, Adilén María Roque Jaime, and Dana Rocío Ávila Lozano. 2011. "The Campesino-to-Campesino Agroecology Movement of ANAP in Cuba: Social Process Methodology in the Construction of Sustainable Peasant Agriculture and Food Sovereignty." *Journal of Peasant Studies* 38, no. 1: 161–91.

Rubalcava, Rosa María. 2008. "Progresa-Oportunidades: Un Programa Social con Compromiso Demográfico y Perspectiva de Género." In *Políticas Sociales y Género: Tomo II. Los Problemas Sociales y Metodológicos,* edited by Gisela Zaremberg, 225–67. Mexico DF: FLACSO.

Ruckert, Arne. 2010. "The Forgotten Dimension of Social Reproduction: The World Bank and the Poverty Reduction Paradigm." *Review of International Political Economy* 17, no. 5: 816–39.

Rutherford, Stuart. 2002. "Money Talks: Conversations with Poor Households in Bangladesh about Managing Money." Working Paper No. 45, Institute for Development Policy and Managing Money, University of Manchester.

———. 2003. "Microfinance's Evolving Ideals: How They Were Formed and Why They're Changing." Paper presented at ADBI Annual Conference, Microfinance in Asia: Poverty Impact and Outreach to the Poor, Tokyo, December 5.

Saad-Fihlo, Alfredo. 2005. "From Washington to Post-Washington Consensus." In *Neoliberalism: A Critical Reader,* edited by A. Saad-Fhilo and D. Johnston, 113–19. London: Pluto Press.

Saavedra, Jaime, and Omar Arias. 2005. "Stuck in a Rut." *Finance and Development* 42, no. 4: 18–22.

Sabatier, Paul A., and Christopher M. Weible. 2007. "The Advocacy Coalition Framework: Innovations and Clarifications." In *Theories of the Policy Process,* edited by Paul A. Sabatier, 189–220. Boulder, CO: Westview.

Sachs, Jeffrey. 2005. *The End of Poverty.* New York: Penguin Press.

Sachs, Wolfgang. 1999. *Planet Dialectics: Explorations in Environment and Development.* London: Zed Books.

Sanahuja, José Antonio. 2001. *Altruismo, Mercado y Poder: El Banco Mundial y la Lucha Contra la Pobreza.* Barcelona: Intermón Oxfam.

Sande Lie, Jon Harald. 2006. "Developmentality: The CDF and PRSP as Governance Mechanisms." Accessed September 12, 2007. http://www2.warwick.ac.uk.

SAPRIN (Structural Adjustment Participatory Review Initiative). 2001. "The Policy Roots of Economic Crisis and Poverty: A Multi-Country Participatory Assessment of Structural Adjustment." Executive Summary. Accessed March 27, 2003. www.saprin.org/SAPRIN_Exec_Summ_Eng.pdf.

Schreiner, Mark. 2003. "A Cost-Effectiveness Analysis of the Grameen Bank of Bangladesh." *Development Policy Review* 21, no. 3: 357–82.

Schteingart, Martha, ed. 1999. *Políticas Sociales para los Pobres en América Latina.* Mexico DF: Global Urban Research Initiative and Miguel Angel Porrúa.

Scott, John. 2010. "Subsidios Agrícolas en México: ¿Quién Gana, y Cuánto?" In *Subsidios para la Desigualdad: Las Políticas Públicas del Maíz en México a Partir del Libre Comercio,* edited by J. Fox and L. Haight, 73–127. Santa Cruz: University of California.

Seligson, Mitchell. 1995. "Thirty Years of Transformation in the Agrarian Structure of El Salvador." *Latin American Research Review* 30, no. 3: 43–74.

Sen, Amartya. 1989. "Development as Capability Expansion." *Journal of Development Expansion,* no. 19: 41–58.

———. 1999. *Development as Freedom.* New York: Alfred A. Knopf.

———. 2003. "La Economía Política de la Focalización." *Comercio Exterior* 53, no. 6: 555–62.

———. 2010. *The Idea of Justice.* Cambridge, MA: Harvard University Press.

Serrano, Claudia. 2005. "Claves de la Políticas Social para la Pobreza." Accessed March 3, 2012. www.unesu.org/piapobreza/Lectura7.pdf.

Serrano, Franklin. 2004. "Relações de Poder e a Política Macroeconômica Americana, de Bretton Woods ao Padrão Dólar Flexível." In *O Poder Americano,* edited by José Luís Fiori. Petrópolis: Vozes.

SGTS and Associates. 2000. "Civil Society Participation in Poverty Reduction Strategy Papers (PRSPS) Vol. I: Overview and Recommendations." Report commissioned by the Department for International Development, October. Accessed March 28, 2005. http://www .dfid.gov.uk/pubs/tiles/cs-prsps-vI.pdf.

Simões, Armando A. 2006. "Los Programas de Transferencia: Una Complementariedad Posible y Deseable." In *Universalismo Básico: Una Nueva Política Social para América Latina,* edited by C. Molina, 293–311. Washington, DC, and Mexico DF: BID and Planeta.

Singh, Anoop, and Charles Collyns. 2005. "Latin America's Resurgence." *Finance and Development* 42, no. 4: 8–13.

Skoufias, Emmanuel, ed. 2000. "¿Está Dando Buenos Resultados Progresa?" In *Informe de los Resultados de una Evaluación Realizada por el IFPRI 2000.* Mexico DF: SEDESOL.

———. 2005. *"Progresa y Sus Efectos Sobre el Bienestar de las Familias Rurales en México."* International Food Policy Research Institute, Informe de Investigación 139. http://www.ifpri .org/sites/default/files/publications/ab139sp.pdf.

Skoufias, Emmanuel, Benjamin Davis, and Sergio de la Vega. 2001. "Targeting the Poor in Mexico: An Evaluation of the Selection of Households for Progresa." Working Paper No. 103, Food Consumption and Nutrition Division of the International Food Policy Research Institute, Washington DC.

Skoufias, Emmanuel, and Bonnie McClafferty. 2001. "Is PROGRESA Working? Summary of the Results of an Evaluation by IFPRI." Discussion Paper No. 118, Food Consumption and Nutrition Division of the International Food Policy Research Institute, Washington DC.

Smith, Stephen. 2005. *Ending Global Poverty: A Guide to What Works.* London: Palgrave Macmillan.

Soares, Sergei, Rafael Guerreiro Osório, Fábio Veras Soares, Marcelo Madeiros, and Eduardo Zepeda. 2007. "Conditional Cash Transfers in Brazil, Chile and México: Impacts upon Inequality." Working Paper No. 35, International Poverty Centre, UNDP.

————. 2009. "Conditional Cash Transfers in Brazil, Chile and Mexico: Impacts upon Inequality." Special issue, *Estudios Económicos*, 207–24.

Sogge, David, ed. 1998. *Compasión y Cálculo: Un Análisis Crítico de la Cooperación no Gubernamental al Desarrollo*. Barcelona: Icaria Editorial.

————. 2002. *Dar y Tomar: ¿Qué Sucede con la Ayuda Internacional?* Barcelona: Icaria Editorial.

Sottoli, Susana. 2008. *Los Programas de Combate a la Pobreza desde la Perspectiva de los Derechos Humanos: Un Estudio de Cuatro Casos en América Latina*. Panama and New York: UNICEF.

Stahl, Karin. 1994. "Política Social en América Latina: La Privatización de la Crisis." *Nueva Sociedad*, no. 131: 48–71.

Stahler-Sholk, Richard. 1997. "Structural Adjustment and Resistance: The Political Economy of Nicaragua under Chamorro." In *The Undermining of the Sandinista Revolution*, edited by G. Prevost and H. E. Vanden. New York: St. Martin's Press.

Stern, Nicholas, and Francisco Ferreira. 1997. "The World Bank as 'Intellectual Actor.'" In *The World Bank: Its First Half Century—Perspectives*, edited by D. Kapur, Vol. 2. Washington, DC: Brookings Institution Press.

Stewart, Francis. 2008. "Human Development as an Alternative Development Paradigm." Accessed March 16, 2008. http://hdr.undp.org/en/media/1.

Stiefel, Matthias, and Marshall Wolfe. 1994. *A Voice for the Excluded: Popular Participation in Development; Utopia or Necessity?* London, and Atlantic Highlands, NJ: Zed Books and UNRISD.

Stiglitz, Joseph E. 1998. "More Instruments and Broader Goals: Moving beyond the Post-Washington Consensus." In *Wider Annual Lectures*, 2. Helsinki: WIDER.

————. 2002. *Globalization and Its Discontents*. New York: Norten.

Streeten, Paul. 1981. *First Things First: Meeting Basic Human Needs in the Developing Countries*. New York: Oxford University Press.

————. 1984. "Basic Needs: Some Unsettled Questions." *World Development* 12, no. 9: 973–78.

————, ed. 1986. *Lo Primero es lo Primero: Satisfacer las Necesidades Básicas en los Países en Desarrollo*. Madrid: Tecnos/Banco Mundial.

————. 1998. "Beyond the Six Veils: Conceptualising and Measuring Poverty." *Journal of International Affairs* 52, no. 1: 1–31.

Sumner, Andrew. 2006. "In Search of the Post-Washington (Dis)consensus: The Missing Content of PRSPs." *Third World Quarterly* 27, no. 8: 1401–12.

Sunkel, Osvaldo, ed. 1993. *Development from Within: Towards a Neostructuralist Approach to Latin America*. Boulder, CO: Rienner.

Sunkel, Osvaldo, and Ricardo Infante. 2010. *Hacia un Desarrollo Inclusivo: El Caso de Chile*. Santiago, Chile: CEPAL

Székely, Miguel. 2003. *Es Posible un México con Menor Pobreza y Desigualdad*. Mexico DF: Secretaría de Desarrollo Social.

Tabb, William. 2004. *Economic Governance in the Age of Globalization*. New York: Columbia University Press.

Tan, Celine. 2007. "The Poverty of Amnesia: PRSPS in the Legacy of Structural Adjustment." In *The World Bank and Governance: A Decade of Reform and Reaction*, edited by D. Stone and C. Wright, 147–67. New York: Routledge.

Teichman, Judith. 2007. "Multilateral Lending Institutions and Transnational Policy Networks in Mexico and Chile." *Global Governance* 13, no. 4: 557–73.

Tetreault, Darcy. 2006. "The Evolution of Poverty in Late 20th-Century Mexico." *Canadian Journal of Development Studies* 27, no. 3: 309–26.

———. 2009. *Pobreza y Degradación Ambiental: Las Luchas de Abajo en Dos Comunidades del Occidente de Jalisco: Ayotitlán y La Ciénega.* Guadalajara: Universidad de Guadalajara.

Thomas, Caroline. 2001. "Global Governance, Development and Human Security." *Third World Quarterly* 22, no. 2: 159–75.

Thornton, Nigel, and Marcus Cox. 2005. *Developing Poverty Reduction Strategies in Low-Income Countries under Stress (LICUS).* London: Agulhas Development Consultants.

Todd, Helen. 1996. *Women at the Center: Grameen Borrowers after One Decade.* Dhaka, Bangladesh: University Press.

Toledo, Victor. 1990. "The Ecological Rationality of Peasant Production." In *Agroecology and Small Farm Development,* edited by M. Altieri and S. Hecht, 53–59. Boca Raton: CRC Press.

———. 1992. "Utopía y Naturaleza: El Nuevo Movimiento Ecológico de los Campesinos e Indígenas de América Latina." *Nueva Sociedad* 122: 234–49.

Toussaint, Eric. 2006. *Banco Mundial: El Golpe de Estado Permanente.* Madrid: El Viejo Topo.

Townsend, Peter. 2007. "The Right to Social Security and National Development: Lessons from OECD Experience for Low-Income Countries." Working Paper No. 18, Department of Social Security, ILO, Geneva.

Toye, John. 1987. *Dilemmas of Development.* Oxford: Blackwell.

Trócaire. 2004a. "Are PRSPS Combating Rural Poverty in Honduras and Nicaragua? Lessons for a New Generation of PRSPs." Accessed March 2, 2012. http://trocaire_org/pdfs/policy/prsp/combatingruralpovert.pdf.

———. 2004b. "The Impact of Poverty Reduction Strategies on the Rural Sector in Honduras and Nicaragua." Accessed March 2, 2012. http://www.trocaire.org/resources/policy-resource/impact-poverty-reduction-strategies-rural-sector-honduras-and-nicaragua.

Tussie, Diana, ed. 2000. *Luces y Sombras de una Nueva Relación: El Banco Interamericano de Desarrollo, el Banco Mundial y la Sociedad Civil.* Buenos Aires, Argentina: Temas Grupo Editorial.

UK Ministry of Defence. 2007. *Global Strategic Trends 2007–2036.* London: 31 Development, Concepts and Doctrine Centre (dCdC).

UNDESA (United Nations Department of Economic and Social Affairs). 2005. *The Inequality Predicament: Report on the World Social Situation.* New York: United Nations.

———. 2009. *Rethinking Poverty: Report on the World Situation 2010.* New York: United Nations.

UNDP (United Nations Development Programme). 1997a. "Governance for Sustainable Human Development." Policy Document, UNDP, New York.

———. 1997b. "Participatory Local Governance." Policy Document, UNDP, New York.

———. 1997c. "The Shrinking State: Governance and Sustainable Human Development." Policy Document, UNDP, New York.

———. 1999. *Human Development Report 1999: Globalization with a Human Face.* New York: Oxford University Press.

———. 2006. *Governance for the Future: Democracy and Development in the Least Developed Countries.* New York: UNDP.

———. 2009. *Overcoming Barriers: Human Mobility and Development.* New York: UNDP.

———. 2010. *Regional Human Development Report for Latin America and the Caribbean 2010.* New York: UNDP.

United Nations. 2010. *The Millennium Development Goals Report 2010*. New York: United Nations.

UNRISD (United Nations Research Institute for Social Development). 2010. *Combatiendo la Pobreza y la Desigualdad: Cambio Estructural, Política Social y la Política*. Geneva: UNRISD.

Uphoff, Norman. 2004. "Social Capital and Poverty Reduction." In *Social Capital and Poverty Reduction in Latin America: Toward a New Paradigm*, edited by R. Atria and M. Siles, 105–32. Santiago, Chile: ECLAC.

Valencia Lomelí, Enrique. 2003. "Transición Hacia la Atención Focalizada de la Pobreza Extrema: Caso Progresa en México." Serie *Estudios de Caso y Experiencias Relevantes de Gerencia Social en América Latina, 8*. Washington, DC: IDB, Instituto Interamericano para el Desarrollo Social y Centro Internacional de Investigaciones para el Desarrollo.

———. 2006. "La Política Social de Vicente Fox: Contexto Histórico y Balance." *Asian Journal of Latin American Studies* 19, no. 1: 81–99.

———. 2007. "Los Debates sobre los Regímenes de Bienestar en América Latina y el Este Asia: Los Casos de México y Corea del Sur." Paper presented at Segundo Congress del Consejo de Estudios Latinoamericanos de Asia y de Oceania. Asia Ocean, Seoul, South Korea, June 21–23.

———. 2008. "Conditional Cash Transfers as Social Policy in Latin America: An Assessment of Their Contributions and Limitations." *Annual Review of Sociology*, no. 34: 475–99.

———. 2009. "Conditional Cash Transfer Programs: Achievements and Illusions." *Global Social Policy* 9, no. 2: 167–71.

———. 2010. "La Ilusión de la Neutralidad Política de las Transferencias Monetarias Condicionadas: El Caso de Oportunidades en México." Universidad de Guadalajara, mimeo

———. 2011. "La Ilusión de la Neutralidad Política de las Transferencias Monetarias Condicionadas: El Caso de Oportunidades en México." In *La Necesaria Reconfiguración de la Política Social de México*, edited by M. I. Patiño Rodríguez Malpica, D. Martínez Mendizábal, and E. Valencia Lomelí, 105–22. León, Mexico: Universidad de Guadalajara/Konrad Adenauer Stiftung/Universidad Iberoamericana León.

Valencia Lomelí, Enrique, and Rodolfo Aguirre-Reveles. 2001. "Discursos, Acciones y Controversias de la Política Gubernamental Frente a la Pobreza." In *Los Rostros de la Pobreza: El Debate*, edited by L. R. Gallardo and J. Osorio, Vol. I, 21–93. Mexico: Editorial Limusa.

Valencia Lomelí, Enrique, David Foust, and Darcy Tetreault. 2010. *Informe Final: Estudio sobre la Implementación de las Recomendaciones de los Estudios Referentes a la Pobreza y Su Erradicación en las Políticas Públicas en México*. Guadalajara, Mexico: Universidad de Guadalajara.

———. 2011. "Sistema de Protección Social en México a Inicios del Siglo XXI." CEPAL-ASIDI. http://www.eclac.cl/publicaciones/xml/8/43778/Sistema-proteccion-social-Mexico2011.pdf.

Valencia Lomelí, Enrique, Mónica Gendreau, and Ana María Tepichín, eds. 2000. *Los Dilemas de la Política Social: ¿Cómo Combatir la Pobreza?* Guadalajara: Universidad de Guadalajara and ITESO.

Valenzuela, Arturo. 2005. "Latin America: A Time of Transition." *Finance and Development* 42, no. 4: 16–17.

Vargas, Óscar René. 2001. *Once Años del Ajuste*. 3rd ed. Manaugua: Consejo Nacional de Universidades de Nicaragua.

Velasco e Cruz, Sebastião. 2007. *Trajetórias: Capitalismo Neoliberal e Reformas Econômicas Nos Países da Periferia*. São Paulo: Editora UNESP.

Veltmeyer, Henry. 2002. "Social Exclusion and Models of Development in Latin America." *Canadian Journal of Latin American and Caribbean Studies* 27, no. 54: 251–80.

———. 2007. *Illusions and Opportunities: Civil Society in the Quest for Social Change*. Halifax: Fernwood.

———. 2009. "The World Bank on 'Agriculture for Development': A Failure of Imagination or the Power of Ideology?" *Journal of Peasant Studies* 36, no. 2: 393–410.

———. 2010. *The Poverty Report: Ideas, Policies and Pathways*. Ottawa: CASID.

———, ed. 2011. *Critical Development Studies: Tools for Change*. Halifax and London: Fernwood, and Zed Books.

Veltmeyer, Henry, and James Petras. 2005. "Foreign Aid, Neoliberalism and Imperialism: In *Neoliberalism: A Critical Reader*, edited by A. Saad-Filho and D. Johnston, 120–27. London: Pluto Press.

Vilas, Carlos M. 1997a. "De Ambulancias, Bomberos y Policías: La Política Social del Neoliberalismo (Notas para una Perspectiva Macro)." *Desarrollo Económico* 36, no. 144: 931–52.

———. 1997b. "La Reforma del Estado Como Cuestión Política." *Política y Cultura*, no. 8: 147–85.

Villatoro, Pablo. 2004. "Programas de Reducción de la Pobreza en América Latina: Un Análisis de Cinco Experiencias." *Series Política Social* 87. Santiago, Chile: CEPAL.

———. 2005a. "Estrategias y Programas de Reducción de la Pobreza en América Latina y el Caribe." Paper presented at XXXI Reunión Ordinaria del Consejo Latinoamericano, Caracas, Venezuela, November 21–23.

———. 2005b. "Los Programas de Protección Social Asistencial en América Latina y Sus Impactos en las Familias: Algunas Reflexiones." Paper presented at the Reunión of Expertos "Políticas Hacia las Familias e Inclusión Sociales," CEPAL, Santiago, Chile, June 28–29.

Vorley, Bill. 2003. *Food, Inc.: Corporate Concentration from Farm to Consumer*. London: UK Food Group.

Vuskovic, Pedro. 1993. *Pobreza y Desigualdad en América Latina*. Mexico DF: CEIICH-UNAM.

Wade, Robert. 1997. "Japón, el Banco Mundial y el Arte del Mantenimiento del Paradigma: el Milagro del Este Asiático en Perspectiva Política." *Desarrollo Económico* 37, no. 147: 351–87.

———. 2004. *Governing the Market: Economic Theory and the Role of Government in East Asian Industrialization*. Princeton, NJ: Princeton University Press.

Wallace, Tina. 2004. "NGO Dilemmas: Trojan Horses for Global Neoliberalism?" In *Socialist Register 2004*. London: Merlin Press.

Weber, Heloise. 2002. "Global Governance and Poverty Reduction: The Case of Microcredit." In *Global Governance: Critical Perspectives*, edited by R. Wilkinson and S. Hughes, 132–51. London and New York: Routledge.

Webster, Neil, and Lars Engberg Pedersen. 2002. *In the Name of the Poor: Contesting Political Space for Poverty Reduction*. London: Zed Books.

Weisbrot, Mark, Dean Baker, Egor Kraev, and Judy Chen. 2005. *The Scorecard on Globalization 1980–2000: 20 Years of Diminished Progress*. Washington, DC: Center for Economic and Policy Research.

Weisbrot, Mark, Dean Baker, Robert Naiman, and Gila Neta. 2001. *Growth May Be Good for the Poor, but Are IMF and World Bank Policies Good for Growth?* Washington, DC: Center for Economic Policy Research.

Weiss, John, and Heather Montgomery. 2004. "Great Expectations: Microfinance and Poverty Reduction in Asia and Latin America." ADB Institute Discussion Paper No. 15, Asian Development Bank Institute.

White, Howard, and Geske Dijkstra. 2003. *Programme Aid and Development: Beyond Conditionality.* London: Routledge.

Wilken, Gene. 1987. *Good Farmers: Traditional Agricultural Resource Management in Mexico and Central America.* Berkeley: University of California Press.

Williamson, John. 1990. "What Washington Means by Policy Reform." In *Latin American Adjustment: How Much Has Happened?*, edited by J. Williamson, 5–38. Washington, DC: International Economics Institute.

Wilson, Francis, Nazneen Kanji, and Einar Braathen, eds. 2001. *Macroeconomic Policy, Growth and Poverty Reduction.* New York: St. Martin's Press.

Winters, Paul, and Benjamin Davis. 2009. "Designing a Programme to Support Smallholder Agriculture in Mexico: Lessons from PROCAMPO and Opportunidades." *Development Policy Review* 27, no. 5: 617–42.

Wittman, Hannah, Annette Desmarais, and Nettie Wiebe. 2010. "The Origins and Potential of Food Sovereignty." In *Food Sovereignty: Reconnecting Food, Nature and Community*, edited by H. Wittman, A. Desmarais, and N. Wiebe, 1–14. Halifax: Fernwood.

Wodon, Quentin. 1998. "Cost-Benefit Analysis of Food for Education in Bangladesh." Background Paper for the Poverty Assessment of Bangladesh at the World Bank, World Bank, Washington, DC.

Wolfensohn, James. 1999. *A Proposal for a Comprehensive Development Framework.* Washington, DC: World Bank. Accessed October 10, 2004. http://www.Worldbank.org/cdf/cdf-text.htm.

Woo-Cumings, Meredith. 1999. *The Developmental State.* Ithaca, NY: Cornell University Press.

Woodroffe, Jessica, and Mark Eliss Jones. 2000. "States of Unrest: Resistance to IMF Policies in Poor Countries." World Development Movement Report. http://www.globalpolicy.org/socecon/bwiwto/imf/2000/protest.htm.

Woodward, David. 1992. *Debt, Adjustment and Poverty in Developing Countries.* Vol. II. London: Pinter Press.

Woolcock, Michael. 1988. "Social Capital and Economic Development: Towards a Theoretical Synthesis and Policy Framework." *Theory and Society*, no. 27: 151–208.

Woolcock, Michael, and Deepa Narayan. 2000. "Social Capital: Implications for Development Theory, Research and Policy." *The World Bank Research Observer* 15, no. 2: 145–270.

World Bank. 1968. *Annual Report.* Washington, DC: World Bank.

———. 1972. *Annual Report.* Washington, DC: World Bank.

———. 1981. *Accelerated Development in Sub-Saharan Africa: An Agenda for Action.* New York: Oxford University Press.

———. 1988a. *Inequality, Poverty and Growth.* Washington, DC: World Bank.

———. 1988b. *Adjustment Lending: An Evaluation of Ten Years of Experience.* Washington, DC: World Bank.

———. 1989. *Sub-Saharan Africa: From Crisis to Sustainable Growth.* New York: Oxford University Press.

————. 1990. *World Development Report 1990: Poverty*. Oxford: Oxford University Press.

————. 1991. *World Development Report 1991: The Challenge of Development*. Oxford: Oxford University Press.

————. 1993. *Annual Report*. Washington, DC: World Bank.

————. 1994a. *Governance: The World Bank Experience*. Washington, DC: World Bank.

————. 1994b. "Honduras: Country Economic Memorandum/Poverty Assessment." http://www.wds.worldbank.org/servlet/WDSContentServer/WDSP/IB/1994/11/17/0000092 65__3961006170721/Rendered/PDF/multi_page.pdf.

————. 1996a. *Sustainable Banking with the Poor: A Worldwide Inventory of Microfinance Institutions*. Washington, DC: World Bank.

————. 1996b. *The World Bank Participation Sourcebook*. Washington, DC: Environmentally Sustainable Development Department, World Bank.

————. 1999. "Can the Poor Influence Policy? Participatory Poverty Assessments in the Developing World." http://www.imf.org/external/pubs/cat/longres.cfm?sk=15200.

————. 2000a. *World Development Report 2000/01: Attacking Poverty*. Washington, DC: World Bank.

————. 2000b. "Tanzania Country Assistance Strategy FY 01–03." Report No. PIN42, World Bank, Washington, DC.

————. 2001. *World Development Report 2000/2001: Attacking Poverty*. Oxford: Oxford University Press.

————. 2002a. "Participation: The Case of Nicaragua." Accessed March 2, 2003. http://www.worldbank.org/participation/NICARAGUA.pdf.

————. 2002b. *Reaching the Rural Poor: A Rural Development Strategy for Latin America and the Caribbean*. Washington, DC: World Bank.

————. 2003a. *Land Policies for Growth and Poverty Reduction*. Washington, DC: World Bank.

————. 2003b. "Nicaragua: Poverty Assessment." Report No. 26128-NI, World Bank, Washington, DC.

————. 2004a. *Partnerships in Development: Progress in the Fight against Poverty*. Washington, DC: World Bank.

————. 2004b. "The Poverty Reduction Strategy Initiative: An Independent Evaluation of the World Bank's Support through 2003." Accessed September 11, 2004. http://inweb18.worldbank.org/oed.org.

————. 2004c. *La Pobreza en México: Una Evaluación de las Condiciones, las Tendencias y la Estrategia del Gobierno*. Washington, DC: World Bank.

————. 2006a. *World Development Report 2006: Equity and Development*. Oxford: Oxford University Press.

————. 2006b. *La Pobreza y Crecimiento: Ciculos Virtuosos y Viciosos*. Washington, DC: World Bank.

————. 2007a. *Meeting the Challenges of Global Development*. Washington, DC: World Bank.

————. 2007b. *Innovaciones Operacionales en América Latina y el Caribe: Mecanismos de Control y de Rendición de Cuentas en Programas de Transferencias Monetarias Condicionadas. Una Revisión de los Programas en Ameérica Latina*. Washington, DC: World Bank.

————. 2008. *World Development Report 2008: Agriculture for Development*. Washington, DC: World Bank.

————. 2009. *PovcalNet: The On-line Tool for Poverty Measurement Developed by the Development Research Group of the World Bank*. Washington, DC: World Bank.

————. n.d. "The PRS Process." Independent Evaluation Group. Accessed October 1, 2010. http://worldbank.org/ieg/prsp/prsp_process.html.

World Bank and IMF (International Monetary Fund). 1999. *Building Poverty Reduction Strategies in Developing Countries.*

————. 2002a. *"A New Approach to Country-Owned Poverty Reduction Strategies."* Accessed November 26, 2002. http://www.wds.worldbankorg/servnet/WDSContentServer/WDSP/IB/2000/05/31.pdf.

————. 2002b. *"Guidance for Joint Staff Assessment of a Poverty Reduction Strategy Paper."* Accessed November 26, 2002. http://povertyworldbank.org/files/IPRSP%Guidance%20 Note%20Sept%207.pdf.

————. 2005. "2005 Review of the PRS Approach: Balancing Accountabilities and Scaling Up Results." Accessed May 18, 2006. http://siteresources.worldbank.org/INTPRS1/Resources/PRSP-Review/2005_Review_Final.pdf.

World Vision. 2002. *Masters of Their Own Development? PRSPs and the Prospects for the Poor.* Monrovia, CA: World Vision International.

Wright, Graham. 2000. *Microfinance Systems: Designing Quality Financial Services for the Poor.* Dhaka, Bangladesh: University Press.

Ynaraja Ramírez, Ramón. 2000. "Bolivia: Una Experiencia en Microfinanzas." *Boletin Economico de Ice*, no. 2655: 25–32.

Yunus, Muhammad. 2001. *Banker to the Poor: Micro-Lending and the Battle against World Poverty.* Oxford: Oxford University Press.

————. 2007. *Creating a World without Poverty: Social Business and the Future of Capitalism.* New York: Public Affairs.

Zeller, Manfred, and Richard Meyer, eds. 2002. *The Triangle of Microfinance: Financial Sustainability, Outreach and Impact.* Baltimore, MD: John Hopkins University Press.

Zeller, Manfred, Manohar Sharma, Carla Henry, and Cecile Lapenu. 2001. "An Operational Tool for Evaluating Poverty Outreach of Development Policies and Projects." Food Consumption and Nutrition Division Discussion Paper No. 111, International Food and Policy Research Institute, Washington, DC.

Zuvekas, Clarence. 2002. "The Honduran Poverty Reduction Strategy." *MACLAS*, XVI. Accessed January 17, 2008. www.maclas.vcu.edu/journal/Vol%20XVI/Index_XVI.html.

About the Contributors

João Márcio Mendes Pereira is a professor of history at the Rural Federal University of Rio de Janeiro. He earned his doctorate from the Fluminense Federal University (UFF) in Niteroi, Brazil. His research interests include contemporary history, international political economy, and political sociology, in particular the history of the World Bank, American and multilateral aid to development, the agrarian question, and rural social movements in Latin America. Recent publications include *A política de reforma agrária de mercado do Banco Mundial: Fundamentos, objetivos, contradições e perspectivas* (Hucitec, 2010) and *O Banco Mundial como ator político, intelectual e financeiro (1944–2008)* (Civilização Brasileira, 2010). His articles are published in academic reviews such as *Tempo Social, Revista de História* (USP), *Revista Brasileira de Política Internacional, Tempo, Topoi, Revista Brasileira de História, Varia História, Revista Brasileira de Educação, Sociedade e Estado,* and *Estudos Avançados.*

Anthony Holland O'Malley is coordinator of International Development Studies at Saint Mary's University (Halifax, Canada) and author, inter alia, of "Critical Analysis and Development" in *Critical Development Studies Handbook* (Fernwood, 2011), "The Dialectics of Class and Community" in *Community-Based Development in Latin America* (Kumarian, 2001), "Banking on Poverty: Assessing the World Bank's War on Poverty" in the *Canadian Journal of Development Studies* (2006), and "Poverty Reduction Programs and Rural Poverty" in the *Poverty Report* (2010). He also coedited the Kumarian publication *Transcending Neoliberalism: Community-Based Development in Latin America.*

Darcy Victor Tetreault is a research professor at the Autonomous University of Zacatecas, Mexico, in the Development Studies Program, and an adjunct professor at Saint Mary's University, Halifax, Canada. He obtained an MA in International Development Studies from Saint Mary's University in 2002 and a

PhD in Social Sciences from the University of Guadalajara, Mexico, in 2007. From 2007 to 2010 he taught and carried out research at the University of Guadalajara, La Ciénega University Center, on issues related to poverty and environmental degradation. He has received several academic awards and distinctions, including the national-level (Mexico) Arturo Warman Prize 2008 for his doctoral thesis, which was published the next year by the University of Guadalajara under the title *Pobreza y degradación ambiental: Las luchas de abajo en dos comunidades del occidente de Jalisco: Ayotitlán y La Ciénega*. His work has been published in scholarly journals and books in Mexico, North America, and Europe. His academic interests include poverty, social policy, international development studies, rural social and socioecological movements, and political ecology.

Enrique Valencia Lomelí has been a professor and researcher at the Universidad de Guadalajara since 1994. He is also the president of the Poverty and Social Policy research working group of CLACSO, the Council of Social Science Programs based in Buenos Aires, Argentina. He has edited and authored various comparative studies and books and scholarly articles on social and economic policy. Recent publications include *Perspectivas del universalismo en México* and "Conditional Cash Transfers as Social Policy in Latin America: An Assessment of Their Contributions and Limitations" (*Annual Review of Sociology*, 2008).

Henry Veltmeyer is professor of International Development Studies at Saint Mary's University (Halifax, Canada) and the Universidad Autónoma de Zacatecas in Mexico. He has authored and edited over forty books on issues of Latin American development, social movements and the state, and the political economy of globalization and local development. Recent publications include *Transcending Neoliberalism: Community-Based Development in Latin America* (Kumarian, 2001), *Socialism of the 21st Century: Possibilities and Prospects* (2011), *Imperialism, Crisis and Class Struggle: The Verities of Capitalism* (2010), *The Cuban Revolution as Socialist Human Development* (2012), *The Critical Development Studies Reader* (2011), and, with James Petras, *Unmasking Globalization* (2001), *Multinationals on Trial* (2007), *Social Movements in Latin America: Neoliberalism and Popular Resistance* (2011), and *Beyond Neoliberalism: A World to Win* (2011).

Index

absolute poverty
  agricultural modernization and, 40
  defining, 39–40
  public policy established for, 41
  relative poverty distinguished from, 41
ACCION International, 140, 141n2
Acquisition of Productive Assets (APA),
  198–99
Agency for International Aid (USAID), 37,
  44, 159
aggregate economic performance, 8
agriculture. *See also* small-scale farming;
  World Development Report 2008: Agri-
  culture for Development
  absolute poverty and modernization of, 40
  capitalist development of, 71–72
  limitations of, 30
  Mexican rural poverty solution through,
    202–3
  Mexican subsidy programs for, 198
  Mexico's neoliberalism policies for, 195–99
  for modernization, 59, 80
  resource scarcity and, 194
  rural poverty and, x
  rural poverty solutions with, 18–19, 30
  TNCs dominating, 208
  transitory nature of, 59
  WDR-08's perspective on migration and
    labor *versus*, 69–70
  World Bank's renewed focus on, 192
"agriculture-based" countries, 67, 69, 192
  increased productivity in, 75, 77
  PRPs for, 77–78

  rural poverty reduction in, 76
  transformation obstacles in structure of, 74
agriculture for development, 59
agroecology
  in Cuba, 217–18
  effectiveness of, 213–14
  as movement, 214–15
  NGO techniques for, 215–16
  as science, 214
  for small-scale farming, 216–18
  in *La Vía Campesina*, 217
Akram-Lodhi, Haroon, 63, 65–67, 81–82,
  163
ANAP. *See* National Association of Small
  Farmers
APA. *See* Acquisition of Productive Assets
apex organizations, MFOs mediated by, 129
Argentina, 167, 184
"assault on poverty," by World Bank, 33–34,
  56
  defending strategy of, 43
  dismantling, 51
  initial elements lacking in, 38
  loan destination changes for, 36–37
Assistance Fund for Social Infrastructure
  (FAIS), 95

BancoSol, 132, 134, 141n7
Ban Ki-moon, 11
BANRURAL, 196–97
Barba Solano, Carlos, 96
basic needs, 45–46, 89–90
basic universalism, 108, 186